How Much Do We Deserve?

How Much Do We Deserve?

An Inquiry into Distributive Justice

✦ ✦ ✦

SECOND EDITION

Richard S. Gilbert

Skinner House Books
Boston

Printed in Canada

Cover design by Suzanne Morgan
Photos by Nancy Pierce / UUA

Note: All Bible quotations are from the New Revised Standard Version.

Library of Congress Cataloging-in-Publication Data

Gilbert, Richard S., 1936–
    How much do we deserve? : an inquiry into distributive justice /
Richard S. Gilbert.—2nd ed.
       p. cm.
    Includes bibliographical references and index.
    ISBN 1-55896-416-9 (alk. paper)
    1. Distributive justice.   2. Income distribution.   3. Economics—
Moral and ethical aspects.

HB523.G54 1990
174—dc21   2001020186

10 9 8 7 6 5 4 3 2 1
05 04 03 02 01

Contents

Foreword

The World Trade Organization protest in Seattle in November 1999 drew an estimated forty thousand people. Forty thousand people came to protest unfair trade agreements; forty thousand people were informed about these complex issues and angry. Environmentalists, trade union workers, human rights activists, people of many different ethnic groups stood together as they have never before stood. For the more than one hundred people that our church sent to Seattle, it was a life-changing event. We knew we had made a difference. We came away convinced that major social changes were underway.

Something new *is* coming. Something new is stirring in the collective psyche. A new consciousness is pushing from within, waiting to be born. It has to do with our spiritual being. And it has to do with justice. It begins with a kind of restlessness and uneasiness, a growing agitation about what we see happening in the United States. Why are so many of our mentally ill wandering the streets? Why did an Oregon food bank have a 17-percent rise in requests in 1999? Why have so many teenagers been cast away, forced to sleep in doorways? Why any of this in such a time of plenty?

I have come to believe that economic inequity—in theological terms, greed—which has become steadily worse over the past few decades, is the root problem that must be addressed. The abuse of economic power manifests itself not only in the lives of the poor but in the lives of the middle class as well. How many of us are working longer hours than ever before? Which of us do not know individuals who have lost their jobs to downsizing after years of faithful service? How many families must have two or more breadwinners just to survive?

But change is in the air. Alternative voices are being heard now—voices like that of Richard Gilbert, who has been issuing a call to conscience throughout his forty years of ministry. In this second edition of *How Much Do We Deserve? An Inquiry into Distributive Justice*, he eloquently guides readers to greater commitment, thoughtfulness, and determination in the cause of social justice. He contends that all people have worth and that a society should be judged not by how much freedom it gives to the strong but by how much care it gives to the most vulnerable. Gilbert proceeds from the principle that all people share the same

4333

fundamental needs and are entitled to have these needs met as a simple human right. He persuasively makes the case that the world's resources would be sufficient for all if distributed in an equitable manner.

We can't do justice work in a vacuum. We need to learn from people who live on the edge: poor people, children who are homeless, migrant workers—people who make us feel shaken and uneasy because their lives are not like our own. We will learn what we must do only when we risk not knowing at all what to do, when we listen to voices we have not yet heard. We have to leave home, in a sense—move away from our comfortable ways of being—to find ourselves and our calling. We need to develop a passionate discontent, an anger that picks us up and shakes us by the neck and won't let us go. The Holy Spirit, you know, is not on the side of order and stability.

So, what are we to do? We must understand that our world is not irrevocably the way it is. The current economic structures have not been divinely ordained. Human beings have made choices, and they can make different choices. We must imagine; we must dream. It's not just those others who are in trouble; it's all of us. We are all one body. We must gather in groups and tell one another about our fears for the world as it is and for ourselves if it changes. If we allow our hearts to speak, we will discover very quickly that we are not alone. And with that knowledge will come the sense of community and caring that will support us on our journey to a better place.

The solution to our social problems will not come from the top. Our politicians will not lead us to this new world. *We* must lead, and *they* must follow. Passionate, creative citizens can create a better way. Gilbert gives us a strong nudge in that direction.

It's pretty clear that capitalism has won out over socialism, but the excesses of capitalism have led us to poverty—material poverty for many and spiritual poverty throughout the land. We need a vision. Scripture doesn't say, "Without a program, the people perish." It doesn't say, "Without a political agenda, the people perish." Scripture says, "Without a vision, the people perish."

Our vision, our changing consciousness, will determine the shape of the world and even what we are able to see. Our passion for justice will rekindle the social imagination. But be wary. To transform ourselves and our society, we must be grounded in something larger than our own egos. Ego will always fail us because it is self-referential. It always asks the question: How will my importance be raised up? What will I get out of this? The way of the Spirit is different. The question becomes: What brokenness needs to be made whole? What am I called to give? Gilbert undergirds his message with a sustaining spirituality.

A new day is coming. There are signs of it everywhere. Gilbert puts the penetrating question to each of us, and to our institutions: *Where will you stand?* Let it not be said fifty years, a hundred years, from now, "Look what terrible injustice was being done—and we said nothing." Much has been given us, and much is required. Let us love mercy and do justice. Let us care for the earth that is our home. If not, what will we say to the children when they ask us about the world we have given them? The challenge is placed before us.

Marilyn Sewell
Senior Minister
First Unitarian Church
Portland, Oregon

Introduction

In his play *A Masque of Reason,* poet Robert Frost imagines a contemporary conversation between the biblical Job and God. At one point, Job asks why he has been singled out to exemplify the principle that what we deserve and what we get are not necessarily connected. God responds that as a society, people can never think things out in the abstract. Rather, they must see them "acted out by actors."

Similarly, economic justice is an abstract issue in many ways. In order to lay the foundation for an exploration of this difficult issue, let me introduce six actors on the public stage who dramatize the discrepancy of desert (or what one deserves) in an affluent society. Considering these individuals' experiences will help us think through the concept of distributive justice.

✦ ✦ ✦

First, meet Donald Hall, a poet. At the age of seventeen, he decided he was a socialist, subscribed to the socialist journal *The Worker,* and at prep school read it as publicly as he could. In his memoir *Life Work,* he relates an incident that raised the issue of class for him in a way that contradicted the view of most Americans that we live in a classless society. His father owned a dairy, which made him a boss's son, a role he theoretically despised. Hall recounts, "I remember crossing the dairy's parking lot walking with my father, who wore a brown suit and brown shoes and brown fedora, past young men my age in ratty clothes washing the mud from trucks. I lowered my gaze, unable to look them in the eyes." Hall concludes that "class in America may be a joke but it is not funny."

✦ ✦ ✦

Our second "actor" is AT&T CEO Robert Allen, who made headlines in 1995 after announcing layoffs of 40,000 employees. (Some 125,000 had already been laid off over the previous ten years.) With questionable timing, Allen's compensation package was revealed at the same time: $5.2 million in cash plus $11 million in stock options (a value that soared, along with AT&T stock prices, when the layoffs were announced). Observers asked: Is *anyone* worth $16 million in compensation? Many observers were astonished to note that AT&T had made less than 1 percent profit that year. Even the *Wall Street Journal* wondered about the justice of Allen's compensation, since in the last decade he had "[blown] upward of $12 billion on losses and acquisitions" in an ill-fated attempt to enter the computer industry. Allen's long-term incentive pay, close to $2 million, came as the company conveniently scrapped the formula of linking this compensation to prior profit rates. This combination of "lackluster performance and stellar pay" is not unusual in the business world. Graef Crystal, a researcher on executive pay, told the *New York Times* that he found no connection between CEO pay and corporate performance. "It's a table of random numbers," he is quoted as saying in a 1996 issue of *Dollars and Sense,* "like throwing darts against the wall."

◆ ◆ ◆

Next, meet Mario G., a refugee from Central Mexico. As described in *The Nation* magazine in 1996, "He has worked for just about every big-name high-tech company in Silicon Valley: Hewlett-Packard, Sun Microsystems, Advanced Micro Devices and Oracle Systems. Windows is his expertise. He washes them." His days are long—sometimes ten or twelve hours—but he never works more than forty hours a week, because then he would have to be paid overtime. Mario G. earns $6.20 an hour before taxes. Mario lives in East Palo Alto, just across the freeway from Stanford University and Hewlett-Packard's corporate campus, but the street outside his house is unpaved. While the high-tech region in which he lives is prospering, Mario G.'s own standard of living is declining. The average family income in the Palo Alto area was about $60,000 in 1996, twice the national average. But almost one-third of the workers in Silicon Valley earned less than $15,000 a year. As Mario observes, "The rich get richer, we get poorer. How can any one man's work be worth 800 times more than mine?" Mario's math is not precisely right, but it is close enough. He is referring to W. J. Sanders III, CEO of Advanced Micro Devices, whose salary last year was 717 times that of an entry-level janitor. The rising tide of the economic boom has not yet lifted Mario and millions like him.

◆ ◆ ◆

Consider the case of Angela Stroud, who for seven years worked in Clayton, North Carolina, for Champion Products, a division of Sara Lee, turning out quality sweatsuits, jerseys, and other sportswear items.

Angela and her co-workers helped make this division an industry leader in supplying uniforms for the NFL, the NBA, and the 1996 U.S. Olympic team. But according to a 1997 issue of *Dollars and Sense,* despite their loyalty and productivity, Angela and 414 other Champion workers "were punted out the factory door," joining 1,400 other Champion employees in North Carolina (62 percent of its statewide workforce) who had lost their jobs in the past five years. Why did all these people lose their jobs? Champion was not losing sales. Nor was Sara Lee unprofitable. Business was booming and profits were good. But the company found that it could substantially increase its profits by shipping production (and Angela's job) to Chihuahua, Mexico, "where 50 cents an hour labor is available and health and safety laws are a cruel joke."

◆ ◆ ◆

Marion Wright Edelman, Executive Director of the Children's Defense Fund, writing in the March/April 1988 issue of *Unitarian Universalist World*, describes the death of a child named Shamal, who

> died in New York City. He was eight months old. The cause of death was poverty complicated by low birthweight, poor nutrition, homelessness, and a viral infection. During his short life he had never slept in an apartment or house; his family was always homeless—he had been in shelters, hospitals, hotels, and the welfare office. He and his mother sometimes rode the subway late at night. Robert Hayes of New York's Coalition for the Homeless said Shamal died because he didn't have the strength to resist the "system's abuse."

While this incident occurred in New York, it could happen in any community in any year.

◆ ◆ ◆

Jim Hightower, a former Texas politician and relentless social critic, wrote a populist manifesto entitled *There's Nothing in the Middle of the Road but Yellow Stripes and Dead Armadillos.* He illustrates the incredible disparity in earnings among Americans by citing the case of a twenty-something giant of a man who happened to be a very good basketball player. After signing a $121-million contract with the Los Angeles Lakers, that man, Shaquille O'Neal was "besieged by the media asking

xiv   How Much Do We Deserve?

about the preposterousness of that sum." O'Neal retorted, "I'm tired
of hearing about money, money, money, money, money. I just want to
play the game, drink Pepsi and wear Reebok."

✦ ✦ ✦

By accidents of fate, these six people are living in six totally different
worlds all within the same country. And while they are different in
many ways, the most striking difference is the economic resources each
possesses:

- ✦ Donald Hall recounts his embarrassment at being born into a family of means; he was unable to face people who were less well
  born, experiencing a sharply divided community despite all claims
  of a classless society.

- ✦ Robert Allen enjoys a superfluity of riches in the wealthiest nation
  the world has ever known, but his former employees wonder
  where their next paycheck will come from.

- ✦ Mario G. immigrated to the United States for economic opportunity yet feels the vast income disparity in the nation's economy; he
  cannot see how he will ever be able to share in its bounty.

- ✦ Angela Stroud shared a small bit of American affluence until her
  job was one of many lost in the great globalization process that
  dominates the worldwide economic race.

- ✦ Shamal never had a chance. He began life without even the minimum requirements for entering the economic race, let alone
  surviving it.

- ✦ Shaquille O'Neal is the big winner, thanks, in large part, to a seven-
  foot, 325-pound body built for playing basketball.

The contrast among these individuals raises perplexing questions:
Did they get their just deserts? Does anyone? What economic rights do
we have, if any? From a moral standpoint, is it possible to determine
how much each of us deserves, or must we submit to the supposedly
value-free, invisible hand of the marketplace?

These questions point to issues that are not merely academic; they
describe the daily lives of 5 billion people around the world, many of
whom are poor and a very few of whom are rich. Getting our just
deserts is a nearly intractable issue fraught with economic, religious,

psychological, and social difficulties. However, the very complexity of the issue and the controversy that it inherently arouses should be no excuse for refusing to address it. How much do we deserve?

IS ECONOMIC JUSTICE AN OXYMORON?

The term *economic justice* has been called an oxymoron, an inherently contradictory phrase. The study of economics—sometimes called "the dismal science"—seems totally divorced from moral analysis. This "soft" science deals with a world of hard data and difficult choices. Since the time of Adam Smith, it has been said that "if all the economists in the world were placed end to end they wouldn't reach a conclusion." At this juncture, however, we must arrive at some economic conclusions, lest the United States evolve into a nation at war with itself.

The secularization of the Western world has resulted in a level of specialization that places economic analysis in the hands of one group of experts and moral analysis in the hands of another. To be sure, economics and ethics seem strange bedfellows. The quantification of economics now dominates normative inquiry.

I recently heard a professor at the University of Rochester's Simon School of Business Management lecture on the economics of health care. At one point, he made an unflattering comparison between the Canadian and U.S. health systems. I asked him how the 44 million uninsured Americans fit into the equation. He demurred, saying that this was a policy question, as if economists live in an abstract world, somehow apart from (and perhaps above) the decisions that affect the lives of real people.

In *The Power of Myth*, Bill Moyers shares the philosophy of the late Joseph Campbell about the values that mark a society:

[There was] a time when . . . spiritual principles informed the society. You can tell what's informing the society by what the tallest building is. When you approach a medieval town, the cathedral is the tallest thing in the place. When you approach an eighteenth-century town, it is the political palace that's the tallest thing in the place. And when you approach a modern city, the tallest places are the office buildings, the centers of economic life. . . . That's the history of Western civilization.

Bill Gates, co-founder of Microsoft and the world's richest man, clearly finds that religious activity does not measure up to economic activity. Gates is quoted in a 1998 issue of *The Christian Century* as saying, "Just in terms of allocation of time resources, religion isn't very efficient. There is a lot more I could be doing on a Sunday morning." And so, at the beginning of this new millennium, it is not poets but entrepreneurs who are the unacknowledged legislators of the world.

This specialization betrays the historical reality that economics arose from the field of moral inquiry. For Aristotle, economics (or *oikonomia*, "management of the household") was a branch of ethics and addressed the question of whether each person in the household received what is required for a fully human life. Redoubtable economist Adam Smith was actually a moral philosopher who believed that moral sentiment would hold in check the very acquisitive human nature that, in turn, drove the economy.

If just and effective economic policies are to be implemented, the normative must be returned to the center of economic discussion and ethics and economics must be considered in a common dialogue. In that dialogue, the economic system should be the servant, not the master, of humanity. Once hidden theological and ethical assumptions should be raised and discussed. No single economic theory or system should be revered as absolute. And every system should have a built-in capacity for self-criticism from the norm of justice, the ultimate characteristic of social ethics. If this dialogue does not occur, we, as a society, will know the price of everything and the value of nothing.

For me, social ethics is grounded in religion. And one of the purposes of religion is to meet basic human needs and affirm basic human rights, for life is holistic. Human beings are unitary. There is no distinction among religious, social, political, and economic persons. These descriptions of our humanity are rather arbitrary, if useful, ways to describe the dimensions of our humanness. *Homo faber* and *homo religiosus* are one person.

Economic justice is a broad term given to widely divergent interpretations. My focus is on *distributive justice*, which is, according to the *Dictionary of Religious Ethics*, the "virtue by which goods and burdens of the community are distributed with due proportion among the citizens." While this definition emphasizes the distributive dimension of the economy, the productive side of the economic equation will be addressed, as well. And even though we live in a global economy, the focus will be on the economy of the United States.

It is my intent to bridge the gap between scholars in economics and theological/ethical disciplines and concerned laity and clergy, as well as other interested citizens. I will do my best to present the sometimes esoteric work of the experts, translating their knowledge into practical guidelines that will be useful in citizen debate and action in a free society. As Robert Kuttner wrote in *The Economic Illusion*, "Economic distribution is far too important to leave to economists."

My goal is to contribute to public debate about social policy, both public and private. In this era of booming prosperity, I will look at both ends of the economic continuum: from welfare legislation, as it affects people who are poor, to taxation, as it affects those who are rich. This examination will also have implications for setting wages and salaries in the private sector. Finally, as a member of the middle class in a middle-class religious movement, I believe lifestyle issues must be raised, revolving around what has been called "the predicament of the prosperous."

HAVE WE LOST OUR CAPACITY FOR MORAL OUTRAGE?

I worry that comfortable Americans, living in this culture of contentment, may have lost the capacity for moral outrage. We constitute a culture both of contentment and contradiction—contentment in the unparalleled prosperity we enjoy at the beginning of the new millennium yet, at a deeper level, contradiction in the islands of poverty we see in an ocean of plenty. The competing issues of materialism and spirituality trouble us at the deepest levels of our being. We who have taken pleasure in our prosperity are vaguely anxious that millions of others, living in our very midst, have not enjoyed the same bounty.

So, are we the deserving and they the undeserving? Is the marketplace the measure of all things? How much inequality of any type can a democracy experience and survive? In a competitive society, what should we do with the "losers"? How much is enough in this winner-take-all economy? Is economics guru Paul Samuelson right when he speaks of "the ruthless economy"? If the person who ends up with the most "toys" wins, just what does he/she win? Must people be cost effective? Are those of us who have benefited from this affluence prepared to critique and transform the very economic structures and policies that have been so good to us? What do we owe each other?

These are the questions that empty the room. No one today wants to think about them, let alone answer them. Yet this feeling of moral and spiritual unease is not new. The prophet Amos warned the people of Israel about being "at ease in Zion," lying upon beds of ivory and stretching themselves on couches, chanting to the sound of the viol, drinking wine in bowls, but who are not grieved for the affliction of Israel.

In the words of a modern prophet, Walt Kelley, in *Pogo*,

There is no need to sally forth, for it remains true that those things which make us human are, curiously enough, always close at hand. Resolve then, that on this very ground, with small flags waving and tinny blasts on tiny trumpets, we shall meet the enemy, and not only may he be ours, he may be us.

✦ ✦ ✦

How Should We Slice the Pie?

> *Ninety-eight out of one-hundred rich men in America are*
> *honest. That is why they are rich. I have some feeling for the poor,*
> *but the number of the poor who are to be sympathized with is*
> *very small. To sympathize with a man whom God has punished*
> *for his sins, thus to help him when God would continue a*
> *just punishment, is to do wrong, no doubt about it.*
> —Russell Conwell, "Acres of Diamonds"

In his "Attack on Distributive Justice" in *Without Guilt and Justice,*
philosopher Walter Kaufmann writes,

> Desert is incalculable. . . . It is quite impossible to say how much
> income surgeons, lawyers, executives, or miners deserve, or what
> kind of housing each deserves, or how much free time per day, per
> week, or per year. It makes no sense to call any particular distribu-
> tion of goods among them "just."

He goes on to cite seven categories that are customarily used in calculating *desert:* what one is, what one has, what one does, what one needs,
what one desires, what one has contracted, and what one has done.
Kaufmann argues that it is impossible in each case to determine desert,
stating that "instead of seeking an ever elusive justice, an autonomous
ethic should minimize brutality and dishonesty."

Despite Kaufmann's useful admonition, a distributive ethic that
informs public policy must be somewhat more specific. Minimizing
brutality and dishonesty is desirable but hardly adequate. It is a necessary but not sufficient condition for justice. Over the years, a number

of serious efforts have tried to stake out a rationale for distributive justice, and these opinions merit our consideration in formulating a contemporary ethic of distribution. Throughout humanity's ethical tradition, critiques of economic justice have generally been more sympathetic to the plight of the poor than the privilege of the rich. Philosophers and theologians have constantly wondered: What should become of the "losers"? And what are the dangers in "winning"? Certain religious and philosophical traditions have, by and large, called for a reduction in inequality and, in so doing, have kept the human equation alive in economic debate.

HINDUISM

Hinduism is the oldest of the organized world religions. Its approach to distributive justice is complicated by its deeply embedded caste system, which includes the so-called untouchables, the *Harijan*, at the very bottom. This issue came to the attention of the rest of the world during the nineteenth and twentieth centuries as Western values penetrated the Asian subcontinent. Reformers such as Rammohan Roy, founder of the Brahmo Samaj movement; Vivekananda, the founder of the Ramakrishna movement; poet Rabadranath Tagore; and, of course, Mahatma Gandhi have met this inherently conservative tradition head on.

Gandhi, though perhaps more universal prophet than Hindu, wrote the following about human equality:

> Men are equal. For, though they are not of the same age, same height, the same skin and the same intellect, these inequalities are temporary and superficial. The soul that is hidden beneath this earthly crust is one and the same for all men and women belonging to all climes. . . . The word "inequality" has a bad odour to it, and it has led to arrogance and inhumanities, both in East and West.

In a kind of Eastern *noblesse oblige*, Gandhi railed against the wealth and prestige into which he had been born. Writing on the relationship between rich and poor, he expressed a distributive ethic that set meeting basic human needs as a priority claim:

> I suggest we are thieves in a way. If I take anything that I do not need for my own immediate use, and keep it, I thieve it from somebody else. . . . You and I have no right to anything that we really have until these three million are clothed and fed better. You and I, who ought

to know better, must adjust our wants . . . in order that they may be nursed, fed and clothed. . . . There is enough wealth to meet everyone's need, but not everyone's greed.

BUDDHISM

According to tradition, soothsayers informed his father that Siddhartha Gautama would grow up to become either the most powerful king in the world or a poor man who would be a great spiritual teacher. That same tradition indicates that although his father sought to protect him from the world, he did venture forth and beheld the *four sights:* a feeble old man, a diseased person, a corpse, and a monk. The Buddha, in a clear rejection of the wealth and privilege to which he had been born, chose the aesthetic path of poverty. His life and subsequent Buddhist history offer sharp criticism of material acquisition.

Buddhist teaching attempts to minimize desire for self-aggrandizement. Its doctrine of *anatman* abandons the notion of being preoccupied with one's self. One's aim in life should not be to accumulate that which pleases the self but to eliminate the desire for those things that do not contribute to the spiritual life. The goal of Buddhism is to become a *Bodhisattva:* a truly enlightened being who seeks wisdom and salvation not only for himself or herself but for others as well. Bodhisattvas postpone their own entry into *Nirvana* to instruct others in the Buddhist way of life. Thus, in economic terms, Buddhism attacks self-seeking individualism and promotes finding salvation by being bound up with the well-being of others.

A popular modern interpretation of Buddhism applied to contemporary society is E. F. Schumacher's essay "Buddhist Economics" in his book *Small Is Beautiful.* He focuses on *right livelihood,* which requires moderation, the *Middle Way,* "to obtain the maximum of well-being with the minimum of consumption."

CONFUCIANISM AND TAOISM

In the *Analects,* Confucius points to moderation in wealth and poverty and a strong communitarian ethic:

> Great Man is conscious only of justice; Petty Man, only of self-interest. . . . I have always understood Great Man does everything possible to help the poor but nothing to enrich the rich. . . . To centralize wealth is to disperse the people; to distribute wealth is to collect the people.

Another great classic from China, the *Tao Te Ching*, comments on the dire consequences of acquiring wealth:

> Amass a store of gold and jade, and no one can protect it. Claim wealth and titles, and disaster will follow. . . . Fame or self: Which matters more? Self or wealth? Which is more precious? Gain or loss: Which is more painful? He who is attached to things will suffer much. He who saves will suffer heavy loss.

Islam, Zakat, and Sadaqah

The Koran has a strong egalitarian bent, along with an emphasis on solidarity, kindness, and justice (16:90). It condemns hoarders of wealth (3:180) and upholds the virtuous who share it (57.7). *Zakat*—one of the five pillars of Islamic faith better known as *alms giving*—is an obligatory act of giving by those with possessions to those without. It is essentially a tax on net wealth (a flat rate of 2.5 percent) and as such forms the foundation of the Koran's proportionate transfer to the poor. The purpose is not to punish productivity but to combine it with a social conscience.

There are two concepts of justice in the Koran—*adl* and *ihsan*—and both deal with the concept of balance. *Adl* suggests that justice comprises the avoidance of excess—hence, the scales of justice. *Ihsan* goes beyond this concept to call for restoring economic balance by making up a loss or deficiency. This concept underlies that of *ummah:* the ideal society in which it is recognized that people are not all equal and that each has different needs. *Ihsan,* then, is the Koran's emphasis on sympathy for the downtrodden and oppressed—an Islamic version of an option for the poor.

The goal of contemporary Islamic economics and ethics is to create a social security system in which every citizen is guaranteed a reasonable level of income, regardless of his/her ability to earn it. Proportionate payments to the poor and proportionate sacrifices by the rich are religious obligations. In this concept, the *vertical axioms* of unity, equilibrium, free will, and responsibility combine with the *horizontal axiom,* social policy.

Zakat is the minimal tax, but it is part of a larger voluntary contribution called *sadaqah*, or "pious giving." Additional taxes are also permitted based on one's ability to pay. Taxation represents the sharing of a community's income between rich and poor. Social justice implies an equitable distribution of income. Wealth is not intended to be held only among the rich; rather, when justly earned, wealth is to be regarded as a bounty from God and spent to redress distributive imbalance.

JUDAISM

The Jewish biblical heritage is rich in references to economic justice. One of the most notable is the Year of Jubilee concept found in Leviticus 25:10–24 (see also Deuteronomy 15:4). According to this historic concept, the land was to be returned to its original owners—without compensation—every fifty years. Doing so was a means to equalize land ownership, the primary source of wealth in those days. There is scholarly debate as to whether this principle was ever practiced. The concept alone, however, is radical in its redistributive ethic. Many current-day religious leaders embraced the concept, calling the year 2000 a Year of Jubilee and demanding that the debts of poor nations be cancelled.

The Hebrew prophets clearly proclaimed opposition to great gaps between rich and poor. Isaiah issued this warning:

> Woe to those who join house to house, who add field to field, until there is no more room, and you are made to dwell alone in the midst of the land. The Lord of hosts has sworn in my hearing: "Surely many houses shall be desolate, large and beautiful houses, without inhabitant." (5:8–9)

The so-called Third Isaiah bespeaks economic restoration in this classic passage:

> The Lord has anointed me to bring good tidings to the afflicted; he has sent me to bind up the brokenhearted; to proclaim liberty to the captives, and the opening of the prison to those who are bound; to proclaim the year of the Lord's favor. (61:1–2)

Amos is unparalleled in his efforts as prophet for the poor:

> Hear this, you who trample upon the needy, and bring the poor of the land to an end, saying when will the new moon be over . . . and the Sabbath . . . that we may buy the poor for silver and the needy for a pair of sandals. (8:4–6)

Micah likewise has harsh things to say about rich oppressors:

> Woe to those who devise wickedness and work evil upon their beds. . . . They covet fields and seize them; and houses and take them away. (2:1–2)

From the time of the Hebrew prophets, Jewish concern for inequality and poverty has been divinely mandated. The ethical monotheism of the prophets understood that God was the creator of the earth and its inhabitants and not indifferent to the plight of his creatures. Historically, the motivation of charity was fundamentally religious—a duty toward God as well as toward one's neighbor.

God's sovereignty is also expressed in the realization that God is not only creator of the earth but also its owner. Individuals of means who fail to provide for those who are poor are essentially asserting an individual claim on property that ultimately belongs to God. The rabbis deemed that refusing to assist the poor was not only unethical but also idolatrous.

More important, God's sovereignty as creator means that all people are created in God's image—not in physical or mental terms, for that would be anthropomorphism, but in moral terms. Human beings should be like God in their capacity to discern right and wrong. Beyond this, God has liberated the Jewish people from poverty and oppression; they are obligated to be grateful by, in turn, liberating others from such bondage. In sum, the virtue of compassion transforms gratitude to God into caring for God's people, especially those who are poor, and including them in the bonds of the community. Compassion as a simple, humanitarian virtue stems from the historical experience of the Jewish people, who have known the slavery to which poverty subjected them.

This inherent dignity of God's creatures carries a vital lesson: Poverty is an affront to humans' worth as creatures of God. Consequently, those people who can are obliged to help others avoid the degradation of poverty. Belief in God as the creator leads directly to the covenant, which is to create a just human community. Doing so is the only means by which Jewish life can be fully realized. Charity is not passed from one individual to another but from the community to the poor. Thus, the covenant was made not between individuals and God but between the Jewish community and God.

CHRISTIANITY

Christian teaching about economics begins with Jesus, who, in the Sermon on the Mount, says that we cannot serve two masters, God and Mammon (Matthew 6:24). Matthew 6:21 says that where one's treasure is, there the heart—the core of one's being—will also be. And First Timothy makes the unequivocal statement that "the love of money is the root of all evil."

The Christian scriptures are emphatic in enjoining wealth and championing the cause of the poor:

> Do not lay up for yourselves treasures on earth. (Matthew 6:19)

> For what will it profit a man, if he gains the whole world and forfeits his life? (Matthew 16:26)

> Take heed, and beware of all covetousness; for a man's life does not consist in the abundance of his possessions. (Luke 12:15)

Jesus' response to the rich young man in search of salvation is also unequivocal:

> Truly, I say to you, it will be hard for a rich man to enter the kingdom of heaven. Again I tell you, it is easier for a camel to go through the eye of a needle than for a rich man to enter the Kingdom of God. (Matthew 19:23–24)

Acts includes several references to the practice among early Christians of holding all goods in common and sharing them according to need:

> And all who believed were together and had all things in common; and they sold their possessions and goods and distributed them to all, as any had need. (Acts 21:44–45; see also 4:32–37)

The point of these passages from Acts seems clear, even in the context of the eschatological hope of the time that the end of the age was imminent. While citing the Bible is no guarantee of truth, there is indisputably a strong biblical tradition of challenging excessive wealth. At the same time, a preferential option for the poor can be discerned, indicating that the bonds of community are paramount.

The early church carried on this tradition in the writings of St. Jerome and St. Ambrose. St. Jerome, it was said, would rather store money in the stomachs of the poor than in a purse. St. Ambrose anticipated St. Thomas Aquinas by indicating that giving to the poor was not charity but simply giving those individuals what they rightfully deserved. Economic resources were to be held in common for the use of all people, not merely the rich. St. Ambrose, in a letter to Bishop Constantius some time in 379 C.E., writes,

> Woe to him who has a fortune amassed by deceit, and builds in blood a city, in other words, his soul. For it is the soul which is built like a city. Greed does not build it, but sets it on fire and burns it.

THE GRECO-ROMAN TRADITION

The Greco-Roman philosophical tradition informed later Roman Catholic and Protestant teaching on economic justice and is instructive today on its own merits. As mentioned earlier, the Greek word *oikonomia* refers to the law or management of the household and deals with the question of whether each person receives what is required for a full life. In his play *Eumenides,* Aeschylus deals forthrightly with matters of economic justice when he has the chorus proclaim,

> But whoever transgresses in daring defiance, and is laden with wealth that he has heaped up unjustly, I say that he shall certainly, in due time, lower his sails when storms of trouble break on him. . . . He is wrecked on the reef of justice, losing the prosperity that had been his throughout all his days, and he perishes unwept, unseen.

In the *Laws,* Plato suggests that limits be placed on both poverty and affluence, preferring equality in property but realizing this is impossible. In discussing the ideal state, he says that when goods are in excess, they produce strife among people and when they are deficient, they produce serfdom. Plato also poses this dilemma:

> The good man must give first attention to the soul, secondly to the body and only thirdly to the pursuit of money. . . . it is impossible for them to be at once both good and excessively rich.

In *The Republic,* Plato goes on to propose four classes of people in terms of their possessions, with minimum and maximum amounts of wealth:

> And having set this [inferior] limit, the lawgiver shall allow a man to possess twice this amount, or three times, or four times. Should anyone acquire more than this—whether by discovery or gift or money-making, or through gaining a sum exceeding the due measure by some other such piece of luck—if he makes the surplus over to the State, he shall be well-esteemed and free from penalty.

Aristotle draws on the maxim attributed to Roman jurist Ulpian: "Justice is the constant and perpetual will to render to each what is due him." Like the work of Plato before him, Aristotle's *Nichomachean Ethics* suggests that goods should be distributed not by arithmetic but by geometric proportion—that is, proportionate equality. Yet there are strong egalitarian strains in Aristotle's writing. He writes about the "unjust man grasping; he must be concerned with goods—not all goods, but those with which prosperity and adversity have to do." Justice has to do with "another's good"—what is advantageous to one's neighbor.

Furthermore, Aristotle's understanding of home economics is stated in these unequivocal words:

> Household management is more concerned with human beings than with the acquisition of inanimate property, and with human excellence than with the excellence of property we call wealth. . . . Justice is a kind of mean . . . while injustice relates to the extremes. . . . Injustice is excess and defect. . . . In the unjust act to have too little is to be unjustly treated; to have too much is to act unjustly.

Elsewhere, Aristotle suggests that anyone with few resources—especially someone with a physical disability that prevents him/her from working—should come before the council to receive aid. And if the individual's claim is approved, he/she should receive public sustenance.

Other Greek and Roman writers echo these sentiments. One of the surviving orations of Lycias proclaims, "All fortune, good and bad, is to be shared in common by the community as a whole." Cicero, in his essay "Moral Duties," warns against the dangers of excessive wealth: "Luxury, which is shameful at every period of life, makes old age hideous." And Greek philosopher Thales provides an apt summary of this strain of the Greco-Roman tradition: "If there is neither excessive wealth nor immoderate poverty in a nation, then justice may be said to prevail."

ROMAN CATHOLICISM

St. Thomas Aquinas actively engages the distributive justice question in *Summa Theologica:*

> All material riches belong in common to the whole human race. . . . The institution of private property exists for the purpose of enabling man to achieve the most effective use of material things.

In situations of extreme deprivation, one can take and consume another's property without violating the Seventh Commandment. Again, quoting Aquinas, "Whatever certain people have in abundance is due, by natural law, to the purpose of succoring the poor."

Poverty is a virtue only when voluntary. It is a natural human right "to live becomingly," having a sufficiency of resources for a decent and virtuous life. All people are entitled to as many material goods as necessary to preserve life. Beyond this, goods are to be distributed to persons as befits their individual stations in society, even though this cannot be determined with mathematical precision. Proportionate equality is the *desideratum.* The right to a decent life has a claim on the superfluous wealth of others.

According to Aquinas, a "just wage" is not to be determined by the "higgling of the market" but by "a considered judgment that looked to the good of the worker and of society as a whole." In the Middle Ages, it was assumed that a worker's wages were sufficient to support a family (prefiguring the Living Wage Campaign). Just distribution occurs according to individuals' needs and merits. And while there is supposed to be an equitable distribution of public benefits and burdens, this is not absolute equality of distribution. Aquinas notes, "Consequently in distributive justice a person receives all the more of the common goods, according as he holds a more prominent position in the community."

However, there is to be both a floor and a ceiling on the acquisition of material goods. Although practical objections to implementing such a goal are formidable, progressive taxation receives Aquinas's blessing. He believes that citizens should be taxed according to their ability to pay: "Distributive justice would demand a progressive tax rate to equalize the sacrifice exacted from the tax payers." The virtuous life requires providing a sufficiency of goods to the many as opposed to leaving property in the hands of a few. Equitable distribution is therefore required. In quoting Ambrose, Thomas Aquinas therefore seems to lay the basis for a preferential option for the poor: "It is the hungry man's bread that you withhold, the naked man's cloak that you store away, the money that you bury in the earth is the price of the poor man's ransom and freedom."

Leo Schumacher, in his study of St. Thomas Aquinas and his economic ethics, *The Philosophy of the Equitable Distribution of Wealth*, draws this conclusion: "The right to private property in his philosophy is subordinate to and harmonizes perfectly with the more basic right of all mankind to the use of the earth and its resources. In case of conflict, the superior right must prevail." St. Thomas himself seems to suggest a zero-sum society when he writes, "One man cannot overabound in external riches without another man lacking them, for temporal goods cannot be possessed by many at the same time."

The Thomistic ethic of distributive justice is somewhat paternalistic, class-bound, and essentially conservative, yet it includes a sense of limit and proportion. Most notably, extremes of wealth and poverty are rejected, charity is mandated, a progressive taxation for more equal distribution of goods is supported, and a sense of community responsibility for the poor is deemed essential.

According to current Roman Catholic thinking, justice—one of the four cardinal virtues—is the moral value by which people give one another their due. And this ethic points toward another: One is to give all that is due until equilibrium is created. In contrast to much Protestant teaching, Roman Catholic doctrine has traditionally placed a strong emphasis on the common good, or *commonweal*. It seeks a middle ground between Western individualism and Marxist collectivism. Neither the individual nor the collective has prior moral claim; rather, there is dynamic interaction between them with an evident and obvious tension.

On the one hand, according to the *Dictionary of Moral Theology*, "This doctrine implies the duty of cooperation toward the common good even at the sacrifice, within due limits, of one's individual good." On the other hand, the "common good must always resolve itself, even though indirectly, into a real good for the members of society." At stake here is an indispensable minimum, a "freedom from want, guaranteeing to every human person the means indispensable to life."

In his 1916 book *Distributive Justice*, John Ryan elaborates six principal canons of distributive justice:

+ *The canon of equality: All who participate some way in the productive process should receive the same amount of remuneration.* Among the Fabian socialists and others, George Bernard Shaw was a champion of this absolute equality. Ryan opposes this canon because it would treat unequals equally.

+ *The canon of need: People are rewarded according to their capacity to use goods reasonably.* This notion would discount the relation between distribution and production and therefore would be incomplete ethically and impossible socially.

+ *The canon of effort and sacrifice: Effort may not be productive and thus, alone, cannot be rewarded. Needs have a prior claim.* Ryan maintains that this canon would be ideally just if we could ignore the question of needs and productivity, which we cannot. This canon cannot be universally enforced.

+ *The canon of productivity: Persons are rewarded in proportion to their contribution to production.* This canon ignores the moral claims of needs and efforts and does not take into account the fact that persons are differently endowed.

+ *The canon of scarcity: Some kinds of labor are more plentiful or scarcer than others.* In addition, some involve superior sacrifice, such as a long period of educational preparation. But persons with such scarce skills may have had unequal opportunity to acquire them; thus, this canon is unfair.

+ *The canon of human welfare:* Ryan contends that this canon takes into account the five other canons and cannot be said to be unjust. It is a decidedly utilitarian view: "Once the vital needs of the individual have been safeguarded, the supreme guide of the canon of human welfare is the principle of maximum net results, or the greatest product at the lowest cost."

Charles Curran, in a discussion of distributive justice and taxation in a 1995 issue of *The Journal of Religious Ethics*, writes that property rights are limited, not absolute. The "goods of creation exist to serve the needs of all." He suggests the following formula: "Goods or advantages are to be distributed according to needs and necessities, while burdens should be distributed according to capacities."

The Canadian Roman Catholic bishops released a statement on economics in December 1983, "Ethical Choices and Political Challenges: Ethical Reflections on the Future of Canada's Socioeconomic Order." The spirit of that document is reflected in the comments made by Pope John Paul II during his September 1984 visit to Canada:

> The needs of the poor take priority over the desires of the rich; the rights of workers over the maximization of profits; the preservation of the environment over uncontrolled industrial expansion; production to meet social needs over production for military purposes.

In November 1986, the Roman Catholic Bishops of the United States issued their own pastoral letter, *Economic Justice for All: Pastoral Letter on Catholic Social Teaching and the U.S. Economy*. Six years in the making, the statement is a strong but hardly radical critique of the American economy. Nevertheless, it is an official expression in the tradition of a preferential option for the poor. It emphasizes solidarity, or the common good, and warns against greed, "the most evident form of moral underdevelopment." The bishops condemned a concentration of privilege that results from more than a mere difference in talent or desire to work but has systemic causes that must be examined. In summary, the bishops assert:

> Distributive justice also calls for the establishment of a floor of material well-being on which all can stand. This is a duty of the whole of society and it creates particular obligations for those with greater resources. This duty calls into question extreme inequalities of income and consumption when so many lack basic necessities. Catholic social teaching does not maintain that a flat, arithmetic equality of income and wealth is a demand of justice, but it does challenge economic arrangements that leave large numbers of people impoverished. Further, it sees extreme inequality as a threat to the solidarity of the human community, for great disparities lead to deep social divisions and conflict.

In coming to the relief of the poor, the affluent must do so not merely out of their "superfluous goods."

The bishops have been attacked by both conservatives and liberals in the Roman Catholic community. From the conservative side, the Lay Commission on Catholic Social Thought and the U.S. Economy critiqued the statement sharply in their own publication, *Toward the Future*. The Commission points to the unparalleled prosperity of the American economy and the benefits of democratic capitalism. In the Commission's view, democratic capitalism has been proven the world's most effective antipoverty program, and efforts to tamper with its invisible hand are fraught with danger. The group recommends the creation of economic justice through individual enterprise, which will result in trickle-down benefits for all.

From the liberal side, the bishops have been criticized by the liberation theology movement, which is most prominent in Africa, Latin America, and Asia. Speaking on behalf of the poor in developing nations, as well as impoverished and oppressed groups in developed nations, liberation theologians view Jesus as the champion of the oppressed. They see history and society from the "underside"—from the perspective of those who have lost out in economic development. God is said to identify with these people and to be allied with them against the rich in their own and other countries. Liberation theologians have a revolutionary consciousness that calls for a radical redistribution of wealth and power in the interest of justice. In their critique, they fault the bishops for working primarily within the paradigm of the capitalist system, which they believe is inherently exploitative. Liberation theologians have often been unhappy with Pope John Paul II but were cheered by his historic 1998 visit to Cuba, during which he warned the Cuban people against embracing the "blind market forces" of global capitalism: "The wealthy grow ever wealthier, while the poor grow ever poorer."

PROTESTANTISM

With the rise of the so-called Protestant ethic came a dramatic change in distributive ethics. Prior to the Reformation, the whole range of economic activities had to stand trial at the bar of religion. As the Protestant ethic and the spirit of capitalism merged, economics and ethics became segregated. Richard Tawney, in *Religion and the Rise of Capitalism*, writes that the "unbridled indulgence of the acquisitive appetite" was a deadly foe of Christianity until the onset of the

Calvinist ethic in the sixteenth century. At that time, worldly wealth seemed to become a virtue in the eyes of deity.

At first, the Calvinist ethic dominated the economic order. The Calvinists had little pity for poverty but distrusted wealth, for both distracted the soul from spiritual life. Tawney writes that the Calvinist ethic "did its best to make life unbearable for the rich." But the shift in values was underway. While medieval writers understood nature as a moral restraint upon economic self-interest, by the seventeenth century, the concentration on divine ordinance shifted to a focus on human appetites and "natural rights were invoked by the individualism of the age as a reason why self-interest should be given free play."

As described by Tawney, the Puritan,

> convinced that character is all and circumstances nothing, sees in the poverty of those who fall by the way, not a misfortune to be pitied and relieved, but a moral failure to be condemned, and in riches, not an object of suspicion—though like other gifts they may be abused—but the blessing which rewards the triumph of energy and will.

In short, the very qualities of economic gain—ambition, energy, diligence, success—continued to fire the pecuniary spirit long after the religious props had been taken away. And so the attitude toward wealth and poverty changed. The pursuit of riches, once condemned as the enemy of religion, was now its ally. The result was an orgy of materialism.

The spirit of capitalism was infused into the Protestant milieu, as illustrated by John Wesley's sermon "On the Use of Money":

> We ought not to prevent people from being diligent and frugal; we must exhort all Christians to gain all they can, and to save all they can; that is, in effect, to grow rich. [For] the bourgeois business man . . . [the Protestant ethic] gave him the comforting assurance that the unequal goods of this world was a special dispensation of Divine Providence, which in these differences, as in particular grace, pursued secret ends unknown to me.

A contemporary case for democratic capitalism must also be noted. While the rhetoric of democratic socialism closely parallels the Jewish and Christian traditions in ethics, it is democratic capitalism in its American form that has, in fact, approximated the values celebrated by these traditions, according to their advocates. They contend that it is the economic power of capitalism, more than the redistribution of wealth, that has caused the standard of living to rise. Democratic capitalism produces an admittedly rough system of justice, distributing reward according to contribution: The adherents of democratic capitalism claim there is an authentic redistribution from people who are well off to those who are less well off.

Idealistic and radical calls for absolute equality of income are dismissed out of hand as simply impractical. While the market is not God, it is the best mechanism for ensuring a middle range of income. For some proponents of democratic capitalism, progressive taxation on the wealthy and transfers to the poor are necessary corrections to the market (this, in keeping with the idea that inequalities should be permitted if they ultimately benefit people who are less well off). Government has a very limited role in this scenario; rather, the market is essentially the means of distribution.

Even so, there is severe Protestant criticism of current patterns of economic distribution. In *The Passion for Equality*, Kenneth Cauthen, former theology professor at Colgate Rochester Theological School, writes, "The economic inequality that prevails is an offense to justice as well as to charity. Poverty, unemployment, and inequality are symptoms of ills that call for drastic cures. . . . Justice requires more economic equality." This critique faults the American tradition of individualism, a kind of social nominalism in which only individuals are real. As long as the rules are fair and equally enforced, individuals should get what they can. Moral virtue is thought to reside in self-interest, "the happy thought that in their strivings the hope of success and the comfort of moral virtue coincided," as Cauthen puts it. Community as a reality is neglected. This tradition of individualism ignores the interdependence that marks modern economic systems and blunts moral perception. Cauthen concludes, "The truth is that we are all in it together." And he paraphrases the Apostle Paul as follows:

> For as in one [physical] body we have many members, and all the members do not have the same function, so we though many are one body as an economic system, and individually members one of another (Romans 12:4–5). Such a holistic understanding of the common good argues not only for equality of opportunity but also a ground for some measure of equality of results. . . . Good created in common should be enjoyed in common.

In reality, anyone who preached any of these religious precepts to the U.S. Chamber of Commerce, the National Association of Manufacturers, the United Auto Workers, or even the Democratic and Republican parties would be laughed out of the hall. Why is there such a discrepancy between the teachings of the great religions and the common economic assumptions of our time? What did these religious people have against wealth and why? Is there something archetypal here?

I believe there is. I see an inherent tension between economic affluence and religion's preoccupation with justice. It is a tension worth exploring.

PHILOSOPHICAL UTILITARIANISM AND ITS VARIANTS

The most influential theory of distributive justice for the American political economy is *utilitarianism,* summarized in John Stuart Mill's well-known formula that "we should always perform that act, of those available, which will bring the most happiness, or least unhappiness, to the greatest number of people."

Mill's classic essay "Utilitarianism," on which modern discussions are based, entertained and responded to a number of criticisms of that ethic. Most consequential for this consideration of distributive justice, however, is his discussion of the connection between justice and utility. For Mill, justice, as a peculiar instinct, was not grounded in any objective reality. "Mankind," he writes, "are always predisposed to believe that any subjective feeling, not otherwise accounted for, is a revelation of some objective reality." Rather, justice becomes instrumental to utility, not a central virtue in and of itself. According to Mill,

> A person is said to have a right to what he can earn in fair professional competition, because society ought not to allow any other person to hinder him from endeavoring to earn in that manner as much as he can. But he has not a right to three hundred a year, though he may happen to be earning it; because society is not called on to provide that he shall earn that sum. On the contrary, if he owns ten thousand pounds three-per-cent stock, he has a right to three hundred a year because society has come under an obligation to provide him with an income of that amount. To have a right, then, is, I conceive, to have something which society ought to defend me in the possession of. If the objector goes on to ask why it ought, I can give him no other reason than general utility.

Mill also provides an illustration of justice requiring utility: "In cooperative industrial association, is it just or not that talent or skill should give a title to superior remuneration? Or is it just that those who do the best they can should do equally well?" Here are two canons of distributive justice, need and effort: "Who shall decide between these appeals to conflicting justice? . . . Social utility alone can decide the preference."

Utilitarianism does not recognize any transcending criterion for justice other than utility, which is based on the logic of seeking the greatest good for the greatest number. When utilitarianism as an ethical system is linked to *laissez-faire* economics in the thought of Adam Smith, it provides the moral foundations for a capitalist economy. Smith contends that the general interest is best served when each actor seeks personal self-interest. An "invisible hand" guides the market, shaping these individual claims into a common good. Not only is this invisible hand a technical gift, it is, in fact, a divine gift, as suggested by Robert Heilbroner in *The Nature and Logic of Capitalism:* "For Adam Smith the force is that of a Deity working its will to direct divine action into socially beneficial paths that men could not discover for themselves with their limited capacity for reason and foresight."

Such a process has built-in inequalities in what we would now call a *zero-sum society.* Adam Smith writes in his classic *The Wealth of Nations,* "Wherever there is property, there is great inequality. For one very rich man, there must be at least five hundred poor, and the affluence of the rich supposes the indigence of many." Smith also warns of the dangers of wealth: "By having their minds constantly employed on the arts of luxury [the people] grow effeminate and dastardly." In short, this is the price of economic efficiency. Clearly, the value of efficiency takes priority over that of equality. Vast discrepancies of wealth may be a necessary evil, but for Smith, they were indeed essential.

A more contemporary version of the utilitarian approach in the context of a market economy is Milton Friedman's *Capitalism and Freedom.* Friedman extols the virtues of freedom in the marketplace, which he believes is the simplest and most just way to arrange an economy for all concerned. Goods and services will find their natural prices, which, because of competition in a free market, will also be their lowest prices. For government to play any role except that of "umpire" would be anathema. Friedman, however, has his own antipoverty program: a negative income tax that operates strictly through market mechanisms and governmental income tax systems.

THE PHILOSOPHY OF ENTITLEMENTS

Social philosopher Robert Nozick, in *Anarchy, State and Utopia*, provides a libertarian view of distributive justice. He has developed a theory of entitlement by which people deserve what they have justly acquired by original acquisition and what has been justly transferred to them from someone else who had justly acquired it.

According to Nozick, if the world were wholly just, the following inductive definition would exhaustively cover the subject of justice in holdings:

1. A person who acquires a holding in accordance with the principle of justice in acquisition is entitled to that holding.

2. A person who acquires a holding in accordance with the principle of justice in transfer, from someone else entitled to the holding, is entitled to the holding.

3. No one is entitled to a holding except by (repeated) applications of 1 and 2.

The complete principle of distributive justice would say simply that a distribution is just if everyone is entitled to the holdings they possessed under the distribution.

Nozick's theory of justice in holdings is historical—that is, dependent on what has actually happened. As such, it stands in contrast to the "current time-slices" theories that are informed by structural principles of distribution, which are based only on current information—in other words, welfare economics. These are end-result or end-state theories, whereas Nozick's theory depends on historical principles. As he sums up, "From each as they choose, to each as they are chosen."

An end-results theory of redistribution inevitably interferes with people's entitlements—their lives and their freedom. According to Nozick, "The socialist society would have to forbid capitalist acts between consenting adults." By contrast, the market does not interfere with people; it is neutral to people's desires. This entitlement theory is set in the context of a *minimal state*, which protects its citizens against foreign and domestic harm, enforces laws and contracts, and very little else. Nozick goes so far as to write, "Taxation of earnings from labor is on a par with forced labor." That is, one's holdings are an extension of one's self, and to interfere with them is to violate the individual. We are not compelled to sacrifice ourselves for the sake of others.

Egalitarian theorists believe the only proper criterion for redistribution is human need. Ultimately, they claim that "society [that is, each of us acting together in some organized fashion] should make provision for the important needs of all its members." Nozick rejects this thesis in favor of a theory of entitlements.

To be sure, Nozick has been widely criticized. Social ethicist Daniel Maguire, in *A New American Justice,* contends that Nozick's libertarianism is simply an old idea within new book covers, a sophisticated version of a "don't tread on me" individualism. What entitlement theorists forget, according to Maguire, is that humans are social individuals and fundamentally sharing animals. No society can survive without this understanding. Nozick's libertarian utopia simply would not work in the real world. As Maguire concludes, "Even Nozick with his dire view of taxes undoubtedly pays them since academics are not forced to practice the nonsense they may write."

Nozick can be faulted at other points as well. He tends to forget that the entitlement system may diminish the coercive power of the state over the individual but neglect the unequal power resulting from unequal holdings. This is passing strange in a theory of human autonomy and the supreme importance of being in charge of one's own life. It would seem that public coercion is wrong but private coercion is acceptable.

Nozick also assumes that private property has always existed. Clearly, there was an original period in which all natural resources were simply there—the common possessions of all people. From this point, individuals claimed private ownership. In his concept of self-ownership, Nozick does not entertain the possibility of world ownership or the idea that the earth's resources are ultimately held in common by the world's people.

The idea that freedom and private property are conceptually connected is an ideological illusion. Nozick rejects *paternalism*—action for another's benefit but against his/her will—if it is state initiated but accepts it if it is privately initiated. By *freedom,* Nozick seems to mean the freedom of private property owners to do as they wish with their property rather than bear any social responsibility for others.

Another theoretician, George Gilder, makes a spirited defense of capitalism as altruistic, taking exception to Ayn Rand's assertion that capitalism and altruism are incompatible and to the quip attributed to John Maynard Keynes that "capitalism is the extraordinary belief that the nastiest of men for the nastiest of motives will somehow work for the benefit of us all." Instead, Gilder asserts that the businessperson's investment is really a gift to the community, for there is no predetermined return. "Altruism is the essence of capitalism," according to Gilder. He would justify large disparities in income because it would create greater production, the results of which would trickle down to the poor.

This rationale has been liberally applied in the so-called supply-side policies of former President Ronald Reagan. The distributive problem, according to *Reaganomics,* cannot and ought not be handled by the state but by the market. A market unrestrained by governmental intervention will automatically allocate resources in a just manner.

In a responding salvo, Robert Lekachman has written *Greed Is Not Enough.* Lekachman critiques Gilder's notion of capitalism as altruistic with this sarcastic remark: "Capitalism is a secular faith. Avarice is a deadly sin as well as the most powerful of economic motives."

A SOCIAL CONTRACT

John Rawls's *A Theory of Justice* is perhaps the most influential philosophical statement of distributive justice available today. It is essentially a social contract theory that uses a hypothetical *original position* to set the rules for a just society. In this situation, people are assumed to be rational, self-interested, and in a basic state of equality. They live behind a "veil of ignorance," each individual unaware of his/her potential place in society or fortune in the allocation of talents and skills; they are challenged to create a society in which everyone has an equal chance of being the most or least fortunate economically.

In this situation, Rawls develops his two principles of justice and two priority rules. The first principle is a forthright statement of basic political equality: "Each person is to have an equal right to the most extensive total system of equal basic liberties compatible with a similar system of liberty for all." The second principle has to do with the arrangement of inequalities in the just society:

> Social and economic inequalities are to be arranged so that they are both (a) to the greatest benefit of the least advantaged, consistent with the just savings principle (a reasonable and adequate amount for future generations) and (b) attached to offices and positions open to all under conditions of fair equality of opportunity.

Hence, preference is to be given to the least advantaged, making this principle a kind of philosophical option for the poor. Rawls's general conception in the form of the "difference principle" can be stated as follows:

> All primary goods—liberty and opportunity, income and wealth, and the bases of self-respect—are to be distributed equally unless an unequal distribution of any or all of these goods is to the advantage of the least favored.

Michael Walzer, in *Spheres of Justice*, understands the distributive issue to be a broad one involving far more than the allocation of economic resources. For Walzer, justice is an issue in understanding membership in a society. He sets the problem in the real world as follows:

> The appeal of equality is not explained by its literal meaning. Living in an autocratic or oligarchic state, we may dream of a society where power is shared, and everyone has exactly the same share. But we know that equality of that sort won't survive the first meeting of the new members. . . . we know that money equally distributed at twelve noon on a Sunday will have been unequally redistributed before the week is out.

Walzer proposes a *complex theory of equality*, to distinguish it from merely dividing economic and other resources equally. He seeks to keep the "spheres of justice" separate so that inequality in one (say, the economic sphere) does not automatically translate into inequality in another.

Using the illustrations of ancient Greece and the medieval Jewish community, Walzer stresses that, as a first priority, every community must provide for the basic needs of its members. In discussing "fair shares," he develops the Talmudic maxim that people who are poor must be helped in proportion to their needs. "Hungry men and women don't have to stage a performance, or pass an exam, or win an election."

Although not all needs can be met, due to an inevitable scarcity, Walzer states that these socially recognized needs should be met before any surplus is distributed. People who accumulate great sums of money "act like tyrants" and distort society. Such provision of goods and services recognizes not only need but also membership. Some goods must be provided by state coercion because not everyone will understand what they need for their own welfare—for example, public health measures such as a pure water supply.

Money, for Walzer, is a "universal pander." In a cutting critique of the market ethic, he denies that it recognizes desert. "Initiative, enterprise, innovation, hard work, ruthless dealing, reckless gambling, the prostitution of talent: all these are sometimes rewarded, sometimes not." His point is not to call for eliminating the market but to recognize that it is a zone of the city, not the city itself. One may relish the market's variety and liveliness yet recognize its limitations and problems.

Walzer believes that, because of huge production and sales oligopolies, consumer sovereignty is a myth. Rather, consumer power has been fragmented and rendered impotent. The increased variety and availability of private goods make the lives of the poor harder. Moreover, as private goods increase, public goods tend to decrease. The problems created by the automobile and the sorry state of public transportation is simply a case in point. Too many people are excluded from effective participation in the market.

A radically *laissez-faire* economy would be like a totalitarian state, according to Walzer, invading every other sphere and dominating every other distributive process. It would transform every social good into a commodity and lead to market imperialism. Walzer calls for three distributions: (1) blocking "desperate exchanges" in the market (those made under economic duress of poverty) and through unions; (2) redistributing money directly through the tax system; and (3) cooperatively controlling the means of production. In proposing these distributions, Walzer argues for a form of decentralized democratic socialism. He puts forth a new version of the social contract in which resources are redistributed with some shared understanding of the needs of society's members. This social contract is a moral bond connecting the "strong and the weak, the lucky and the unlucky, the rich and the poor." It creates a union that transcends all differences.

Walzer contends that the United States maintains one of the "shabbier" systems of providing security and welfare in the world. It fails to live up to his three principles: (1) that the commonly understood needs of the citizens must be met; (2) that goods are to be distributed in proportion to need; (3) and that the underlying equality of membership must be maintained. He cites health care as an area of the free enterprise market system in which wealth still determines the quality of services available. He argues for national health insurance on the grounds that the doctor's market freedom ought not to be decisive.

Needed goods are not commodities and thus are not to be provided in the competitive market but as public goods.

Walzer summarizes his three principles of distributive justice in a revised version of the Marxist (socialist) maxim: "From each according to his ability (or his resources); to each according to his socially recognized needs. This, I think, is the deepest meaning of the social contract." Walzer is, in fact, arguing for a form of democratic socialism. Socialism defines its distributive principle in this way: "A just distribution system is one in which everyone produces according to his ability and receives according to his need." This slogan originated with French socialist Louis Blanc, not Karl Marx, who did not feel the need for such a principle. For Marx, matching goods and needs in a communist society, with an abundance of goods, would be a simple political process.

The social contract school of thought holds that economic justice in distribution is essentially an agreement within a free society to meet the basic needs of all people by limiting individual liberty to the smallest extent possible.

Toward the Beloved Community of Earth

As the Reverend Marilyn Sewell said at the General Assembly of the Unitarian Universalist Association in 2000, "The Holy Spirit is not on the side of order and stability." This has been the essence of religious and philosophical traditions over the years and indicates my own sense of moral outrage that the United States has so badly failed its citizens who are poor. The ethical and spiritual lives of those who are prosperous are at risk, given the unjustifiable gaps in income and wealth that exist in this country. The *Beloved Community of Earth* is a vision of a world in which justice prevails, one that grows out of a sense of spirituality.

I affirm the preferential option for the poor as a way of declaring my identification with them. This value also suggests that human beings were not given life for the purpose of self-indulgence but so that they could meet a responsibility to their neighbors, especially those who are powerless. "To be is to be for others," as Unitarian Universalist theologian Gene Reeves has put it.

Traditional theology, like history, is written by society's "winners." But upon reviewing theology from the underside one realizes that it has its own validity and is, by its very existence, a critique of first-world affluence and the theology it has created. David Hollenbeck, S.J., in his book *Claims in Conflict,* suggests three ethical principles that give greater articulation to the preferential option for the poor:

1. The needs of the poor take priority over the wants of the rich.
2. The freedom of the dominated takes priority over the liberty of the powerful.
3. The participation of marginal groups takes priority over the order that excludes them.

CRITIQUING THE CRITIQUES

I reject an apologia for democratic capitalism that gives virtually unqualified praise to any system that, by its very nature, creates "winners" and "losers." I am suspicious of the dogmatic zeal of those people who would deify the merely human contrivance of the system. What's more, I am skeptical of the "tough love" attributed to the capitalist system by the "winners" in the struggle for the prize. Concepts of economic justice should demand a constant critique of the imperfections of any merely human social system and provide the motivation and the analysis for criticism. The Protestant principle stands as a perennial question over our economic arrangements and reminds us that the passion for justice is a constant imperative.

Utilitarianism, which espouses "the greatest good for the greatest number," is a calculating ethic that makes no reference to any kind of transcendent judgment. This type of "ethics by aggregation" does not provide a floor, by which the least well-off are guaranteed some decent minimum standard of living. Given the terms of utilitarianism, slavery could be justified under the utility criterion, and that is prima facie wrong. Utilitarianism can also be faulted for defending short-run inequalities for greater future goods, reminding us of John Maynard Keynes's quip that "in the long run we are all dead."

The social contract theory proposed by Rawls, with its "difference principle," is a major step forward from utilitarianism but still inadequate. Rawls does not provide a substantive theory of distribution but a formal procedure for just distribution based on an "original position" schema. However, this experiment in thought does help us address the real problem of distribution. For Rawls, economic inequalities can be justified only when they work to benefit the least advantaged. But he does not explain issues such as how this is to be determined, what comprises a fair share, and how much inequality is to be tolerated.

Walzer comes closest to my own view with his modified social contract theory. His emphasis on the moral claims of living in community and his focus on human needs above discretionary consumption are instructive. Goods needed for basic human security should not be subjected to the vagaries of the marketplace but must be the first charge against the resources of a community.

A Personal Perspective

There is a conflict between America's religious faith in economic justice and the workings of the market. We are told by every religion and philosophy known to humankind that material acquisition is not the pursuit of happiness, but the marketplace gives us the opposite message.

What kind of theology can address this dilemma? My own theological framework is founded on the idea that there is a power beyond ourselves, one that functions in the cosmos as creation, in nature as creative evolution, and in humanity as history. Moreover, we, as humans, live with and strike bargains with this power. A purely utilitarian ethos does not do justice to the power that gives us life and being. Nor does such an ethos recognize those values that transcend the workings of the marketplace.

We are part of this creating, sustaining, transforming power. In the cosmos, it is a creative power that has provided the cosmic context that is life. We act in gratitude for that precious gift. In nature, that creativity has produced a finite planet for whose destiny we are responsible. We thrive as human beings as we are able to discern the ecological laws of that creative process and live in harmony with them; we suffer environmental disaster when we do not.

Historically, we are co-creators of human destiny. As creatures of finite freedom, we are free to assume responsibility for human destiny but fated by limitations in our capacity to shape history. We are also free to pursue our individual purposes but fated as creatures of earth who depend on it and one another. History should be understood in a prophetic sense as subject to human intervention and direction. We are not subject to the vague dispensations of some fateful invisible hand of the market to determine our economic destiny. The Beloved Community of Earth should be the ideal, transcending the reality in which we live.

Justice is the foundational value in social ethics. It is predicated on the inherent dignity and worth of every individual. Theologically, that has been understood through the phrase *children of God* in the Jewish and Christian traditions. In more universalistic language, it is based on the idea of reverence for life. From a philosophical stance, justice means that people are treated as ends, not means. And in a political entity, it means that people are "endowed with certain inalienable rights . . . life, liberty and the pursuit of happiness." As articulated by its secular covenantal Constitution, the United States exists "to provide for the general welfare." Human dignity, then, is at the core of justice. In economic terms, an unfair distribution of goods and services dehumanizes people, thus undermining their basic human dignity.

I submit four propositions that argue for the justice of more equitable distribution of income and wealth. Justice is informed by three principles—freedom, equity, and community—and undergirded by a fourth principle—a fundamental religious impulse. Economic justice has a spiritual foundation.

Economics is more than the calculus of self-interests that are presumably vectored into some vague common good. I contend that great disparities of income and wealth are spiritually as well as morally debilitating. What is my warrant for these claims? I cannot prove the nature of cosmic creativity, nor do I presume to know the will of God, however defined. My theology is not apologetic but confessional. It seeks not conversion but clarity. It is simply elaborated in the interest of serious conversation to determine if it has appeal. My theology is based on William Jones's *functional ultimacy,* which claims that while we are not ontologically ultimate—the supreme beings of creation—we are functionally ultimate. We must make these determinations for ourselves.

My ethics and economics call for an intuitive response to economic injustice, drawing on a vast religious tradition that, if I read it correctly, finds fault with conspicuous consumption in the face of desperate human need. It also draws on the American traditions of freedom, egalitarianism, and social contract (secular) and covenant (religious). It calls on our basic human sensibilities, which can be summarized in the term *reverence for life.* Since we cherish our own lives, we can safely assume that other similar creatures also cherish their lives. If our mission is to revere life, then our fate is caught up in that of our neighbors in an interdependent community. With this intellectual, theological, ethical framework for an intentional discussion of real issues that face real people, we turn to the realities of poverty in the midst of plenty.

Our economic lives today move too rapidly. It is time to pause and allow our religious sensibilities to digest, interpret, and address what has happened. There is a story of an African safari whose guides, after several hours of exhausting travel, suddenly sat down. When the American hunter asked what they were doing, the leader of the natives said, "We come so far, so fast. We must stop and let our souls catch up." So must we.

Distributive Injustice
in Practice

*Most middle-class Americans are class-passing by pretending to be
what they're not: well-off. They live in houses they can't afford,
drive cars they don't own, and wear clothes they've bought on
credit. Worst yet, toward the end of each pay period, many
use their charge cards to buy food. My term for their condition
is middle-class poverty. This late-20th-century phenomenon
has crippled the American soul.*

—Thandeka, *Unitarian Universalist World*

While the American economy has been inordinately successful in
production, it has been decidedly less successful in distribution. Poverty
exists in the midst of plenty and has become so much a part of the landscape that most Americans have become inured to its stark reality. It is
the new American apartheid. There are "dinners without appetites at
one end of the table and appetites without dinners at the other," in the
words of nineteenth-century Senator Charles Sumner.

Economist Paul Samuelson's familiar metaphor from his classic
text *Economics* aptly describes the growing divide that marks the American economy:

A glance at the income distribution in the U.S. shows how pointed is
the income pyramid and how broad is its base. "There's always
room at the top" is certainly true; this is so because it is hard to get
there, not easy. If we make an income pyramid out of a child's
blocks, with each layer portraying $1,000 of income, the peak would
be far higher than the Eiffel Tower, but almost all of us would be
within a yard of the ground.

This static imagery points to what has been described as the new American apartheid—a divided society in which the rich are getting richer, the poor are getting poorer, and the middle class is essentially stagnating. In Matthew 25:29, we read, "To those who have shall more be given, and to those who have not shall be taken away even what they have." That, I submit, is the description of first-century reality, not the prescription for a twenty-first-century Beloved Community.

The facts are sobering. Think of the national annual income as a pie (see Figure 1). The richest quintile (or 20 percent) of U.S. families gets nearly half the pie, and the second richest gets almost another fourth. That leaves just one-fourth of the pie for the remaining 60 percent of the population. Specifically, the poorest quintile survives on less than 4 percent of the pie, the second poorest gets less than 10 percent, and the middle quintile gets 15 percent. Also keep in mind that these figures do not include unearned income, typically enjoyed by the wealthy, which would greatly increase the disparity.

· The inequality among levels of family income declined from 1947 to 1980. But by 1984, the disparity had returned to the 1964 level—a reversal that has been dubbed "the Great U-Turn"—and it continued to grow from 1984 to 1999. Even more disturbing is the fact that this disparity increased during a time of unparalleled economic growth.

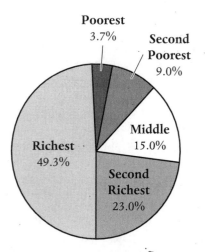

FIGURE 1   *Household Income Distribution by Quintile: 1999*

Source: Based on U.S. Census Bureau data, September 26, 2000.

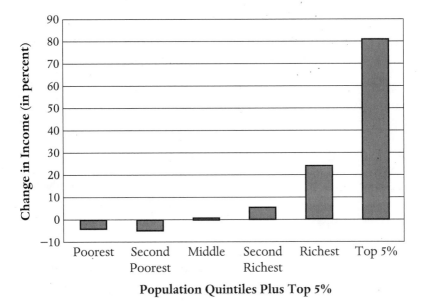

FIGURE 2   *Family Income Growth: 1981–1999*

Source: Based on U.S. Census Bureau data, October 6, 2000.

That growth was enjoyed, however, only by those individuals in the top income brackets (see Figure 2). From 1981 to 1999, the top 5 percent of the population saw just over an 80-percent increase in family income. The richest 20 percent of the population saw nearly a 25-percent increase in income, and the second richest saw a modest 5-percent increase. But again, the remaining 60 percent of the population did not fare so well: They experienced barely perceptible gains or even losses in income. Hence, the much-maligned reformist epithet—"The rich get richer and the poor get poorer"—is founded in fact.

Income inequality can be measured in several ways. The *Gini coefficient of income equality* is a technical measure widely utilized. When the coefficient G equals 0, it means that perfect income equality exists. For instance, each 10 percent of the population earns 10 percent of the total income, each 20 percent earns 20 percent, and so on. The higher the coefficient, the greater the inequality. Among U.S. households, the Gini coefficient increased from 0.376 in 1947 to 0.457 in 1999.

We can more easily measure inequality by examining shares of family income. According to a U.S. Census Bureau 2000 report

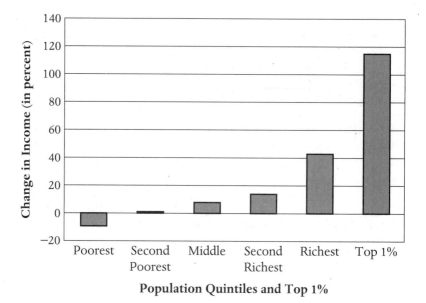

FIGURE 3   *Percentage Change in After-Tax Income: 1977–1999*

Source: Based on Congressional Budget Office data as interpreted
by the Center on Budget and Policy Priorities.

(adjusted for 1999 dollars), between 1977 and 1999, the after-tax income
(adjusted for inflation) of the poorest quintile of American families
actually declined by 9 percent whereas that of the richest quintile grew
by 15 percent (see Figure 3). But again, the greatest disparity is found in
examining the performance of the top 1 percent of American families:
The after-tax income of that group increased by 115 percent.

The long-term trend in income distribution shows increasing
inequality. The middle 60 percent of the U.S. population, which has a
mean (average) income between $29,482 and $68,000, has received a
declining share of "the pie" over the last thirty or so years—from 53.6
percent in 1970 to 47.6 percent in 1998. The mean annual income of the
poorest quintile of the population has barely changed (from $12,093 in
1970 to $12,526 in 1998), while the mean annual income of the richest
quintile has risen 63 percent (from $89,682 to $140,846). And once again,
the top 5 percent of the population has enjoyed tremendous gains: a 55-
percent increase in annual income (from $131,450 to $217,355).

The increase in income disparity illustrated by these figures is even more disturbing when considered in this context: The 1999 figures for the bottom three quintiles are the lowest percentages recorded since the U.S. Census Bureau began collecting such data in 1947, and the figures for the top two quintiles are the highest percentages recorded.

Figure 4 shows trends in the percentage of income received by each 20 percent (quintile) of the U.S. population in selected years from 1969 to 1999. In sum, only the top quintile saw an increase in the percentage of income received, from about 43 percent to nearly 50 percent. And of course, a gain by this top group meant varying degrees of losses by the four remaining lower groups.

These data do not include capital gains income, which accrue primarily to the affluent. If capital gains were included, the income of the top quintile would be substantially higher. According to a 1998 Internal Revenue Service (IRS) study, reported by the Center on Budget and Policy Priorities (September 4, 2000), 72 percent of capital gains

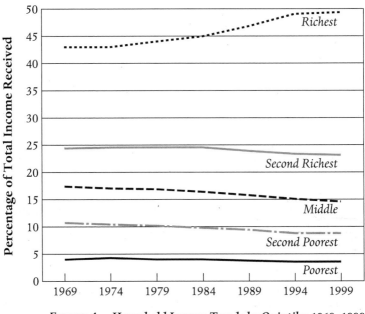

FIGURE 4   *Household Income Trends by Quintile: 1969–1999*

Source: Based on U.S. Census Bureau data, October 20, 2000.

income that year went to income tax filers with gross adjusted incomes of $200,000 or more. In addition, census data do not record earnings above $999,999, which means an individual who makes $5 million is recorded as making only $999,999. When considered in calculating personal income, both of these factors would increase the degree of income disparity.

Despite historic economic growth in the United States during the 1990s, the poverty level declined only slightly, from 13.3 percent in 1989 to 11.8 percent in 1999; the latter was the lowest rate since 1979. The actual number of people living in poverty declined from 34.5 million in 1998 to 32.3 million in 1999; this was still 2.1 million above the 1989 level, which was the last comparable period of economic expansion. The decline in poverty was concentrated in U.S. cities, where 1.8 million of the 2.2 million drop occurred.

DOES A RISING TIDE LIFT ALL BOATS?

This pattern of growing income inequality represents the largest transfer of wealth in human history—the transfer, of course, percolating up rather than trickling down. These figures tell an incontestable story: The United States is subject to the "iron law of maldistribution," i.e., income inequality is steadily increasing.

Thus, a rising tide does not seem to lift all boats. The yachts are riding high, to be sure, but the day-sailors are just keeping afloat. The rowboats, however, seem to have sprung leaks or been washed ashore. In short, the trickle-down theory is certainly damp, if not all wet.

Furthermore, as Frank Levy points out in *Dollars and Dreams,* measures of income inequality that come from census data may be understated, since "we know with certainty that significant proportions of doctors, lawyers, dentists and others in high-income occupations refuse to give income numbers to the census." And at the other end of the income continuum, while the share of income going to the poorest quintile varied within a range of 1 percent (or $1,500), that refers to all family income for a group that receives only about 5 percent of the total to begin with—a big difference to the persons involved.

Furthermore, according to the U.S. Department of Commerce, in a September 1998 press release, "An increase in the number of married women in the workforce contributed to a 150 percent increase in the real median income of married-couple families between 1947 and 1997." In other words, had two-earner families not become the norm in American society, income inequality would have been much greater over this period. Although women still earn far less than men do, the pattern is changing. But in 1999, the percentage of female-to-male earnings, which had been increasing, fell slightly from 73 percent to 72.3 percent.

In terms of actual dollar amounts, according to a September 2000 U.S. Census Bureau press briefing, the average (mean) annual income in 1999 for U.S. households followed a consistently inequitable pattern. The average annual income for the poorest quintile of U.S. households was $9,940, and that for the highest quintile was $135,401. For the top 5 percent, the average annual income was an astronomical $235,392.

An increase in income disparity also exists between rich and middle-class households. Data from the same census report of average (mean) annual income show that the third (or middle) quintile had an annual income of $40,879 and that for the fourth (or second-highest) quintile was $63,555. And while these income figures are respectable, they are approximately one-third and one-half, respectively, of the income level enjoyed by the top quintile ($135,401). Moreover, these figures are conservative, since they factor in only federal taxes, not state and local taxes, which tend to be regressive. These figures also do not include the value of in-kind benefits or transfer payments, but doing so would equalize the pattern by only 8 percent.

These data confirm the opinion of a number of observers who have noted a decline in the American middle class. In 1987, Frank Levy made a statement that is just as true today as it was then: "The middle of the income distribution is not getting much smaller, but it is growing a little poorer—despite more two-earner families." He also asked this question: "Are we living as well today as we did in 1973?" According to Levy, "The answer is no. We appear to be doing better, but this is only because we have borrowed against the future in ways that must eventually be repaid."

A September 1998 U.S. Census Bureau report corroborates Levy's words:

> Until recently, the income of each new generation was higher than the previous one. This trend reversed beginning with the generation of men who were 25–34 in 1987; their median income was lower than that of same-age men from the previous generation (20 years earlier).

Thus, the so-called baby boomers have, in many cases, become worse off than their parents. Economist John Miller, of Wheaton College, reports in a 2000 issue of *Dollars and Sense* that despite the longest economic expansion in U.S. history, "It took until 1998 for the expansion to add back the purchasing power workers lost in the relatively mild recession at the beginning of the decade."

Even more dramatic is the real decline in weekly wages that occurred from 1973 to 1998. According to data from the U.S. Bureau of Labor Statistics, real wages rose approximately 10 percent from 1967 to 1973, from $457 to $502. But over the next twenty years, real wages fell from $502 to a low point of $421 in 1993, increasing again just slightly to $442 in 1998.

The Reverend Galen Guengerich, of All Souls Church (Unitarian) in New York City, dramatizes the American income and wealth disparity in the opening of a 1998 Sunday morning sermon:

> Take a walk through the neighborhood around All Souls Church in Manhattan. You soon see the problem. The wealthiest census tract in New York City begins just seven blocks from All Souls; the average household income in that 12-block area is just over $300,000 per year. The poorest census tract begins only a few blocks farther away; the average household income in that area is about $5,000 per year. In the faces of the people you meet and the houses where they live, you see a city divided against itself, a painful and unsettling contrast between wealth and want, hope and despair, opportunity and oblivion. You see the difference, in other words, between the privileged and the impoverished.

OF CAMELS AND NEEDLES

Evidently, the castigation of the wealthy by Amos and Jesus and his followers has not discouraged the American pursuit of riches. The disparity in wealth is much more pronounced than that in income. Think of *income* as the annual influx of resources that provides at least the necessities of life, whereas *wealth* is a kind of surplus that provides further opportunities, prestige, status, political influence, and leisure. For the average family, wealth is more a safety net—a cushion—than a source of social and political power.

Edward Wolff examines this phenomenon in his book *Top Heavy: A Study of the Increasing Inequality of Wealth in America.* He shows that the richest quintile possesses nearly 85 percent of the total wealth, while the lowest quintile statistically has 0 percent. The wealth possessed by the other three quintiles totals only 15 percent, demonstrating a concentration far greater even than the concentration of income. The second-richest quintile has 11 percent of the wealth; the middle quintile, 4 percent; and the second-poorest, 1 percent. Whereas the top 1 percent have 13 percent of total income, they own 39 percent of total wealth. The bottom 80 percent of the population have only 15 percent of the wealth and 50 percent of the income.

. According to the Economic Policy Institute, as presented in Meredith Bagby's *Annual Report of the United States of America*, the wealthiest 1 percent of the population owned 40 percent of all economic assets in 1997, up from 19 percent in 1976. In their book *Shifting Fortunes: The Perils of the Growing American Wealth Gap*, Chuck Collins, Betsy Leondar-Wright, and Holly Sklar state that the top 5 percent of the American population now hold more than 60 percent of all household wealth. The next 9 percent have maintained about 30 percent of the wealth, and the bottom 90 percent have seen their share drop from 51 percent in 1976 to 29 percent in 1995.

The soaring stock market of the late 1990s was a major factor in this increase of wealth among the wealthy. The wealthiest 1 percent of Americans own nearly half (46 percent) of all publicly held stocks and just over half (54.2 percent) of public and private bonds; the next 9 percent own 44 percent of all stocks and 34.3 percent of bonds. Clearly, not much is left for the bottom 90 percent of the population to own: namely, 10 percent of stocks and 11.5 percent of bonds.

And even though the percentage of Americans who own stock has almost quintupled since 1952, about half (mostly through retirement plans) own only a small fraction of the stock. Nearly two-thirds of American families (59 percent) have more equity in their homes than in the market, according to the June 2000 report of the Joint Center for Housing Studies at Harvard University. We have witnessed a second Gilded Age.

According to *Forbes* magazine in 1998, there were 387 billionaires in the world. Richard Barnet and his colleagues at the Institute for Policy Studies, quoted by Martin Marty in *Context* in 1995, have calculated that the combined wealth of these people equals the income of the bottom 45 percent of the entire population of the world, or 2.5 billion people. Furthermore, the wealth of the super rich is expected to accelerate. The combined worth of those individuals with assets of more than $1 million was over $17.4 trillion. The wealth of the mega-rich was predicted to grow by 10 percent annually to reach a total of $23.1

trillion by the end of 2000. Europeans and North Americans account for 59 percent of the total worth.

To put this in a somewhat more human perspective, consider that the three richest officers of Microsoft Corporation have more assets— namely, about $140 billion—than the combined wealth of the forty-three least-developed nations in the world, whose total population is over 600 million. The United Nations Human Development Report of 1998 drew a similar conclusion in considering how to provide for people's basic needs:

> The additional cost of achieving and maintaining universal access to basic education for all, basic health care for all, reproductive health care for all women, adequate food for all and safe water and sanitation for all is roughly $40 billion a year. This is less than 4 percent of the combined wealth of the 225 richest people in the world. . . . The three richest people have assets that exceed the combined GDP of the 48 least developed countries.

In today's economy, there is no reasonable sense of proportion. In its 1997 development report, the United Nations pointed out that a handful of wealthy individuals had the combined personal resources to guarantee every poor person in the world clean water and basic education—for the next ten years! The cost of such a project would be $80 billion—less than the combined net worth of the seven richest persons in the world. These individuals have the means "to close the gap between the annual income of poor people and the minimum income at which they would no longer be poor."

In compiling its 1999 list of the 400 richest people in the United States, Forbes used $500 million as the minimum income criteria. Of these 400 elite individuals, 170 were billionaires. In 1999, there were just under 3 million households with a net worth of $1 million or more. The top 1 percent had a net worth of $2.5 million or more, and the top 10 percent with assets of $368,000 or more owned an estimated 68.3 percent of the nation's wealth.

The Forbes data have been analyzed in terms of a metaphor used by populist Jim Hightower in his book There's Nothing in the Middle of the Road but Yellow Stripes and Dead Armadillos. He describes Forbes magazine heir Steve Forbes: "He was born on third base and thought he hit a triple." Based on that remark, the advocacy group United for a Fair Economy took a look at the "Forbes 400," asked how these individuals came by their wealth, and published the results in a 1997 study,

"Born on Third Base," quoted in *Economic Apartheid in America,* by Chuck Collins:

> But how many of our wealthiest citizens actually started life in the batter's box and faced the pitcher? And how many started life on first, second or third base? How many were born crossing home plate and inherited their way directly onto the Forbes 400 list? . . . 30.1% started in the batter's box—includes individuals and families whose parents did not have great wealth or own a business with more than a few employees (H. Ross Perot was born of a horse trader and into a comfortable but by no means affluent family). 13.9% were born on first base—includes individuals who biographies showed signs of a wealthy or upper class background, but did not apparently have assets of more than $1 million. (Bill Gates' parents were comfortable professionals and he went to Harvard University, but quit for better prospects. He got a head start in life, but the success of his venture did not depend on substantial family money or assets). 5.75% were born on second base—members inherited a small company or wealth worth more than $1million, but less than $50 million. (Poultry magnate Frank Perdue inherited his father's egg farm and hatched millions in chickens). 6.85% were born on third base—includes people who inherited substantial wealth, in excess of $50 million, but not enough to qualify for members in the Forbes 400 (Kenneth Feld inherited Ringling Brothers Circus in 1982 when it was worth millions but took it to the big top); (born on Home Plate) J. Paul Getty, Jr. inherited the oil fortune from his father. David Rockefeller is the great grandson of Standard Oil founder John D. Rockefeller. . . . It is likely . . . that the analysis understates the number of Forbes 400 members who belong in the "Home Plate" and "Third Base" categories.

Perhaps nowhere is the increasing gap between the rich and the poor (and that between the rich and the middle class) as obvious as in the relationship between a Chief Executive Officer's (CEO's) pay and that of an average worker. In April 1999, *Business Week* released its forty-ninth annual executive pay "scorecard." The magazine reported that CEO pay (including salary, bonuses, long-term compensation, and exercised options) had increased 442 percent from 1990 to 1997. The article quoted the fictitious character Gordon Gekko in the film *Wall Street*: "Greed is good! Greed is right! Greed works! Greed will save the USA!"

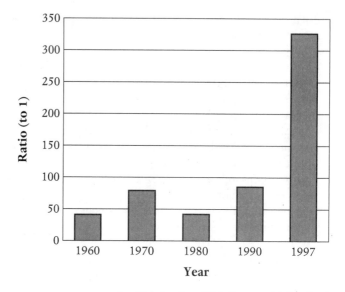

FIGURE 5   *CEO Pay as a Multiple of the Average Worker's Pay: 1997*

Source: Based on data from *Business Week* annual report on executive pay.

According to *Business Week*, the average top executive in a major American corporation made 326 times the pay of the average American manufacturing worker in 1997 (see Figure 5). This was about a fourfold increase since just 1990, when the average CEO made 85 times the salary of the average worker. And that figure had doubled since 1980.

In 1965, a CEO made forty-four times the average factory worker's salary. If factory workers had received comparable pay raises between 1980 and 1995, they would now be paid $90,000 a year. Minimum wage workers would be paid $39,000.

American CEOs are compensated far more generously than those in other industrial nations (see Figure 6). According to Mishel, Bernstein, and Schmitt in *The State of Working America*, CEOs in other industrial nations make around half of what American CEOs do. For instance, in 1997, the average CEO in France made 58 cents for each dollar paid to an American CEO—and the French were second to the Americans.

In *Wealth, Income and Equality*, Dutch economist Jan Pen develops a graphic metaphor to convey the extent of wealth disparity in West-

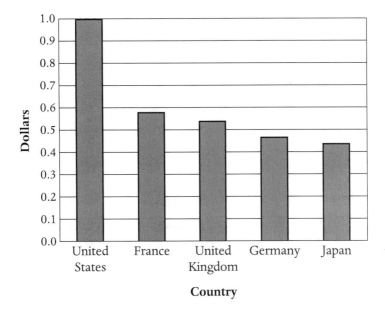

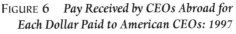

FIGURE 6   *Pay Received by CEOs Abroad for Each Dollar Paid to American CEOs: 1997*

Source: Based on data from Mishel et al., *The State of Working America: 1998–1999.*

ern democracies. He asks the reader to imagine a parade of people in which everyone's height is proportional to his or her individual wealth. Thus, a person of average wealth is represented by a person of average height. The parade begins with the smallest (the poorest) at the front, with the rich bringing up the rear in a one-hour parade. The first marchers are actually buried several feet beneath the ground, since they have negative net worth; that is, they owe more than they own. For approximately twenty minutes, a group of invisible marchers passes by; these individuals own no wealth. After half an hour, there are dwarfs, people about six inches tall, whose wealth comprises household furniture, a car, and perhaps a small savings account.

"But a surprise awaits us," writes Pen. "We keep on seeing dwarfs. Of course they gradually become a little taller, but it's a slow process." Only at about twelve minutes before the hour do we begin seeing people of average height, for more than three-quarters of the world's population have fewer assets than average. In the last few minutes, "giants loom up . . . a lawyer, not exceptionally successful, eighteen feet tall." In the last few seconds, there are people so tall we cannot even see their heads; these are the corporate managing directors, who are one hundred yards tall. Pen continues,

> The rear of the parade is brought up by a few participants who are measured in miles. . . . Their heads disappear into the clouds. . . . The last man, whose back we can see long after the parade has passed by, is John Paul Getty. . . . His height is inconceivable: at least ten miles; perhaps twice as much.

Up the Down Escalator

While the stock market has boomed and the economy has produced increasing numbers of millionaires and billionaires, it has also increased the number of people living in poverty. What is astonishing at the cusp of the millennium is that in the wake of the longest economic expansion in American history, poverty remains a pesky and persistent problem. What is equally disturbing is that the so-called poverty gap—the money needed to bring all people above the poverty line—has remained at $65 billion despite the *decrease* in poverty. Slightly fewer people are poor, but they are poorer.

There has been considerable controversy over the definition of *poverty*. The U.S. Census Bureau's poverty statistics are based on a *market basket* measure devised by Mollie Orshansky in 1965, which establishes a poverty threshold by multiplying the cash value of a minimally adequate diet by three. In 1982, the Census Bureau proposed a redefinition of poverty. Counting government food, housing, and medical assistance as income would have pushed many poor people above the official poverty level.

This long-standing attempt to redefine poverty down was bitterly attacked by the late social critic Michael Harrington as "statistical prestidigitation." In his essay "Solving Poverty with Statistics," he points out that if the income of the poor were so adjusted, then the poverty level and the income of those above it would also have to be adjusted in a comparable way. For example, if a single elderly person eligible for Medicaid and Medicare lived in New York State, the insurance value of this coverage, counted as income, would have been $6,336 in 1987, even if this person never used these programs. However, given that the poverty line in 1987 was $5,447, this person would not have been considered poor, even if he/she did not have a single dollar of other income to buy food and shelter. As summarized by Harrington, a "person who endures a long, miserable terminal illness can rise—statistically—into the middle class through the expensive process of dying."

Since the size of the market basket has not been adjusted to reflect increases in average consumption among other members of the population, the U.S. Census Bureau poverty rate represents an absolute measure of economic deprivation. The National Academy of Sciences has suggested a new approach to measuring poverty. After an in-depth, three-year study of the method of measuring poverty, *Measuring Poverty: A New Approach,* issued in 1995, an expert panel proposed a new measure that would redefine the poverty line based on the cost of food, clothing, and shelter, with a small amount added for other expenses. These figures would be updated annually and adjusted from place to place based on regional differences in the cost of housing. The basic criterion was that part of the family's income that was available for consumption, including not only cash income but also noncash government benefits the family received (except for health insurance). It would also deduct from income those mandatory expenses that reduced income for consumption: income and payroll taxes, work expenses including child care, out-of-pocket payments for medical care, and child support payments made to another household. As Kathryn Porter of the Center on Budget and Policy Priorities pointed out in 1997, "When all these adjustments are taken into account, the number of people counted as poor would likely increase."

The U.S. Census Bureau has established poverty levels for families of different sizes (see Table 1). Whereas the poverty level for a family

Family Size	Poverty Level
1	$8,350
2	$11,250
3	$14,150
4	$17,050
5	$19,950
6	$22,850
7	$25,750
8	$28,650

TABLE 1   *Poverty Levels for Families of Different Sizes*

Source: Federal Register, February 15, 2000.

of one is $8,350, that for a family of four is $17,050, or only *double* the single-person amount.

Another intriguing way of measuring poverty is to use British economist Peter Townsend's *deprivation index,* which is spelled out in the April 11, 1982, *New York Times* in the article "Poverty Is More than Being Flat Broke." The deprivation index is not a purely statistical measurement, which Townsend believes measures only physical needs. People, he contends, are primarily social creatures, and the twelve criteria he suggests are about relationships with fellow citizens. People's deprivation, he argues, increases exponentially with a decline in income, and there is a low point at which people "can no longer operate as citizens or as neighbors." Translated into cash terms, Townsend finds his deprivation index about 150 percent of the basic benefit level in Great Britain. We might think of poverty not as the possession of little, but as the nonpossession of much.

The essential point for our purposes, however, is that all these measures reflect the same pattern over the past thirty years. As shown in Figure 7, the *number* of people living in poverty declined sharply from 1960 to the mid 1970s, from 40 to 25 million people. It then increased sharply in the early 1980s, reaching 33 million in 1985, and then dropped again just slightly to 32.3 million in 1999. Interestingly, in terms of *percentages,* the poverty level has remained stubbornly consistent—around 12 percent—since 1970, despite economic ups and downs.

And among those persons living in poverty, the number who are under 50 percent, under 100 percent, or under 150 percent of the poverty line is disturbing. Another 20 to 30 million people can be said to be living in want while still more are quite vulnerable to poverty. For instance, the death or sickness of a family member or the loss of a job could plunge them below the poverty line.

An examination of poverty levels among different age groups reveals several more trends. Poverty among people who are elderly (over sixty-five) has been reduced in the United States, from nearly 25 percent in 1970 to around 10 percent in 1999. The poverty rate among children under eighteen has increased, however, from 15 percent in 1970 to around 20 percent in 1995 and then falling slightly to 17 percent in 1999.

The real unknown in our current understanding of poverty is the impact of the Personal Responsibility and Work Opportunity Reconciliation Act of 1996. We know that the numbers of people on welfare are down nationwide, but little information seems available about what is happening to those people who have left welfare programs. Some clearly are getting jobs and leaving welfare (though it is debatable

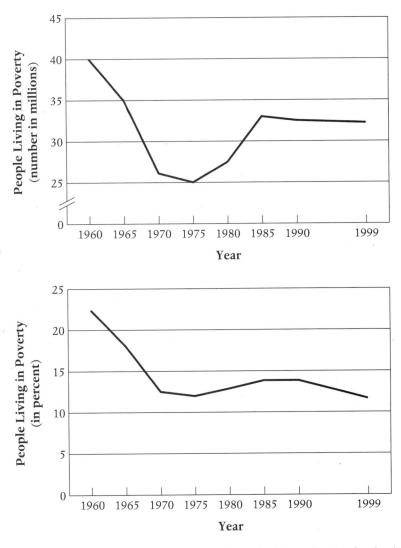

FIGURE 7   *Poverty in the United States by Number (top)*
and Percentage (bottom): 1960–1999

Source: Based on U.S. Census Bureau data, October 24, 2000.

whether their standard of living is better or worse). We do not know
the fates of the others, and no one dares forecast what will happen
when the five-year cumulative lifetime limits for receiving welfare payments begin to expire in 2002.

Also worth noting in this summary of American poverty is the comparison of income distribution and poverty levels in the United States with those of other industrialized democracies. The United States ranks embarrassingly low on this measure of equitable income distribution and comparative poverty rates. "The Luxembourg Income Study," as reported in the Fall 1995 issue of *Too Much* (published by United for a Fair Economy), compared the world's thirteen top industrial nations in terms of the incomes of the richest and poorest segments of their populations (see Figure 8). In the United States, the richest 10 percent made nearly six times the income of the poorest 10 percent. Not surprisingly, this was the greatest disparity among all the nations studied.

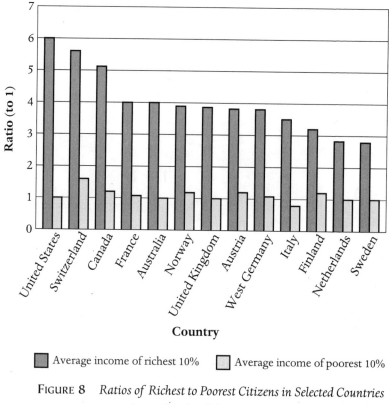

■ Average income of richest 10%   ▫ Average income of poorest 10%

FIGURE 8   *Ratios of Richest to Poorest Citizens in Selected Countries*
Source: Based on "The Luxembourg Income Study," 1995.

Mishel et al., in *The State of Working America,* reveal that the United States has far and away the highest poverty rate among industrialized democracies. Comparative poverty rates for children are even more striking. These authors find that the poverty rate among American children was 25 percent (1994 data). The nation with the next-highest poverty rate was Great Britain (19 percent; 1991 data), followed by Australia and Canada (both 15 percent; 1989 and 1991 data, respectively). The Scandinavian countries of Finland and Sweden shared the lowest poverty rate among children: 3 percent (1991 and 1992 data, respectively). Even American adults are much more likely to experience poverty than their counterparts in the other five countries mentioned. Thus, the world's richest nation has a poor record in distributing its wealth broadly among the populace.

WHO ARE THE POOR?

Who are the poor? To begin, the poor are not always the same group of people. In the 1960s, the so-called culture of poverty concept depicted the poor in biblical terms: "The poor you always have with you." Today, there are more poor people, to be sure, but they are not necessarily those who have been poor before.

Peter Gottschalk and Shelden Danziger, in *The Inequality Paradox,* find that in the short term, workers in the bottom quintile of the income distribution experienced very little income mobility. In the early 1990s, 75 percent of those individuals who started in the lowest quintile of family income were still in that group one year later. Analysis of a longer period of time revealed improved income mobility; even after more than twenty years, however, almost half of the poorest workers remained at the bottom of U.S. income distribution. Forty-seven percent of those who were in the lowest quintile in 1968 were still there twenty-three years later, and another 25 percent had only moved up to the second quintile of income distribution.

Income mobility actually declined between the late 1960s and the early 1990s. In 1968–1969, the percentage of people remaining in the same quintile was 62.7 percent. In 1990–1991, the percentage was 65.9 percent. Thus, the probability of staying in the same quintile of the income distribution "pie" has increased, a circumstance that exacerbates rather than ameliorates income inequality.

In 2000, the U.S. Census Bureau reported that less than 50 percent of those people living below the poverty line in the 1980s remained there for more than a year. Virtually all of the poor individuals who were employed full time rose above the poverty level. But as Meredith Bagby points out in her 1998 *Annual Report of the United States of America,* "There is evidence that income mobility may be slowing. One study at the University of Michigan found that before 1980, more than a third of low-income families moved up to the middle class over a five-year period. After 1980, only a quarter did."

In demographic terms, who are the 32.3 million poor people in the United States? Along lines of race and ethnicity, the U.S. Census Bureau reports that, in 1999, the poverty rate among black people was 23.6 percent (or 8.4 million individuals); for Hispanics, 22.8 percent (7.4 million); for Asians and Pacific Islanders, 10.7 percent (1.2 million); for American Indians and Alaska Natives, 25.9 percent (700,000); and for non-Hispanic white people, 7.7 percent (14.9 million).

Demographic details of sex and marital status also prove interesting. In 1998, there were 10.6 million nonelderly poor women compared to 6.9 nonelderly poor men. Nearly 11 million of the poor lived in married-couple families. Over 3.8 million of the poor lived in female-headed families, and nearly 30 percent of female-headed families lived in poverty. The increase in the number of poor women has been called the *feminization of poverty.*

However, the fastest-growing group in poverty is the so-called working poor. According to a March 2000 report from the Center on Budget and Policy Priorities, "Income and Poverty Trends 1998," some 9 million people worked—over 6 million less than full time and nearly 3 million full time—and still lived below the poverty line. In 1979, the first year that data on working poor were available, 12.1 percent of full-time, year-round workers earned too little to lift a family of four out of poverty. By 1995, the figure was 16.1 percent. The percentage of the poverty level for a family of three with a full-time minimum-wage worker in 1968 was 111 percent, and in 1996, it was 82 percent. The minimum wage was increased to $5.15 per hour in 1996, but with the 1996 welfare reform law and restrictions of other government benefits for the working poor, it seems that working even full time is no longer a sure route out of poverty. The minimum wage would have to be increased to over eight dollars an hour to lift families above the 1999 poverty line.

A September 2000 press release from the U.S. Department of Commerce reveals alarming statistics. While nearly one in seven Americans is poor, almost 17 percent of American children under 18 are poor, a total of 12.1 million, down from the recent peak of 22.7 in 1993 and the lowest number since 1979. In terms of race and ethnicity, 36.7 percent of all black children, 34.4 percent of all Hispanic children, and 15.1 percent of all white children are considered poor. Children make up 39 percent of the poor but only 26 percent of the total population. The poverty rate for children under six living with a female head of household with no male present was 50.3 percent.

As summed up by Senator Daniel Patrick Moynihan in the Children's Defense Fund's "Analysis of the Fiscal Year 1987 Federal Budget and Children," "The United States in the 1980s may be the first society in history in which children are distinctly worse off than adults." Unfortunately, his words are as true today as they were then.

In its 1999 *Kids Count Data Book,* the Annie E. Casey Foundation finds that 5.6 million children—more than one-third of all kids living in poverty—belonged to working-poor families, reflecting a 30-percent increase between 1989 and 1994. Surprisingly, only 14 percent of all children in working-poor families were born to teenage mothers. About half of the families were two-parent households in which at least one parent worked all year. Some 7.6 percent of all children live in working-poor families in which one parent works most of the year but does not earn above the poverty level.

Clearly, the vaunted American work ethic is still more rhetorical than real. Work does not necessarily lift one out of poverty.

MISLEADING ECONOMIC INDICATORS

Writing in the *Saturday Review* in 1968, political economist A. A. Berle analyzes the limitations of replacing the Gross National Product (GNP) with the Gross Domestic Product (GDP) as an economic measure, thus developing a value system with which to critique GNP as the definitive measure of the economy:

1. People are better off alive than dead.
2. People are better off healthy than sick.
3. People are better off literate than illiterate.
4. People are better off adequately housed than inadequately housed.
5. People are better off in beautiful than in ugly cities and towns.
6. People are better off if they have opportunity for enjoyment—music, literature, drama and the arts.
7. Education above the elementary level should be as nearly universal as possible through secondary schools, and higher education as widely diffused as practicable.
8. Development of science and the arts should be available to all.
9. Leisure and access to green country should be a human experience available to everyone.

Another set of economic data comes from the federal government when it periodically publishes its *leading economic indicators,* six quantitative measurements that purport to indicate how the economy will fare six months down the road—namely, claims for unemployment insurance, weekly hours worked, new factory orders, money supply, and consumer expectations. The market and the public at large place a great deal of stock in these figures. The stock market, in particular, lives and dies, experiences its bulls and bears, on the basis of these leading (or perhaps misleading) economic indicators.

These figures are supposed to evaluate economic performance, but they tell only part of the story and can therefore be misleading. They measure things and numbers, not human welfare. They do not point to the quality of the people's lives, even though people's livelihoods hang in the balance when policies are based on these indicators. The fact is that the high priests of economic management and their catechism give us figures that do not necessarily reflect the social and economic well-being of most Americans.

The Gross Domestic Product (GDP), for instance, essentially counts money changing hands. It includes not only life-enhancing activities, such as medical research and educational programs, but also activities that indicate a lowered quality of life, such as polluting and clean-up activities, crime-fighting devices, lawyers' fees from divorces, and much more. Even activities and products with negative purposes and effects point in the direction of a greater and grander economy. The economy produces "illth" as well as wealth, to quote nineteenth-century writer John Ruskin. Are we on the deck of wealth on a sinking ship of illth? Are we living in a statistical Potemkin village that hides the economy we are actually experiencing?

The GDP has no evaluative mechanism to determine whether a given financial transaction brings good or ill. Rather, the GDP is like a calculating machine that can add but not subtract. If we consider only the fact that money is changing hands, the economic hero is the terminal cancer patient going through a divorce; the happiest event is a hurricane or earthquake; and the most desirable habitat is a Superfund clean-up site. These misleading economic indicators add up all the transactions that occur without distinguishing income from expenses, assets from liabilities.

Even depleting natural resources enhances the GDP by portraying the depletion of capital as current income. It treats the earth like a business being liquidated. Pollution shows up twice in the GDP: first when it is produced and then again when it is cleaned up. A car-locking device called the Club added $100 million to the GDP in just one year. The O. J. Simpson trial added $200 million to the GDP, and Prozac adds billions each year. Thus, the current view of economics focuses on what can be measured. If something cannot be measured, it will not be counted.

In addition to GDP, there are other means of measuring economic health. Among them is the *GPI,* or *Genuine Progress Indicator,* as elaborated in *The Social Health of the Nation,* by Marc Miringoff and Marque-Luisa Miringoff. These authors survey the incidence rates of twenty societal factors: infant mortality, high school dropouts, poverty among the elderly, life expectancy, child abuse, child poverty, teenage suicide, health care coverage, average weekly wages, inequality, violent crime, teenage drug use, teenage births, alcohol-related traffic fatalities, affordable housing, and unemployment, among others. Upon analysis, the Miringoffs' data revealed an upward curve in the GPI from the 1950s to the 1970s but then a gradual decline of roughly 45 percent. Interestingly, the GDP continued an upward trend, showing no decline.

Given this discrepancy, I submit that the GPI is a better indicator of economic health than the GDP. Traditional leading economic indicators do not necessarily reflect actual human well-being. Social health indicators, however, provide a much more useful snapshot of how people are doing.

We can also understand inequality and poverty in terms of the human suffering they produce. Economic inequity is not merely an academic concept but a reality that causes real human pain and loss. It is especially important to see the trends in human suffering as a function of increasing inequality.

HEALTH CARE

Health care is one vital indicator of the social well-being of a nation. The United States spends far more per capita on health care than any other nation on Earth: 14 percent of the GDP (or $3,724 per person), which is $1,000 more than the next highest-ranking country, Switzerland, spends. Unfortunately, the outcomes for Americans do not reflect that investment.

A World Health Organization report of June 2000 ranks the United States twenty-fourth in the average citizen's healthy life expectancy at birth, which was 70 years; Japan was first at 74.5 years. And while the richest Americans are the world's healthiest people, the poorest 2.5 percent of Americans are some of the unhealthiest. Poor

Americans have a healthy life expectancy that is characteristic of individuals in sub-Saharan Africa in the 1950s. Due to this disparity among its population, the United States ranks thirty-second in the degree of variation in life expectancy. A sizable percentage of Americans die prematurely.

Traditionally high rates of tobacco-related disease along with high homicide and injury rates also lowered the American score. The United States ranked only fifteenth on an overall index designed to measure a range of health goals, including the population's overall health, health inequalities, how well the health care system performs, how well people of varying income levels are served, and how costs are distributed. The United States' efficiency score was 84 percent, behind virtually all of the countries in Western Europe as well as Israel, Morocco, Chile, Saudi Arabia, and Costa Rica.

The method of financing health care in the United States is cited as one reason it lags behind other developed nations. According to the U.S. Census Bureau report of September 2000, 42.6 million Americans did not have health insurance coverage in 1999 (15.5 percent of the population), up from 31 million (12.9 percent) in 1987 but also the first drop since 1987. The number of uninsured children was 10 million (13.9 percent), down from 11.1 million (15.4 percent) in 1998. Some 19.7 percent of all children and 57.8 percent of poor children are covered by Medicaid. Both the number and percentage of uninsured poor remained unchanged from 1998 to 1999: 10.4 million (32.4 percent).

Since the 1996 welfare law went into effect, many families who are eligible for Medicaid mistakenly think they are no longer covered and therefore are not enrolled. And many other families lack health insurance because many employers fail to provide it. In 1999, 62.8 percent of workers were covered by their employers, up only slightly from 62 percent in 1998.

According to the 1997 National Survey on Health Insurance, conducted by the Kaiser Family Foundation of California and New York's Commonwealth Fund, 52 million working-age adults, or roughly one-third of the workforce, have no health insurance or recently experienced a gap in coverage. Some 59 percent of adults in families with annual incomes of less than $20,000 are uninsured, and in families with annual incomes of between $20,000 and $35,000 (the median family income), the rate is 31 percent. An estimated 51 percent of all uninsured adults reported that they do not have insurance because they cannot afford to pay for it themselves.

The Annie E. Casey Foundation, in its *1999 Kids Count Data Book,* reports that the infant mortality rate for children born into poor families in the United States was 13.5 deaths per thousand live births—more than 50 percent higher than that for children born into families with incomes above the poverty line (8.3 deaths per one thousand live births). Moreover, the Children's Defense Fund (CDF) reports in a 2000 press release that over the past forty years, the United States has fallen from sixth place to a tie for last place in infant mortality among twenty industrialized nations. And this downward trend shows no signs of slackening, according to CDF. Many experts attribute this decline to cutbacks in funding for prenatal and maternal health care.

In a 1986 lecture, Arnold Relman, former editor of the *New England Journal of Medicine,* noted that quality health care for the poor is declining steadily. The health care provided by the free market does not provide equity. Instead, the United States is moving toward a three-tiered health system: (1) deluxe, private service provided by for-profit hospitals and private physicians for the upper class, (2) standard, economy service and prepaid basic insurance plans for the middle class, and (3) inferior, inadequate service for the people who have no health insurance and insufficient funds to secure adequate care on their own.

Legislative efforts to ensure Americans of access to quality health care have failed consistently. Conservatives warned us that enactment of the Clinton Health Plan of 1993 would lead to increasing health care costs and a bureaucratic mess. And they claimed that a single-payer system would be even more expensive and disrupt the doctor/patient relationship. The irony is that these dire results have indeed occurred, but not for the reasons we were warned about. Instead, the culprit has been the competitive marketplace. Health Maintenance Organizations, or HMOs, have not turned out to be our salvation.

A friend of mine, a doctor, told me a story that illustrates what is happening. He attended a meeting of medical personnel in which they were addressed by a local hospital administrator. My friend was struck by the rhetoric used by the official, who talked not so much of patient care and service delivery as of the bottom line, of market share and "winning" in the competition for patients. This administrator apparently sounded more like the CEO of a NYSE or NASDAQ company than a health care executive.

Rene Reixach, a lawyer specializing in health care who addressed a March 2000 conference sponsored by Interfaith Impact of New York

State, spoke of why health care in Rochester, New York, his city, was once so successful:

> The ethos of this town has been: There are community goods that ought to be supported. [But now] business leadership in this community—and [Eastman] Kodak is certainly in the forefront—concluded that there ought to be a more competitive health care system. You know, "Competition is good, and we ought to have more of it." And that's become the standard business mantra.

"Why not let the market decide?" he was asked.

> Because historically, when you have an unfettered market in health care, you just end up with enormous duplication and expense. Each facility or entrepreneurial provider . . . says, "Gee, this is an opportunity. I want one of these." But the result of that is you end up with one of everything. In Grand Rapids, Michigan, they had three hospitals, and each one had a helicopter. Grand Rapids isn't that big a place."

He cited the competition between F. F. Thompson Hospital in Canandaigua and the Clifton Springs Hospital, which are 12 miles apart, each acquiring expensive radiation oncology services, an illustration of health care Balkanization. When asked "How do the Canadians do it?" Reixach replied,

> They have a different culture. People don't jaywalk in Canada. If there's a stoplight, you're supposed to stop and wait for it to turn. We don't believe that. While our Declaration of Independence touts "life, liberty and the pursuit of happiness," a very individualistic goal, Canada's founding document affirms a communal emphasis on "peace, order and good government."

In a 1992 issue of *Public Citizen*, Marilyn Dunlop reports that a Canadian man was handed an invoice showing the cost of his care when he was discharged from the hospital; it was significant enough to be treated as a news event, covered throughout Canada. His bill for $2,269—covering a two-day stay in a Toronto hospital for investigation of an irregular heartbeat—was stamped "Do not remit. Paid on your behalf by the citizens of Canada."

Across the border in the United States, however, health care is treated more and more as a commodity and less and less as a basic human right of citizenship. Is health care a commodity? Is everything for sale? Or is health care a human right?

HOUSING AND HOMELESSNESS

We might ask the same about housing: How many Americans are homeless? There is no easy answer to this question because the question itself is misleading. In most cases, homelessness is a temporary situation. The more appropriate question is: How many people experience homelessness at some time?

There are two basic methods of measuring homelessness: (1) *point-in-time counts,* which reflect the number of people who are homeless on a particular day or week, and (2) *period prevalence counts,* indicating the number of people who are homeless over a given period of time. The point-in-time approach suggests that on any given day, there are between 500,000 and 600,000 homeless people in the United States. According to a 1998 study by the National Coalition for the Homeless using the period prevalence approach, about 1.2 to 2 million people experience homelessness during one year. An estimated 12 million adults have been homeless, in the most literal sense, at some point in their lives. Furthermore, data indicate a dramatic increase in homelessness over the past two decades.

Who are the homeless? The typical homeless person in the United States is a child, and the typical homeless family is a single, twenty-year-old mother with two children under the age of six. Thus, children and families make up the fastest-growing segment of the homeless population. According to a 1997 study by the U.S. Conference of Mayors, children under eighteen made up 25 percent of the urban homeless population. Emancipated teens comprised 4 percent of that population, and persons between thirty-one and fifty comprised 51 percent. The homeless population was 56 percent African American, 29 percent Caucasian, 10 percent Hispanic, 2 percent American Indian, and 1 percent Asian American. Over the last decade, the group in which homelessness increased the most was families with children, who comprised about 40 percent of the homeless population. Families in general comprised 36 percent of the homeless population. Single men comprised 47 percent and single women, 14 percent.

A 1990 Ford Foundation study finds that 50 percent of homeless women and children were fleeing abuse and that 40 percent of homeless men had served in the armed services. The U.S. Conference of Mayors study also finds that a significant number of urban homeless were veterans (22 percent). A 1996 survey by Paul Kroegel, "The Causes of Homelessness," indicates that 20 to 25 percent of the single adult homeless population suffer from some form of severe and persistent mental illness. In 1995, the Bureau of Primary Health Care reported that 22 percent of the people who are homeless were diagnosed with substance abuse disorders.

Why are so many people in the United States homeless? One of the major causes is the growing shortage of affordable rental housing and simultaneous increases in poverty and near poverty. According to the U.S. Department of Housing and Urban Development (HUD), in its 1999 study "Waiting in Vain: An Update on the American Rental Housing Crisis," housing consumes an inordinate amount of the typical poor family's income. More than half of the poor renter households spent over 50 percent of their income for housing. A disproportionate number of these people are particularly vulnerable: 1.5 million are elderly, 4.5 million are children, and more than 1.1 million are adults with disabilities.

An estimated 1 million Americans are on waiting lists for public housing in forty cities. And the decrease in affordable housing has only been compounded by declining government support for such programs. In April 1999, the U.S. Department of Housing and Urban Development reported, "Despite 6 years of unprecedented economic growth, worst case housing needs remain at or near the all-time high of 5.3 million households." Equally disturbing is the fact that contracts of Section 8 rental housing subsidies are expiring and many landlords are opting not to renew because they can make more money in the private market, setting the stage for an even more serious housing shortage.

The problem has been further exacerbated by the decline in public assistance brought on by welfare reform legislation, the Personal Responsibility and Work Opportunity Reconciliation Act of 1996. The program known as Aid to Families with Dependent Children (AFDC) has been replaced with a block grant program called Temporary Assistance to Needy Families (TANF). Current TANF grants are below the poverty level in every state and in most states, below 75 percent of the poverty level. General Assistance (GA) to individuals in need also has been reduced or eliminated in most states, despite evidence that the availability of GA reduces homelessness. In addition, the 1996 legislation denied Supplemental Security Income (SSI) eligibility to both legal and undocumented immigrants, leaving them more vulnerable to homelessness. Tracy L. Kaufman, in a study for the National Low Income Housing Coalition called "Out of Reach: Rental Housing at What Cost?" notes that the entire maximum TANF grant in 49 states and 357 metropolitan areas does not fully cover the fair market rent for a two-bedroom apartment. In 14 states and 69 metropolitan areas, the entire maximum SSI grant does not cover the fair market rent for a one-bedroom apartment.

The greatest irony in the American housing crisis is that the single-largest federal housing assistance program is the entitlement that allows homeowners to deduct their mortgage interest from their income for tax purposes. For every dollar spent on low-income housing programs, the federal government loses four dollars to housing-related tax expenditures—a total of $82 billion in 1999 alone. And understandably, the benefactors in this arrangement are households in the top quintile of income distribution, most earning more than $125,000 annually.

In sum, government assistance to the middle- and upper-income populations, provided through tax breaks buried in the internal revenue code, has been far greater than public expenditures to house the poor. Yet the latter, more visible programs have borne the brunt of public opposition. Once again, public policy is shamefully regressive.

HUNGER IN AMERICA

In 1985, the Physicians Task Force on Hunger in America, of the Harvard University School of Public Health, contended that hunger in the United States was on the rise: "The problem of hunger in the United States is now more widespread and serious than at any time in the last ten to fifteen years." Furthermore, the task force declared that the cause of this rapid spread was the weakening of programs that had virtually ended hunger in the previous decade: "Hunger has returned to our nation primarily due to governmental failure." The report also cited a number of supporting studies. During the Reagan administration (1980–1988), the Presidential Commission on Hunger denied the possibility of measuring hunger and became the lone dissenting voice in the increasing conviction that hunger in the United States is rampant.

A 1987 update of the Harvard report indicated 20 million Americans were hungry, especially infants, the elderly, and blue-collar workers diverted into the service sector. Larry Brown, chair of the Physicians' Task Force, says, "Economic growth has not reduced hunger in any significant way because of the nature of that growth. The economic pie has gotten bigger, but the unevenness of that growth leaves millions falling further behind." In 1993, Second Harvest, a food distribution group, estimated that 25 million Americans suffered from hunger, 50 percent more than in 1985, according to the Center on Hunger, Poverty and Nutrition Policy at Tufts University.

The turn of the century saw little change. Despite an economic boom of nearly a decade, a 1998 report by the Tufts Center estimates that nearly 35 million Americans live in hungry or "food insecure" households. Working families comprise a growing percentage of food bank customers, but the majority are still destitute seniors on fixed incomes, single mothers, and people with disabilities and diseases who cannot support themselves. One volunteer, a probation officer, said, "A lot of cases I deal with in court are kids who steal because they're hungry."

A 1997 study by the U.S. Conference of Mayors finds hunger and homelessness on the rise for the thirteenth consecutive year and predicts that the situation will worsen as more poor families are denied welfare. The demand for food increased by 16 percent, the largest increase in five years. According to the report, one in five persons seeking food were turned away last year. The problem of hunger was especially evident among families with children. Nearly 60 percent of the hungry live with their families, and nearly 40 percent of the people seeking food aid were working.

In a 2000 U.S. Census Bureau/U.S. Department of Agriculture study, the Food Research and Action Center (FRAC) reports that 31 million Americans—12 million children and 19 million adults—"still suffer from hunger or live on the edge of hunger." Even though that figure is down by 3.5 million from 1995, it is a disappointingly modest decrease, considering the economy's growth. FRAC concluded that "while many families are moving from welfare to work, their earnings are low and often they do not receive the food stamps for which they are eligible, leaving parents and children as vulnerable or more vulnerable to food insecurity than before."

According to Sharon Daly of Catholic Charities USA, as quoted in a 1997 issue of USA Today, "Agencies and parishes are having to turn people away. The shelves are bare." The situation of one family, as reported in the same issue, illustrates the hunger predicament:

Michelle Lenesky, 5, was helping her mother, Lisa, sort through the tomatoes at a food bank run by the Rapture Church in Lothian, Maryland, less than an hour south of the nation's capital. It was a drizzly day, and Lisa looked nervously at the washed-out sky. Her husband is a construction worker, pouring concrete for roads and buildings and bridges. It's a tough, dirty job. And when the weather is bad, there is no work, and no check. "You never know," she said. "He might come home today because it's raining." Lisa works, too, as a part-time waitress, serving meals for a caterer, but when she's away she worries about Michelle and her 10-year-old brother: "You can't leave other people with kids these days. Know what I mean?" When all goes well, the Leneskys get by. But if one thing goes wrong—a sick child, a broken truck, even a worn-out pair of shoes—their fragile budget can crack open. "The kids," says Lisa, "always need something." Lisa visits the food bank most Fridays, stocking up on staples like bread and lettuce and tomatoes, and that cuts her food bill at the market by about $60 a week. With that additional cash, Lisa can afford a few extras—new clothes for the children, a birthday present for her sister. "It's real important," she says of her weekly trips to the church. "It helps a lot."

Hunger among the elderly is a national disgrace. Some 6.5 million either cannot afford food or must choose, at times, between buying food and other necessities, according to a 2000 issue of the *American Association of Retired Persons Bulletin*. The Older Americans Act theoretically provides support services, but the funding has not kept pace with need. Conventional wisdom says private charity will fill the gap. As stated by Heritage Foundation senior fellow Dan Mitchell, "If it's worth doing, the private sector can do it." The private sector is not doing it in many places, unfortunately. This anecdote from the March 27–29, 2000, *USA Today* illustrates the problem:

Randall Mueck's job at San Francisco's meal clearinghouse is to decide who will get food and who will wait. In mid-January, 411 of the city's homebound elderly were on Mueck's waiting list, 100 more than a few months earlier. All qualify for a hot, home-delivered meal under the federal Older Americans Act, but there isn't enough money to feed everyone. Seniors who move up fastest are those in the custody of adult protective services, the dying and the very old. Twenty-five percent of the people asking for food are over 90. "I try to think of all 411 and fit someone in accordingly," Mueck explains. "Age is going to bump somebody way up."

CRIME AND PUNISHMENT

While the causal connection between poverty and criminal behavior is widely debated, a few issues seem clear. According to an April 1998 story from the Associated Press, the United States has the highest number of incarcerated individuals in the industrial world. By mid 1997, 567,079 people were lodged in the nation's 3,328 local jails, up 43 percent from 395,554 in mid 1989.

The U.S. Justice Department's Bureau of Justice Statistics conducted a study about what sorts of lives jail inmates led before incarceration, and the results were disturbing, to say the least. Forty-eight percent of female inmates and 13 percent of male inmates had been sexually abused at least once in their lives. Some 27 percent of the women and 3 percent of the men said the abuse had included rape. Large numbers of the inmates grew up in single-parent homes or were children of dissolute parents. Thirty-six percent say they had been unemployed before their most recent arrest. During the month before being arrested, 20 percent of the inmates had been seeking work, 16 percent had not been seeking work, and almost half reported earning less than $600 a month. More than half of the inmates report having used illegal drugs in the month before committing their crimes, which was up from 44 percent in 1989. Eric E. Sterling, of the Criminal Justice Policy Foundation, responded to the study in a 1998 press release:

> It's a cycle we could break, but it involves some expense. As a society, we haven't put our resources there. . . . Poverty often means that kids in trouble are not able to get therapy or counseling. Not to blame their parents, but there is a lack of resources and a social indifference to the problems of poor kids.

In his book *The Rich Get Richer and the Poor Get Prison,* criminologist Jeffrey H. Reiman states that it is anomalous for the richest nation in history to have such a huge incarcerated population. He points to the small but powerful portion of the population who have convinced the middle class that crime is primarily a function of moral culpability, not social conditions. Meanwhile, the so-called prison industrial complex is one of the major growth industries in the American economy. In fact, communities with high rates of unemployment vie for the privilege of being the site for a new prison, which brings high-paying construction jobs followed by civil service positions that typically provide good wages and benefits. The American prison industry is big business.

Public Schooling

Jonathan Kozol's books *Death at an Early Age* and *Savage Inequalities* are searing portraits of the price American public schoolchildren pay for living in poverty. In a 1995 interview with Elizabeth Mehren in the *Los Angeles Times,* Kozol speaks of the poverty-stricken people he encountered:

> They are strong in their faith of God, they believe in the decency of others, and they are not yet soiled by the knowledge that this country doesn't like them. I don't think the problem is that we have insufficient information or cleverness to solve the problem of children in poverty. The problem is that we lack the moral and theological will to act on what we know.

I had occasion to walk to work recently when my car was disabled. It proved a fortuitous event, for on my way, I met Walter, an eleven-year-old African American boy who lives in the city. He was heading for Rochester's School Number One, which was on my route to the church. We walked together and talked about the World Series, but eager for more substantive conversation, I asked him what he wanted to be when he grew up. His response was "a professional basketball player." Since very few individuals can earn a living that way, I asked what might he want to do if he could not play basketball. Without a pause he said, "a professional football player." Our conversation continued, but I couldn't help but wonder what would become of Walter. And given what I know of the statistics of growing up black and male in the United States, I was disturbed at the prospect.

One November morning, I spent time at Abraham Lincoln School, PS 22, which was built in 1916. A high-security fence surrounds the parking lot, and drug paraphernalia and spent cartridges can occasionally be found on the grounds of this aged building. Any visitor to the school will see a sign announcing free breakfast programs for students, which serves as a reminder that 60 percent of them live in poverty. I have learned other details of these students' lives from people who volunteer at the school. One volunteer told me of how she had befriended a child and visited his home one summer day, only to be shocked by the abject poverty she found. She had become very fond of this boy and was deeply disappointed when in his teens, he had a run-in with the law. Another volunteer told of a twelve-year-old, street-smart, man/child who had been taken to the police station in handcuffs after the arrest of his brother and sister. A second boy had been apprehended during a stereo shop burglary, caught carrying out a bag of cookies. A young girl had told a volunteer that she hoped she would get pregnant like her fifteen-year-old big sister, whom she admired, as this would keep her safe from their angry father, who had recently been released from prison.

These youths' stories constitute a microcosm of life in impoverished urban America. Money is not all that is needed to remedy these "savage inequalities." Politicians say that a nation that "sees money as a cure for all that ails it is a society in peril" and urge people to volunteer. Nonetheless, money is an essential part of the solution. Head Start, as well other government-sponsored programs, consistently finds that recent education expenditures have produced positive results. Why, then, are children's programs so often called "budget busters"? In a 1991 issue of the *Washington Post National Weekly Edition*, secretary of education Lamar Alexander described the Reagan administration's America 2000 education plan as "a bold, comprehensive and long-term strategy." But two pages later in the written plan, a footnote says, "No additional amounts are added to the total Department of Education budget to fund America 2000."

UNEMPLOYMENT, UNDEREMPLOYMENT, AND LOWER WAGES

Former secretary of labor William E. Brock was prophetic when he said in the *Washington Post National Weekly Edition* in 1988, "The leaning-down of American business over the last six years has been very substantial. There are an awful lot of companies that were very fat, and this has been good for them. Tough on people, but we have more competitive companies as a result."

Labor market opportunities for large segments of the workforce have eroded, and the availability of public assistance has decreased. The official unemployment rate is relatively low—around 4 percent—but what about the underemployment rate, which includes people who are unemployed, those who are involuntarily part-time employed, and those who have given up looking for employment? According to a study by the Economic Policy Institute, cited in Mishel et al.'s *The State of Working America*, the underemployment rate stood at 8.9 percent in 1997. Among those considered underemployed were 4 million involuntary part-time workers, 1.1 million marginally attached workers, and 0.3 million who are frustrated and have given up looking for work. The underemployment rate is higher than the unemployment rate due chiefly to these factors: an increase in joblessness among relatively unskilled and uneducated workers, labor market transformations (such as deindustrialization), declining rates of unionization, and the globalization of the economy.

In addition to those who are underemployed, many Americans now work in nonstandard work arrangements—for example, as independent contractors, temporary employment workers, day laborers, and regular part-time workers. The Economic Policy Institute estimates that nearly one-third of the American workforce is employed in these nonstandard work arrangements, all of which offer lower wages, fewer benefits, and less job security than traditional arrangements.

What's more, the falling official unemployment rate does not distinguish between kinds of workers. Mishel et al. point out that while unemployment figures are at near-record lows, they do not tell the full story. When involuntary part-timers, discouraged workers, and others only marginally attached to the workforce are factored in, the employment picture is much less optimistic. Less than three-quarters of all workers are regular, full-time employees. And the number of temporary workers, who usually do not receive benefits, has more than doubled since 1989.

Another factor in keeping poverty high is declining or stagnating wages. Despite the recent increase in the minimum wage, it is still 15 percent below its average purchasing power when adjusted for inflation. Consider this sobering example: A worker making minimum wage would have to work eighty-six hours a week to afford a two-bedroom apartment that would cost only 30 percent of his/her income, which is the standard the federal government uses to define affordable housing. Moreover, 40 percent of American households with "worst-case housing needs"—that is, those that pay over half their income in rent, live in severely substandard housing, or both—include at least one working person. A 1997 study of twenty-nine U.S. cities finds that one in five homeless persons is employed. Thus, working is no guarantee of adequate housing.

Not only has the minimum wage not kept pace with inflation, it has not kept pace with productivity. Despite occasional increases, the minimum wage has steadily lost ground over the years. While fewer and fewer people rely upon it, the minimum wage helps to shore up wages in general. Whereas the minimum wage in 1970 would almost lift a family of four out of poverty, now it is barely 65 percent of the poverty level for a family of the same size.

Even while the stock market has boomed, real wages have fallen. In all the euphoria about the vigorous and growing U.S. economy, people have not looked hard enough at the figures. The reality belies a false optimism. There is a separation of classes in this country, as identified by Robert Reich in *Tales of a New America*. He describes the "fortunate fifth," an elite group that deals in computerized information transfer and enjoys unprecedented wealth. In contrast, the Americans at the bottom of the pay scale watch their jobs being exported and are forced to take low-paying service jobs to feed their families.

GOVERNMENT POLICIES

Government policies account for a substantial degree of the income inequality and resultant poverty in the United States. Although the effective tax rate for a middle-class family of four has changed very little since 1980, effective tax rates for the wealthy have increased and the poor have been hit with regressive taxes at the local, state, and federal levels. Income taxes are moderately progressive, but regressive taxes hurt the poor. And as income goes up, the percentage paid in payroll taxes declines with a very regressive effect.

Despite the fact that the federal government does not tax poor people into poverty and even enhances their income with the Earned Income Tax Credit, state governments are not so generous. According to a Center for Budget and Policy Priorities report, "State Income Tax Burdens on Low Income Families in 1999," twenty states continue to levy income taxes on poor families of four, eighteen continue to levy income taxes on poor families of three, and thirty-two states still tax near-poor individuals.

With the passage of welfare reform legislation in 1996, the federal government is now spending less on income security for the poor. And the individual states, who are now charged with welfare reform, have mixed records. In comparison to other Western nations, the United States spends the least on income redistribution. Once again, public policy that is generally not known to or understood by the public penalizes the working poor and undermines economic incentives for them to move out of poverty.

CAUSES OF INCREASING INEQUALITY AND POVERTY

At this juncture, it should be clear that the increasing inequality of income among Americans is indisputable. Furthermore, the human suffering that results from this inequality is palpable. The causes are clear: the decrease in government transfer payments (especially in the wake of 1996 welfare reform); regressive taxation policies, which hit the poor disproportionately hard (in particular, the payroll tax); the stagnant or declining wage scale; the increased incidence of so-called tiered jobs (low-paying entry and service jobs next to high-paying, high-tech jobs); and globalization, which tends to export manufacturing jobs to other nations.

The sharp reductions in poverty in the 1960s resulted from a combination of economic growth, declining unemployment, and large increases in transfers. The stable poverty rate in the 1970s can be attributed to several offsetting factors: Growth slowed and unemployment rose while cash and in-kind transfers decreased. After 1979, declining economic growth, rising unemployment, and lower real transfer levels all contributed to greater poverty. And despite the economic recovery of the 1990s, nearly two-thirds of Americans have made little economic progress—some have even lost ground.

Inequality Abstracted and Personified

The realities of poverty cannot be fully described by statistics. Numbers cannot portray the pain, fear, anger, and sorrow that come with sickness, hunger, joblessness, and homelessness. While we cannot precisely quantify the personal suffering of millions, poverty oppresses morally and spiritually as well as physically. The beautiful theory of economic recovery and the myth of good times for all persist in spite of the brutal facts.

However, the harsh realities have not escaped PBS-TV producer Bill Moyers. In his series *Surviving the Good Times,* he takes us inside the lives of two working-class families in Milwaukee. Eric Alterman, writing in the April 24, 2000, issue of *The Nation,* describes the effect of these stories:

> In the life stories of the Neumann and Stanley families, viewers see layoffs, lost benefits, hospitalizations and family fights, as well as a mother watching the first child on either side of her family graduate from high school. . . . the program's painful irony was that these families embody exactly the values to which our political culture pretends to pay tribute. Tony Neumann loses his union job when Briggs and Stratton picks up and moves south to chase cheap labor. We observe the way his loss of self-respect eats away at his ability to be a good father and husband. The family turns to their church for

spiritual support. When Tony does get a job, he is so deep in debt that he has to accept work on the night shift, creating another kind of family burden. His teenage daughter complains that she sees her father for one hour a day, when he is "crabby and irritable" and no help with her homework. His wife becomes an armored-truck driver, and they grumble that they never sleep together anymore: "It stinks." Across town, Claude Stanley's son joins the Navy in the hope of going to college afterward, while the family is stuck with usurious credit-card fees as the only way to pay his older brother's first-semester tuition. These people's burdens increase every time Alan Greenspan raises interest rates just enough to keep Cisco soaring. Talk about invisible. . . . This may sound like a joke, but when was the last time you heard a TV analyst—even a PBS-TV analyst—comment on a Fed rate rise from the perspective of the Stanleys and the Neumanns?

Having seen distributive injustice in action and having noted the human suffering that stems from income inequality and poverty, it remains for us to develop a religious rationale for greater equity. The "brutal facts" are writ large across the nation, but few stop to read.

Perhaps that is how it should be. In a competitive society, there are "winners" and there are "losers." Have the "losers" rights other than to compete in the contest? Can it then be argued that we can properly use such a morally laden term as *economic rights*? Is there a moral imperative that equates economic rights with human rights?

Human Rights and Economic Rights

We have come to a clear realization that true individual freedom cannot exist without economic security and independence. "Necessitous men are not free men." People who are hungry or out of a job are the stuff of which dictatorships are made. In our day these economic truths have become accepted as self-evident. We have accepted, so to speak, a second Bill of Rights under which a new basis of security and prosperity can be established for all—regardless of station, race or creed.

—Franklin D. Roosevelt, State of the Union, 1944

Roosevelt included in his "second Bill of Rights"

+ The right to a useful and remunerative job in the industries or shops or farms or mines of the nation;

+ The right to earn enough to provide adequate food and clothing and recreation;

+ The right of every farmer to raise and sell his products at a return which will give him and his family a decent living;

+ The right of every businessman, large and small, to trade in an atmosphere of freedom from unfair competition and domination by monopolies at home and abroad;

+ The right of every family to a decent home;

+ The right to adequate medical care and the opportunity to achieve and enjoy good health;

+ The right to adequate protection from the economic fears of old age, sickness, accident, and unemployment;
+ The right to a good education. . . .

> All of these rights spell security. . . . America's own rightful place in the world depends in large part upon how fully these and similar rights have been carried into practice for our citizens. . . . I ask the Congress to explore the means for implementing this economic bill of rights—for it is definitely the responsibility of the Congress so to do.

President Roosevelt's concern with basic human rights was echoed by his wife, Eleanor Roosevelt, in her work with the United Nations. She discovered that what were discussed as "the rights of men" were not necessarily applicable to women in some parts of the world.

The phrase *rights of man,* used especially during the American and French Revolutions, had itself replaced the term *natural rights,* which were based upon natural law. This latter concept was founded on the assumption that moral law is as inherent in the God-given natural process as are the laws of nature.

According to the *Westminster Dictionary of Christian Ethics, human rights* can be defined as follows:

> A set of justifiable or legitimate claims with at least six features: (1) they impose duties of performance or forbearance upon all appropriately situated human beings, including governments; (2) they are possessed equally by all human beings regardless of laws, customs, or agreements; (3) they are of basic importance to human life; (4) they are properly sanctionable and enforceable upon default by legal means; (5) they have special presumptive weight in constraining human action; and (6) they include a certain number that are considered inalienable, indefeasible, and unforfeitable.

Human rights are thus moral claims that individuals make on other individuals or governments. These rights are prelegal and prepolitical. Civil rights, on the other hand, are given by the political order and can be repealed by that order. They have the force of law. The enactment of civil rights laws for African Americans in the 1960s is the clearest example of this. There was a time, obviously, when black Americans did not have civil rights. This is not the case with *human rights,* however, which transcend law. Until recently, black people in South Africa did not have civil rights, but they have always had human rights. In fact, the latter was the justification for seeking the former.

Thus, human rights are derived not from political institutions but from moral law. They are not repealable. They are, to use Jefferson's phrase, "inalienable rights." In the Jewish and Christian traditions, human rights are given by God; no human action can contravene this divine mandate. In more philosophical traditions, human rights come from the inherent worth of people as ends, not means.

Human rights are, by their very nature, universal—valid for all people in all places and in all times. They are not dependent on race, religion, class, nationality, or any other status other than common humanity. Human rights belong to people simply by virtue of their being human. They are not *earned* but *given.* Human dignity is their source—that is, they derive from human nature, from which no one or nothing may detract. That human dignity may derive from theological or philosophical sources. Human rights exist without reference to a particular religious tradition, as debate over theological justification may detract from the very essence of human rights. They are under-girded by a universalistic ethic that regards human beings as having paramount importance.

Human nature is here understood as finite freedom in community. Human beings share the finitude of the animal kingdom as biological creatures (that is, their existential nature as limited creatures). But human beings are also spiritual creatures with the freedom to actualize their potentialities as members of a community (that is, their essential nature as spiritual beings). Humans have basic needs as physical beings, the fulfillment of which is essential not only for their survival but also to provide the conditions in which they may flourish as spiritual beings. Abraham Maslow's *hierarchy of needs,* ranging from survival (food, shel-ter, clothing, etc.) to self-actualization (spiritual), is instructive here.

Furthermore, human rights have to do with what is right. They are normative for human behavior. They create a moral imperative to be sought in human society, establishing ethical guideposts by which civil rights, laws, and individual and social actions are to be judged. Human rights are a standard of measurement. This normative nature of human rights implies human duty to behave in such ways as to actu-alize human rights in social conditions. Rights imply duties on the parts of persons and states. Rights not only presume mutuality in a society of members, they require it. Human rights place the burden of proof on those who would deny them.

HUMAN RIGHTS IN AN ECONOMIC CONTEXT

> It is a paradox that the nation that did so much to articulate and cod-
> ify human rights in its foundation documents has so consistently
> resisted the effective functioning of an international framework to
> protect these principles and values.

The *nation* referred to in this quote is the United States. This less-than-
flattering description came from the October 1998 Amnesty International report on the fiftieth anniversary of the Universal Declaration of
Human Rights.

How do we Americans see our country and its place in the world?
Americans have a rich human rights tradition; we see ourselves as the
biblical "city set on a hill." Some would say, however, that it is hypocritical for us to champion political and civil rights while we do not yet
recognize the economic rights embedded in the Declaration of Independence—that is, the rights to enjoy an adequate standard of living,
to be educated, to join a trade union, to have rest and leisure. Personal
liberty cannot exist without economic security. Someone who is hungry or homeless cannot be truly free. Political and economic rights are
indivisible. You cannot have one without the other.

Is it a human rights violation that in the United States—the wealthiest nation in the history of the world—more than 33 million people
live in poverty, nearly half of them children? Is it a violation of human
rights when millions of Americans are hungry and homeless and when
nearly 43 million have no health insurance? Is it an affront to basic
human rights that one in eight Americans is denied the basic human
right to a decent standard of living? Clearly, economic rights do not
have a prominent place in the American pantheon of values.

In *Equality and Efficiency: The Big Tradeoff,* economist Arthur Okun
writes,

> In short, the domain of rights is full of infringement on the calculus
> of economic efficiency. . . . Society refused to turn itself into a giant
> vending machine that delivers anything and everything in return for
> the proper number of coins. When members of my profession some-
> times lose sight of this principle, they invite the nastiest definition of
> an economist: the person who knows the price of everything and the
> value of nothing. Society needs to keep the market in its place. The
> domain of rights is part of the checks and balances on the market
> designed to preserve values that are not denominated in dollars.

It remains to be seen, however, if *economic rights* are *human rights* in the sense described by Okun. The issue was brought to the fore with the 1948 United Nations (UN) Declaration of Human Rights. That document, along with UN covenants for political and economic rights, has sparked wide controversy. Articles 3 through 20 essentially address what are generally referred to as political and civil rights—the so-called *liberty rights,* which is the term I will use. Articles 22 through 27 essentially address social and economic rights, which I will call *welfare rights.*

Critics of the UN declaration make a rather sharp distinction between liberty rights and welfare rights. The welfare rights section includes references to social security, an adequate standard of living, medical care, rest, leisure, and even periodic holidays with pay. Critics charge that international politics were responsible for adding these economic rights to the more traditional political and civil rights, presumably inserted under pressure from the then-Soviet Union and its allies. They could hardly claim to uphold the civil and political rights but could claim to ensure economic rights—social security, medical services, and guaranteed education.

These same critics suggest that it is impossible to move from philosophizing about human rights to taking action to ensure them. By reducing human rights to the status of ideals, the whole effort to protect them will be undermined. A *right,* critics claim, is not an *ideal.* Rather, a right closely resembles a duty, and the first test of both is practicability. The liberty rights are not difficult to institute and protect. It is not costly to protect one's rights to life, liberty, and property. These rights can be protected by legislation, since they are primarily rights against government interference in the activities of citizens. However, the case is quite different when it comes to welfare rights. For a government to enforce them would require enormous resources, which most nations do not have and have no means of acquiring.

A second criticism of economic rights as human rights is the test of *paramount importance.* Okun suggests that it would be our duty to rescue a drowning boy (if we were there at the time of the accident); however, we would have no comparable duty to give Christmas presents to all the children in his neighborhood. Being entitled to periodic vacations with pay is a claim that fails the test of paramount importance; although it may be desirable, it does not have the status of a right and thus confuses the issue.

Thus, critics distinguish between two interpretations of the term *ideal:* something that one should aim for but that cannot be immediately realized versus something that can be and should be respected here and now. Economic and social rights can be acquired, but they are not human rights that inhere in the person.

While I appreciate the critique, I find fault first with the test of paramount importance and practicability. Granted, the right to enjoy holidays with pay may be an example of an economic right that is not of *paramount* importance, but that does not prove that no economic right is important. I maintain that the rights to a nutritionally adequate diet, to work in decent and healthy conditions, and to financial security in the event of disability are *all* claims of paramount importance.

It may be true that some human rights claims merely reflect the preferences of individuals or groups, but these claims can be distinguished from basic human needs, which are far more important to human dignity than holidays with pay. The test of paramount importance should be applied to those goods that a person cannot be deprived of without experiencing serious harm to his or her well-being or personal dignity.

Second, the *practicability* argument derives from Immanuel Kant's dictum that "Ought implies can." This view contends that there are *prima facie* rights that, when all things are considered, can be overridden by conditions. This does not, however, take away from the moral urgency to try to provide such rights. Moreover, there is the time element, making a claim on the possibility of providing these human rights only in the present. Do we not have the responsibility to shape a social order that will implement rights at some point in the future? This sense of possibility adds a moral urgency that is missing from the views of those who believe economic rights are simply impractical.

Third, critics of economic rights do not consider the variety of contexts in which the question of possibility may be asked. The issue is whether to accept the conditions of scarcity as given, as built into the nature of things, and state that economic claims must yield because they cannot be satisfied.

The adequacy of legislation to meet liberty rights claims is a fourth response to the critic's position. Any American looking at U.S. history should be able to see that it is not easy to legislate rights of any kind. Our painful history of slavery ought to demonstrate that point. Protecting basic human rights—civil and political, or economic—is a costly business. Economic and social claims should be used as a guide to morally significant social policies and as a moral norm for assessing their results. To be sure, guaranteeing certain economic benefits may be limited at all stages of a society's growth, but we should recognize the prior moral claim so they can be met as conditions allow. Moral urgency will then be preserved.

In an issue of *Nomos* dedicated to human rights, Susan Moller Okin finds the dichotomy between liberty and welfare rights a false one for three reasons:

1. It is generally presumed that while liberty rights require only action against the state by law to preserve personal liberty, welfare rights require positive and costly state action. Okin suggests that liberty rights also require positive and costly state action in a whole system of law enforcement, courts, and prisons along with a foreign policy and national defense.

2. People need protection not only from government intrusion but also from the harm done by the growth of economic institutions. Thus, in order to protect human rights, economic as well as political action is required. Some sense of economic rights is part and parcel of this.

3. No human rights can be regarded exceptionless all the time, and the problem of practicability can affect both kinds of rights. Okin further argues that the right to subsistence (welfare rights) is more universal than the right to privacy (liberty rights). Some rights, she claims, are prerequisite for the enjoyment of others. "It is surely unlikely that people would choose to starve or to be constantly exposed to physical danger rather than to be denied the right to speak freely, to own property, or to be educated."

Exceptions must be allowed for both welfare rights and liberty rights based on certain conditions. For example, it is difficult to ensure welfare rights in a condition of scarcity and perhaps impossible to allow the liberty of free speech to someone yelling "Fire!" in a crowded theater. There is also a lack of resources for both kinds of rights. Welfare rights do not fail because they cannot be realized in every case; even so, they do not cease to be rights because one can only "strive to ensure" meeting them, in the language of the Universal Declaration of Human Rights.

Okin also contrasts the classic *liberal equality of opportunity* with *social welfare substantive equality*. The notion of liberal equality of opportunity sees freedom based on equal liberty, with emphasis on the freedom of persons to be left alone to use their economic resources as they see fit. Conversely, the idea of social welfare substantive equality understands freedom to be denied to those who without sufficient resources to maintain even basic well-being have no capacity to exercise such freedom.

The relationship between liberty and welfare rights is complicated. Consider the examples of two South American nations, Chile and Venezuela. Marxist Salvador Allende was democratically elected president of Chile in 1970. While some of his socialist reforms were popular, the nation's economy was deteriorating. Following the overthrow of the Allende government by dictator Augusto Pinochet (with covert American help) and the installation of a free-market approach, the country was in economic shambles and a repressive military dictatorship held power until 1990. In contrast to Chile, Venezuela has had a formal democracy and the highest per capita income in Latin America, but it has paid little attention to meeting basic human needs.

A basic strategy for human needs does not address income redistribution only but also a direct enhancement of the quality of life of people living in poverty. This enhancement should be met more through governmental services than through private income. Without this specific targeting, basic human needs will go unmet and inequality will continue to promote the national security state. The moral claim of economic rights as human rights is dramatized in this claim: The right of peasants to eat supersedes the right of elites to have exotic vacations.

ECONOMIC RIGHTS AND POLITICAL RIGHTS

Political and economic rights cannot be dichotomized. Human rights provide some minimal protection for people who are helpless, giving the poor a means of escaping some of the forces that would otherwise harm them. Economic human rights specify the line no one is allowed to sink beneath—the point where basic life begins. They constitute a minimal demand on the rest of humanity and must be satisfied before other rights can be enjoyed.

There is a distinction between *having* and *enjoying* a right. One may have a right—such as the freedom to associate—but one needs to have voluntary associations in order to enjoy that right. Freedom of mobility is essential, but without the means to move, it is quite academic. It is comparable to providing people with meal tickets but not food.

In *The Politics of Freedom*, political scientist C. W. Cassinelli argues that a democratic government and a strong, broadly based middle class are essential to one another. To ensure the health of this form of polity, it is necessary to bring those individuals who remain underprivileged into the middle-class standard of living and political outlook. According to Cassinelli, "Domestic stability depends upon the belief of lower strata that they can advance to a moderate level of material well-being and social acceptance." The interdependence of liberty rights and welfare rights can be summarized in these words: "In the long run, liberty and welfare are absolutely dependent upon each other, for when the government is representative both are present, and when the government is not representative both are absent."

The American experiment has addressed a wide range of issues, but it has been most ambivalent on that of economic rights (that is, welfare rights). In the American tradition, human identity has been strongly related to one's work status. In tracing the religious roots of human rights in the United States, one finds no revealed set of economic rights, despite the sentiment so eloquently presented in Franklin Roosevelt's speech. The elevation of Adam Smith's "hidden hand" to the equivalent of providence cuts off American economics from what is human and what is entailed in providing for human rights in the economic sphere.

In the beginning of his book on human rights, *Creeds, Society and Human Rights*, theologian Max Stackhouse suggests that modern intellectual history has sought to root basic human rights not in religion, philosophy, politics, or law but in very empirical biophysical needs, "what is necessary for biophysical survival." Stackhouse asserts that "material needs are holy—they are what makes humans whole and they are inviolable."

Economic rights have had a hard time in American history. In fact, only recently (and reluctantly) has the United States begun to entertain some semblance of economic rights. Attempts to provide for income security (e.g., unemployment insurance, food assistance, pensions) made little headway before World War I. It was difficult to find an approach to social protection that was compatible with the American stress on individualism and *laissez-faire*. Providing worker's compensation was the first measure, as it was easy to identify people as victims of injury and thus entitled to income assistance.

Veterans were among the next group to receive social protection. Economic historian Gaston V. Rimlinger was prompted to write on this topic in the Fall 1983 issue of *Daedalus:* "It is intriguing to ponder why the nation was prepared to be quite generous to those who had served in uniform, yet was willing to disregard the often much greater needs of other citizens; why, in other words, the patronage state was legitimate but not the welfare state."

In contrast to the redistributive model adopted by the Scandinavian countries in the post–World War I period, the United States tried to minimize redistribution. The right to benefits in the Scandinavian nations was an expression of social solidarity, whereas in the United States, everything was based on a *quid pro quo* approach. Namely, benefits were based on what Rimlinger calls a "contributory contractual relationship. For political and ideological reasons, the planners sought to design a social security system that interfered as little as possible with free market allocation."

The American system dealt more with the faults of the market system than with trying to provide people with a guaranteed standard of living as a matter of right. Thus, the American system provided a random right to income but not necessarily for the people who most needed it. Welfare in the United States has almost always been means tested (available only to those with incomes below a certain minimum) rather than available by virtue of one's citizenship. This means-testing did help to smooth some of the harsher edges of the market but reduced economic inequality only marginally. In place of an inherited class society, we have created our own class society out of the rough machinations of the market, in which freedom is primary and equality distinctly secondary.

ECONOMIC RIGHTS AS A SUBCATEGORY OF HUMAN RIGHTS

I contend that economic rights (welfare rights) are a subcategory of human rights. Liberty rights and welfare rights cannot be easily dichotomized. In fact, there is a considerable interdependence between them. On the one hand, a hungry person cannot be a free person in that being hungry puts him/her at a disadvantage in serving as a citizen in a democratic state. It is the height of hypocrisy to tell the poor that although they are starving, they are free. On the other hand, political freedom is necessary for citizens to advocate for their basic human needs as part of the human rights due in a democratic society.

The American ethos, shaped predominantly by the Protestant ethic, has long emphasized civil and political rights at the expense of economic rights. It has stressed formal political freedom at the expense of substantial economic rights, prompting the late Whitney Young, President of the Urban League, to say of the post–civil rights era that black people now had a "fistful of rights and empty stomachs."

In his book *Equality and Efficiency*, economist Arthur Okun began to sketch out the meaning of welfare rights in the American setting in discussing the right to survival:

> The case for a right to survival is compelling. The assurance of dignity for every member of the society requires a right to decent existence—to some minimum standard of nutrition, health care, and other essentials of life. Starvation and dignity do not mix well. The principle that the market should not legislate life and death is a cliche. I do not know anyone today who would disagree, in principle, that every person, regardless of merit or ability to pay, should receive medical care and food in the face of serious illness or malnutrition. Attitudes about this have changed dramatically during the past century.

Okun finds this consensus has not been written into U.S. statute books, however. Americans are still somewhat ambivalent about the issue of providing welfare rights. Yet what Okun suggests seems minimal. Moreover, he makes no mention of other human rights listed in the UN declaration: a right to work, just and favorable working conditions and protection against unemployment, equal pay for equal work, just compensation, rest and leisure, basic education, and participation in the cultural life of the community. In an affluent country, there is a "civilizing surplus" beyond the subsistence minimum, and this surplus makes possible this full range of welfare rights to all U.S. citizens. The issue is entitlement.

To What Are We Entitled?

In the Middle Ages, St. Thomas Aquinas wrote about a "just wage," which was not determined by the machinations of the market but by a considered judgment that looked to the good of the worker and of society as a whole. In practical terms, this was a wage that would be sufficient for the worker to maintain self and family. We might call that the *living wage*. It is an entitlement worth considering.

Entitlements are commonly understood as public sector payments to people that do not represent contractual compensation for goods or services. Examples include Social Security, Medicare, Medicaid, food stamps, unemployment compensation, veterans' benefits, farm aid, federal pension systems, and what is pejoratively known as welfare. In addition, we probably should include as entitlements tax expenditures (which are unearned in the normal meaning of that word) that go to specified groups of people. People receive these entitlements because of characteristics such as age, income, and other identifiable conditions.

When entitlements are debated at the highest levels of government, business, labor, and religion, some interesting conflicts emerge. For example, in March 1995, *Washington Post* columnist David Broder found Senator Phil Gramm's opposition to entitlements for the poor disingenuous. Some time before, Gramm had appeared on *Meet the Press* and stated, "We have gone too far in creating an entitlement society." Broder noted that without entitlements, the senator would have lived a much different life. He was born in a military base hospital in Fort Benning, Georgia, where his father lived on a veteran's disability pension—an early entitlement program. He went to the University of Georgia, where his tuition and expenses were paid by the War Orphans Act, another entitlement sponsored by the very senator Gramm replaced. His graduate work in economics was paid for by the National Defense Education Act. Gramm then taught at Texas A&M, a state-supported school, until he became a member of Congress. Broder concluded, "Maybe he'll go all the way to the White House. A presidential pension would certainly round out his life of warning against government handouts."

Former New York Representative Rick Lazio once suggested that all Americans who receive housing subsidies should be required to perform eight hours of community service a month to "remind people to give of themselves." One wonders why he would limit this noble opportunity to poor people living in public housing. By far, the greatest beneficiaries of federal housing programs are those middle-class and wealthy taxpayers who deduct the interest on mortgage payments from their income taxes. Of this $162-billion entitlement, about half goes to the richest 5 percent of Americans, according to the National Low Income Housing Coalition, as reported in a 2000 issue of *Dollars and Sense.*

Others have suggested making a public service requirement directly proportional to the *amount* of benefits someone receives. Should this happen, many people would likely be surprised at just who would be performing compulsory service. It would be interesting to observe big-business CEOs cleaning up highways or tutoring students in inner-city schools.

Meanwhile, during the 2000 presidential campaign, George W. Bush chided the Republican Party for stressing wealth at the expense of tackling social ills. In one speech, he accused House Republicans of trying to "balance the budget on the backs of the poor" by delaying payments to the working poor under the earned-income tax credit. "There are human problems that persist in the shadow of affluence. . . . Prosperity alone is simply materialism." Writing in the *New York Times* on October 6, 1999, Bush said, "Too often, on social issues, my party has painted an image of America slouching toward Gomorrah. . . . Too often, my party has confused the need for limited government with a disdain for government itself."

Other surprising voices have weighed in on the entitlement controversy, usually in the context of proposing to end welfare as we know it. The conservative English journal *The Economist* reminds us, in its January 11, 1997, issue that "more than 85% of [U.S.] social welfare programs go to middle and upper classes, both young and old." Food stamps and housing vouchers did lift some 27 million Americans out of poverty in 1995. Again, from *The Economist,* "In a society as rich as America's it is no wonder that a welfare state that spends almost 9 out of every 10 dollars on the prosperous does not find enough for the needy."

And then there is billionaire Donald Trump. Early in the 2000 presidential campaign, when Trump was testing the waters as a candidate, he made the interesting proposal that the federal government should levy a 14.25-percent tax on wealth to raise $5.7 trillion, thereby erasing the national debt, rescuing Social Security, and slashing taxes for the middle class. Doing so would have increased his personal tax bill by at least $725 million, given his net worth of $5 billion.

Some may call such a measure confiscatory and economically dangerous, but it is as intriguing as the proposal made by Ralph Nader in a 1998 statement to the Associated Press. He called for Bill Gates, Warren Buffett, and other wealthy Americans "to sponsor, plan, and lead a conference of billionaires and multibillionaires on the subject of National and Global Wealth Disparities and What to Do about Them." (I expect this will happen only when our nation's people and their leaders have a revelation more powerful than that of Moses before the burning bush or Paul on the road to Damascus, more enlightening that Buddha beneath the Bo Tree or Mohammed receiving the Koran from the angel Gabriel.)

And so we return to the question: To what are we entitled, in terms of the material blessings of this life? It is far from an abstract philosophical question. It is not only a moral but also a spiritual issue. Harvard psychiatrist Robert Coles worries that affluent American children are permeated by a feeling of entitlement—that the world and its bounties belong to them by right. To borrow from Jim Hightower and his book *There's Nothing in the Middle of the Road but Yellow Stripes and Dead Armadillos,* these youngsters may be among those who, being born on third base, think they have hit a triple.

In *Facing Up: Paying Our Nation's Debt and Saving Our Children's Future,* Pete Peterson, former Reagan administration Secretary of Commerce and self-described Republican "fat cat," points out that most entitlements flow to the affluent. He warns that "the worst aspect of entitlement addiction is how it subtly fixes our attention on how much we are going to get—and how it obscures any thought of what we have received from others and what we wish to pass on in our turn." He proposes an "endowment ethic," by which we would restrain our sense of entitlement and concentrate more on how we might endow the future. And he proposes an "affluence test" that would review entitlement expenditures to ensure that the public does not subsidize the already affluent.

Economist John Kenneth Galbraith, in a 1992 issue of *Harper's* magazine, wrote about the contented majority,

> Where the impoverished are concerned, government support and subsidy is seriously suspect because of its adverse effect on morals and working morale. This, however, is not true of government support to those of comparative well-being. No one is thought to be damaged by Social Security payments or their prospect. Nor is a depositor, by being rescued from a failed bank. Nor if one is employed in the defense industry. The comparatively affluent can withstand the adverse moral effect of being subsidized and supported by the government; not so the poor. . . . The first and most general expression of the contented majority is its affirmation that those who compose it are receiving their just deserts. . . . Good fortune being earned and rewarded, there is no equitable justification for any action that impairs it, such as new taxes or subsidies to the poor.

In the late twentieth and early twenty-first centuries, prosperous Americans have adopted the mantra "I deserve it." According to a study in a 1995 issue of *Harper's,* 70 percent of Americans believe their financial situation is "at least somewhat" reflective of "God's regard" for them. Here is an entitlement ethic that equates one person's prosperity with virtue and another's poverty with vice.

A cartoon comment in a 1994 issue of *Dollars and Sense* stands this whole matter of entitlements on its head: Two men are on their coffee break, talking. One says, "We've got to stop the handouts, the something-for-nothing attitude, the dependency that passes from one generation to the next!" The other asks, "So you're for cuts in welfare checks?" The first replies, "I'm for hikes in the inheritance tax."

The debate over entitlement is brought down to earth in the Living Wage Campaign, a nationwide effort to require the government to pay a living wage to its employees and to require that its contractors pay a living wage. A living wage goes beyond the provisions of the minimum wage, which leaves a family of three or more in poverty, even if it has a year-round, full-time worker.

Again, to what are we entitled? Many people—aware and unaware—enjoy blessings they do not deserve, either by the sweat of their brow or the work of their brain. And many people have been blessed by a living tradition from which they draw material comfort and spiritual blessings. As Ralph Waldo Emerson said,

> We are not born free; we are born with a mortgage. That mortgage is a debt—a debt that we owe to the past and to the future. While we live we pay interest and then pass it on to the next generation. That's how churches, communities and nations survive; by accepting what has been bequeathed and passing it on to those that come after them. This ritual of receiving and giving is an act of Thanksgiving.

I contend that not only are economic rights human rights and that basic human needs ought to be met as a matter of right, but also that current U.S. patterns of distribution violate these basic human rights.

✦ ✦ ✦

Liberty and
Responsibility

> *Liberation is costly. Even after the Lord had delivered the
> Israelites from Egypt, they had to travel through the desert.
> There was starvation and thirst and they kept complaining.
> They had to bear the responsibilities and difficulties of freedom.*
>
> —Desmond Tutu, *Hope and Suffering*

Proposition One: In a given society, the greater the equality in income
and wealth, the more the freedom. *Freedom,* in this sense, means the
human capacity for self-determination.

In economic discussion, the meaning of *freedom* has too often been
related solely to the operations of the free market. Freedom in economic terms does contribute to other kinds of freedom: political, religious, social. However, freedom is also a function of the alternatives
for action from which a person may choose. Freedom from government interference in the marketplace must be balanced by freedom for
choosing among viable economic options.

Freedom to pursue economic ends is always in tension with the
sense of responsibility or trusteeship. That is, the goods of earth do not
belong to human beings; we are merely their trustees. Nature is not a
commodity but a sacred trust emerging from the creative process of
which we are part. Earth's bounties are not private commodities but
the common inheritance of all humankind. The economy is a wholly
owned subsidiary of the environment. The earth is more important
than the stock market. This tension sets one of the equations of the
justice model. How does capitalism square with democracy?

Milton Friedman, among others, argues that freedom is the paramount virtue in the economic as well as the political sphere. Furthermore, he asserts that economic freedom is necessary for political

freedom. People must be free to accumulate and pool resources and thus make themselves independent of the power of the state. Friedman goes on to define that power as the intrusion of government in the free marketplace. In *Capitalism and Freedom,* he writes, "Our minds tell us, and history confirms, that the great threat to freedom is the concentration of power."

This theme is also addressed by Robert Benne in *The Ethic of Democratic Capitalism.* Benne builds on Reinhold Niebuhr's idea of an *equilibrium of powers* in democratic society to argue for a separation of the economic and political spheres, thus enhancing economic freedom. This is applied in the *Protestant principle,* by which power is used to check power, thereby preventing its concentration and guaranteeing political liberty. Benne stresses the emergence in democratic capitalism of *voluntary associations,* which are countervailing powers in democratic equilibrium. He writes, "Under free market capitalism the major economic tasks of American society are performed without direction from the political centers of power." Such economic freedom can be said to constitute freedom itself. Benne continues, "We can choose our vocation. . . . We are free to choose how our money is spent. . . . Market arrangements . . . are an important support for political freedom of dissent." He is not certain of the cause / effect relationship of economic freedom and other modes of freedom: "It is difficult to say whether the free market economic system is a cause or an effect of this dynamic equilibrium in the social and cultural spheres of life. No doubt it is a mixture of both."

Along these lines, it is interesting to note that the social democracies of Western Europe have combined strong democratic political institutions with substantial governmental involvement in the welfare state. Clearly, there are relationships among the various forms of freedom, but it is exceedingly difficult to argue from cause to effect.

What Friedman (and to a lesser extent, Benne) does not consider is the coercive nature of other great concentrations of power—corporations, for instance—that have been created by the very freedom they extol. In the corporate configuration of power, in which most of the stock is controlled by relatively few persons, a handful of people make decisions that ultimately affect many. The central issue in campaign finance reform is the powerful hold that big money has over politicians.

Under the current globalization regime, corporations stretch around the globe and face minimal restraint from governments, national or international. Yet the large numbers of persons affected by corporate decisions have little or no power to challenge them. There is no referendum, for example, when a corporation decides to leave a community, taking thousands of jobs with it. Such action severely limits the freedom of the newly unemployed. Consider what happens when a low-level worker, whose life has been centered on doing a particular job in a particular location, receives a command from an economically powerful employer, backed by the threat of termination. The effect of this command is functionally indistinguishable from one backed by the political authority of the state. The restrictions of the market on personal freedom can be quite as coercive as that of the state—maybe more so. Citizens can vote an oppressive power out of political office, but workers have little, if any, say in the operations of their corporate managers. Should not all people have an equal right to participate in the decisions that affect their lives?

There is a danger that the radically *laissez-faire* U.S. economy could become a totalitarian state, transforming every social good into a commodity. It is market imperialism when wealthy men and women wield not only economic but also political power. American corporations are great concentrations of power—essentially, private governments in which the workers are often subjects. The corporation, then, is a one-party system of private government that is largely beyond internal democratic control.

Milton Friedman counters this view:

> The great advantage of the market . . . is that it permits wide variety. It is, in political terms, a system of proportional representation. Each man can vote, as it were, for the color of tie he wants and get it; he does not have to see what color the majority wants and then, if he is in the minority, submit.

To justify the distribution of income in a free market society, Friedman cites this ethical principle: "To each according to what he and the instruments he owns produces." Economist Scott Gordon rebuts Friedman in *Welfare, Justice and Freedom*:

> Property ownership may be distributed in a highly unequal fashion, but the corporate form permits the pyramiding of power and the concentration of that power in a few hands to a much greater degree than does the property itself. The control of the modern corporation rests in the hands of a small minority of legal owners; it may in fact be effectively exercised by its managerial officials who need not be shareholders at all.

It is curious how Friedman rationalizes that freedom is more limited by government than by great corporations, which are accountable only to their stockholders (and to them only marginally). In other words, the *laissez-faire* market distributes its resources, including freedom, unequally.

THE MARKETPLACE AS A VOTING BOOTH

Milton Friedman makes use of the metaphor of the marketplace as a voting booth. But in doing so, he overlooks a very elementary point: While a political democracy is based on the principle of one person, one vote, the principle of the market system is one dollar, one vote. Scott Gordon counters, "If the ration coupons of political power were for sale, we would live in a plutocracy, not a democracy. . . . Whenever economic power is concentrated it threatens political freedom."

The idea of the free market is that people are free to cast their votes, in effect—to signal the market to produce what they desire. However, to communicate effectively to the market, one must have adequate discretionary resources. The market responds most strongly to those who have the most economic votes to cast. Those who have few votes necessarily have less market freedom. Again, we see that inequality of wealth means not all persons are equally enfranchised.

Moreover, the concentration of wealth distorts the market by creating *needs* that are, in fact, *desires* of affluent individuals. In a situation of great inequality, the affluent have an inherent penchant for creating new needs, which is a condition for the artificial scarcity of luxury goods. The human spirit, wallowing in affluence, becomes insatiable.

Even conservative columnist George Will realizes that the freedom of the affluent to purchase large cars, for example, yields to the energy crisis as government regulations stipulate mileage on car fleets. In his April 19, 1977, column "Do the Rights of Man Include a Buick?" Will concludes, "Neither Detroit nor Washington is recognizably the City of God. But Washington is the seat of government and is responsible for stipulating the national interest. So increasingly, it will discourage some ways of pursuing happiness."

Unfettered economic freedom has also had a moral cost in the United States. Although both the Protestant ethic and Adam Smith's form of market utilitarianism assumed moral restraint on covetousness, all pretense of that has disappeared. And despite George Gilder's attempt to see the capitalist's striving for gain as an altruistic act and one lay Roman Catholic group's extolling creative enterprise as virtue, it seems clear that altruism, as such, has a limited role in market decisions. The traditional confidence that is placed on the natural capacity of the market to check self-aggrandizement is misplaced. Greed will not take care of itself. The acquisitive spirit needs to be tamed and channeled, not celebrated.

In the words of Max Stackhouse, the invisible hand of Adam Smith's market is "actually a secular and little-examined version of 'providence.' . . . Thousands now work, and work hard, with little inner conviction except for gain." Stackhouse believes that theological talk of covenant or moral law is strictly personal in character. Yet this loyalty to the market, which has now lost its sense of "godliness and holiness, still claims the loyalty of most Americans. . . . Americans hold to the system with the zeal of successful fanatics, fighting the growing suspicion that they may be wrong."

One practical example of the impact of inequality on freedom is in the political realm. In "The Big Tilt: Participatory Inequality in America," appearing in a 1997 issue of *The American Prospect,* authors Sidney Verba, Kay Lehman Schlozman, and Henry E. Brady conclude that income position markedly affects voter participation. People who make $15,000 per year are only 60 percent as likely to vote as those making $75,000, only 50 percent as likely to go to a protest or get in touch with a government official, and only 10 percent as likely to make a campaign donation. Contributors at the top gave nearly fourteen times as much as those at the bottom. According to the authors, "Public officials actually receive more messages from the advantaged suggesting a curtailment of government social programs than messages from the disadvantaged urging an expansion of them." Why? Because it takes resources to vote—measured in time, energy, or money—or even just to get to the polls. Another factor is that the poor are usually less educated, and level of education correlates closely with likelihood to vote. And then, there is political alienation—people's discouragement as to whether voting will have any meaningful consequences for their lives.

Verba, Schlozman, and Brady conclude,

> . . . when it comes to political participation, class matters profoundly for American politics. As long as inequalities in education and income persist, as long as Americans have unequal opportunities to develop and practice civil skills, and as long as citizens increasingly donate money rather than time to politics, the voices heard through the medium of citizen participation will be loud, clear, and far from equal.

Campaign finance reform has emerged as a related issue in the debate over the democratic process. Opponents to such reform hold that any restriction on contributions will violate the First Amendment. Yet in a political process in which money drives the media campaign machinery, money speaks too loudly. Does the large contributor have more free speech rights than the person who does not or cannot contribute at all? Certainly, both rich people and poor people have the formal freedom to vote, but we know who has the greater influence on the candidates. Campaign finance reform was an issue in the 2000 presidential campaign, which broke all previous spending records. The public appears to want reform; the politicians apparently do not.

In this light, how credible is the following comment by New York State Senate Majority Leader Joseph Bruno about the loopholes in laws that provide lobbyists with great latitude quoted in a 1998 edition of the *Rochester Democrat and Chronicle?* "When vested interests spend money, they are not buying anything. They don't buy a vote. That's nonsense. That's stuff that these do-gooders talk about. It doesn't mean a thing." If so, one wonders why special interest groups waste their time and money on lobbying. Few people really believe that large contributors donate their money just to exercise their democratic rights. Surely, they want something for their money—and they get it. The resistance to campaign finance reform from those who benefit from the current system is simply one more example of the intrusion of money and the market into other spheres.

FREEDOM AS A FUNCTION OF POSSIBILITY

The late Adlai Stevenson said in a September 6, 1952, campaign speech, "A hungry man is not a free man." Freedom should be understood not only as absence of coercion, as Friedman seems to suggest, but as a function of possibility. One is free insofar as he/she has actual options from which to choose. The poor are severely limited in choices. In his novel *The Red Lily,* Anatole France writes of "the majestic equality of the laws, which forbid rich and poor alike to sleep under the bridges, to beg in the streets, and to steal their bread." Likewise, the American economy gives freedom to both the rich and the poor to drive Rolls Royces through the streets.

Providing greater income equality maximizes individual liberty in a society by granting wide dispersal of freedom to choose. In this context, *freedom* is the ability to engage in purposeful activities. In a money economy, one's freedom is curtailed to the extent to which he/she can participate in market choices. This is a direct function of financial resources. Given this, what good are market alternatives if one does not have the resources needed to acquire them? Is there not more potential freedom in the marketplace when ten people each have $10 to spend than when one person has $100 to spend? This, incidentally, is very nearly the ratio of income between the top and the bottom quintiles in income in the United States. The game of Monopoly—in which only one player wins and all the rest lose—is an enjoyable and instructive pastime, but it is best understood as *play,* not transferable to real economic life.

Economic insecurity restricts people's freedom of action. When people are concerned about their economic security, they are less likely to exercise their freedom. For instance, the worker who is worried about keeping his / her job is less likely to risk speaking out on company policy or even joining a union. Given this, it is difficult not to say that economic liberty is espoused loudest by those who are already the "haves" in the marketplace. It seems to be a convenient ideology of the more fortunate to keep their freedom for prosperity, while allowing the less fortunate their freedom for poverty. As Arthur Okun writes, "Neither rights to ownership of any class of physical assets nor rights to after-tax income are given constitutional safeguards." And as Schumacher quotes philosopher Mortimer Adler, "Anyone who is made dependent for subsistence upon the will of others is an economic slave."

Another example of how inequality restricts freedom is "the overworked American," made popular by Harvard sociologist Juliet Schorr in her book of the same title. Most Western European workers are granted four to six weeks of vacation by law, but American workers usually have only two (at least to start). The *Annual Employment Outlook (Statistical Annex)* of the Organization for Economic Cooperation and Development reported in 1997 that compared to other Western countries, the United States is a nation of workaholics. German workers, for instance, worked 20 percent fewer hours than did Americans in 1997.

What is striking is that in 1970, Americans and Europeans worked roughly the same number of hours. The Europeans used their economic growth to increase leisure, but the Americans did not. In fact, Americans today work 6 percent more than they did three decades ago. One cause of this may be the greater income inequality among Americans, according to economists Linda Bell of Haverford College and Richard Freeman of Harvard University, as reported in a 1998 issue of *Dollars and Sense:* "The bottom rungs of our inequality ladder are so undesirable, and the middle rungs so insecure, that American workers scramble more to keep away from the bottom." Roughly two-thirds of

Americans said they made a point of working hard, even if doing so "interferes with the rest of their life."

Bell and Freeman cite this example, comparing one German and one American worker:

> Wilma in Germany and Carol in the United States. In Germany, pay differences are small, job security is high, unemployment benefits are good, and there is national health care. If Wilma works fewer hours and takes long vacations, she might be less likely to get a promotion or a pay raise, but can still maintain a reasonable standard of living. Carol, in contrast, faces high wage inequality, little job security, and limited unemployment benefits. If Carol doesn't put in extra hours she risks falling into the ranks of the working poor, or losing her job—with little safety net available. So Carol works longer hours than Wilma.

This "fear of falling" severely limits the freedom Americans have to live their lives as they choose. To the degree that financial resources are unequal, economic freedom, as well as social freedom, is proportionately limited.

In this model of distributive justice, freedom has positive as well as negative dimensions. The negative dimension of freedom can be understood as freedom from coercion by governmental or other institutions or individuals. In this regard, the American economic system has made an important contribution in creating countervailing centers of power to challenge the monopoly of governmental power. The positive dimension of freedom is a function of the opportunities people have to exercise it. This is what John Rawls calls the "worth of freedom" in his book *A Theory of Justice,* and it can be distinguished from freedom as a formal category. I contend that when financial resources are not distributed equally in a money economy, freedom is restricted for many.

FREEDOM, RESPONSIBILITY, AND THE ENVIRONMENT

The idea that freedom implies responsibility is far more than a cliché in terms of the operation of freedom in a limited environment. What responsibilities enhance freedom in a finite world?

There is another value that modifies freedom—*stewardship;* the more inclusive term is *trusteeship.* This concept approaches the relatively new concept of *ecojustice,* the delicate balance between concern

for distributive justice and the integrity of the environment. Our freedom as humans to exploit the earth for our own purposes has its limits
in the finite resources of nature as a fragile ecosystem.

The concept of *limits* as a major economic category had its incep-
tion in the 1974 Club of Rome report *The Limits to Growth,* which issued
a warning that the combination of overpopulation, pollution, depletion
of nonrenewable resources, and looming scarcities threaten the earth's
very survival. Furthermore, the report continued, such cataclysmic
problems cannot be solved by the marketplace or any technological fix.
The Club of Rome called this scenario "the world problematique."

Even though the computer projections of the club's report and
others subsequent to it have been called into question, the grounds it
established for economic decision making have been deemed revolutionary. The economic triumphalism demonstrated by the free market
economies of the West and the command economies of the former
Soviet bloc—each faithful to the idea that salvation comes through economic growth—has been debunked. The idea that an economy could
grow out of its problems is no longer considered a dogmatic certainty.

In the aftermath, it has become clear that not only the world's poor
but nature itself was victimized by a rapacious economic ethic that
saw the earth as merely instrumental to human needs. Lynn White's
classic 1967 essay "The Historical Roots of Our Ecological Crisis"
attributes this attitude to the Book of Genesis, with its command from
Yahweh to humankind to "be fruitful and multiply, fill the earth and
subdue it" (1:28). When some reinterpreted this dominion as meaning
the responsibility of stewardship, it became a central controversy in
theological circles. Regardless of whether the world's environmental
problems grew out of the biblical tradition or some more comprehensive causes, the finitude of the planet is a given in today's economic and
ecological debates. After all, one definition of *economics* is "the allocation of scarce resources."

The Worldwatch Institute's annual "State of the World" report
synopsizes the interface between ecology and economics. The Institute's researchers collect reports on both economic and environmental
trends and synthesize them in an annual review. And today, political
and economic leaders around the world regard this review with increasing seriousness. For example, in the *State of the World 2000,* executive
director Lester Brown notes,

> For the first time, the number of people in the world who are
> overnourished and overweight rivals the number who are under-
> nourished and underweight—some 1.2 billion.

He goes on to issue this warning:

> Unfortunately, the expanding global economy that is driving the Dow Jones to new highs is, as currently structured, outgrowing those ecosystems. . . . The market is a remarkably efficient device for allocating resources and for balancing supply and demand, but it does not respect the sustainable yield thresholds of natural systems.

Brown concludes,

> There is no middle path. The challenge is either to build an economy that is sustainable or to stay with our unsustainable economy until it declines. It is not a goal that can be compromised. One way or another, the choice will be made by our generation, but it will affect life on Earth for all generations to come.

LIFEBOAT ETHICS

Spaceship Earth has a limited carrying capacity, and there are—or should be—limits to its growth. Ecologist Garret Hardin develops a powerful metaphor in his 1968 essay "The Tragedy of the Commons," in which he likened the earth to a pasture in which all of the shepherds graze their flocks. Overgrazing by one flock will have inevitable repercussions for others. Some flocks will go hungry if others get more than their fill. Hardin later created even more controversy with his 1974 essay "Lifeboat Ethics," in which he argued that the people of the developed world are like shipwrecked passengers in a lifeboat, obliged to save themselves even at the expense of passengers from the developing world, drowning in the sea around them. It is a grizzly scenario, to be sure.

At the 1972 International Conference on the Human Environment at Stockholm, sponsored by the United Nations, a rift developed between delegates from developed and developing nations. The limits-to-growth movement was charged with being a "hobby of the rich," a new method for stifling growth that would guarantee the superior economic position of the already affluent nations while consigning the poor nations to continued poverty. As summarized by theologian Roger Shinn, in an essay from *For Creation's Sake: Preaching Ecology and Justice,* the delegates from the developing world seemed to be saying,

> You rich have mounted the ladder of economic success and dangled before us the hopes that we could follow you. Now you want to kick over the ladder that you told us to climb. After getting yours, you say that the world's resources are too limited for us to get ours.

In *The Zero-Sum Society,* economist Lester Thurow suggests much the same scenario, applied to the U.S. economy. While there is surely room for growth, there are finite economic resources. Moreover, the accumulation of these resources by some is to the detriment of others. In an economic zero-sum game, those individuals who have unlimited freedom to accrue resources do so at the expense of those who must do without or with very little. This finitude argues for the redistribution of scarce resources.

FREEDOM AND TRUSTEESHIP IN TENSION

We are in need of a new ethical/economic paradigm that will fully take into account freedom within limits. I suggest the concept of *trusteeship* in tension with *freedom*. The idea of trusteeship suggests the application of an investment principle to economic life in general. Under what I call the *prudent person principle,* trustees of other people's investment resources would exercise the judgment that a prudent person would exercise if the resources were his/her own. Economic decisions should be made in the context of what a prudent person would do in the face of limited resources for this and for future generations.

In a sermon printed in a 2000 issue of the Church of the Larger Fellowship (Unitarian Universalist) bulletin *Quest,* Michael A. Schuler notes the values of the prudent person principle by citing an imprudent politician and a prudent child. He quotes a nineteenth-century Wisconsin state senator, Timothy Howe, "who vigorously opposed measures to restrict logging in Wisconsin's northern forests." Chided for his lack of concern for posterity, he replied, "The generation yet unborn have done nothing for me, so I do not care to sacrifice too much for them."

Schuler goes on to tell the story of Severn, the preadolescent daughter of Canadian ecologist David Suzuki. In 1989, the family had visited the Brazilian rain forest for several weeks and could see the devastation caused by gold miners and others who were exploiting it. Severn indicated she and some of her friends wished to attend the 1991 Rio Earth Summit because, in her words, "I think all those grownups will be talking about our future and they need us there to act as their conscience." An American philanthropist heard about this remark and contributed $1,000 for the trip. When other donations were added, the sum grew to $20,000, enabling the youths to attend as members of a nongovernmental organization, the Environmental Children's

Organization. Severn was invited to address one of the plenary sessions, where she said, in part,

> You teach us how to behave in the world. You teach us not to fight with others; to work things out; to respect others; to clean up our mess; not to hurt other creatures; to share; not to be greedy. Why, then, do you go out and do the things you tell us not to do?

In the words of an old Kenyan proverb, "Treat the earth well. . . . It was not given to you by your parents. It was loaned to you by your children."

There is an implicit theological assumption here: The earth and its resources are not private property but the common possession of all. To the extent that we *can* possess resources, they should be held in trust for the community of humankind, both in a contemporary and in a futuristic sense. In *For Creation's Sake,* Roger Shinn tersely states this point in traditional theological language: "There is no such thing as private property—or, for that matter, government property—in any absolute sense. 'The earth is the Lord's.'"

Given the finitude of resources of which we are the trustees, some rather radical implications must be considered. The success of this new paradigm of trusteeship necessitates placing limitations on economic freedom, yet traditionally it has been assumed that virtually no such restraints are appropriate. The practice of economic freedom must also be considered against a scarcity of resources. Economics as the management of scarce resources requires restraint not only in an economic sense—economic production cannot proceed without adequate resources and an environment conducive to human habitation—but also in a theological sense. The earth should be thought of less like a mine, which is to be exploited until devoid of resources, and more like a garden, which we tend and renew. In short, the earth has a moral claim on us.

Furthermore, maintaining such a trusteeship requires looking to the future. The irresponsible consumption of finite resources will condemn generations to come to a privation stemming from our excesses. In the Native American tradition this is known as the Seventh principle: conserving and preserving resources unto the seventh generation to follow.

A CASE FOR REDISTRIBUTION

Finally, this trusteeship necessarily requires a redistribution of scarce resources. Meeting the needs of the poor through an ever-expanding pie is not only unlikely but also fraught with ruinous environmental hazards. If 1 billion Chinese were to live as wastefully as over 272 million Americans currently do, the world would be an ecological catastrophe. Hence, a distributive ethic will seek a just and sustainable society, in which excess is replaced by sufficiency and prodigality by frugality.

Jean Mayer, former president of Tufts University and an expert on hunger, writes prophetically in a 1970 issue of *Psychology Today*,

> It's the rich—in a relative sense, the people less likely to starve—who wreck the environment. Rich people occupy much more space, consume more of each natural resource, disturb the ecology more, litter the landscape with bottles and paper, and pollute more land, air and water with chemical, thermal and radioactive waste. . . . It might be bad in China with 700 million poor people, but 700 million very rich Chinese would wreck China in no time. It's the spread of wealth that threatens the environment.

To which I add: Imagine a world full of SUVs. However, the "free" market answers, as one of the Henry Fords is reported to have said, "Minicars make miniprofits."

Our economic freedom, then, should not be understood as license to accumulate personal goods and services as if we own them for ourselves. Rather, we should consider ourselves as trustees who have the freedom to merge our talents with the natural and other human resources for the good of all. We utilize our freedom as trustees of the Beloved Community of Earth. Freedom, as a human value, cannot stand alone; it must always exist in tension with trusteeship. It is merely one dimension in a set of values that undergird the common good. It is only one of the principles of justice.

♦ ♦ ♦

What Is a
Fair Share?

*These reasonings have no logical connection: "I am richer than
you, therefore I am your superior." "I am more eloquent than you,
therefore I am your superior." The true logical connection is rather
this: "I am richer than you, therefore my possessions must exceed
yours." "I am more eloquent than you, therefore my style must
surpass yours." But you, after all, consist neither in
property nor in style.*

—Epictetus, *Encheiridion*

Proposition Two: In a given society, the greater the equality in income
and wealth, the greater the equity (or fairness). A second principle of
justice is *equity,* by which each person is entitled to a fair distribution
of economic benefits. I argue not for absolute equality of distribution
in which wealth and resources would be meted out evenly among
all people, but for equity, in which all people are presumed to have
human dignity.

Equity is in constant tension with efficiency. What is a just balance
between the fair distribution of resources and the incentives that stem
from inequality of results? Would economic leveling and a policy
providing equality of results eliminate the incentives that emerge from
the desire to be unequal—to have more? And without sufficient incentives, will production be so curtailed that insufficient goods and
services will be expected to provide for the needs of all? How can we
achieve a just balance?

In *Politics,* Aristotle writes, "All men think justice to be a sort of
equality." That may or may not be true, but it is clear that there is no

consensus on what kind of equality might be implied by justice. An egalitarian would say no social inequalities can be justified, a view that prompted Henry Wallich to write, in *Inequality and Poverty,* "An egalitarian society promises to be virtuous, frugal and dull."

In theological terms, there is a concept of equality that is normative. In *The Dictionary of Christian Ethics,* we read that "in some ultimate 'ontological' sense they [people] are equal, and that this equality is more important than their empirical differences." In the Jewish and Christian views, this concept of equality means that all people are children of God.

A vigorous humanist expression of this attitude is given by Walter Lippmann in *Men of Destiny:*

> There you are, sir, and there is your neighbor. You are better born than he, you are richer, you are stronger, you are handsomer, nay you are better, kinder, wiser, more likeable; you have given more to your fellow men and taken less than he . . . and yet—absurd as it sounds—these differences do not matter, for the best part of him is untouchable and incomparable and unique and universal. Either you feel this or you do not; when you do not feel it, the superiorities that the world acknowledges seem like mountainous waves at sea; when you do feel it, they are slight and impermanent ripples upon a vast ocean.

INEQUALITY IN THE MARKETPLACE

The implications of this understanding of moral equality are not readily apparent in the economic sphere. In fact, the moral ideal of democracy, in which all people are created equal and stand equal before the law, seems contradicted by that of a capitalist market economy, in which inequality is the very fuel that feeds the mighty market engine.

According to economist Philip Green, whose article "The Future of Equality" appeared in a 1981 issue of *Current,* inequality is inherent in the workings of the free market system. "The ethos of capitalism is systematized inequality. From cradle to grave we subsist in a world of unequal incentives and rewards, of sharply stratified and omnipresent hierarchy." Despite this, the most passionate proponents of *laissez-faire* policies believe that, given its head, the market will equalize itself. Green surmises that this view is "the homage that vice self-consciously pays to virtue."

In *Generating Inequality,* Lester Thurow articulates the market economy's theory of distribution as one of *marginal productivity.* Reward is given for merit, the skill one demonstrates as an economic actor. However, this theory assumes the market economy is a game with strict rules, perfect competition, complete knowledge, and absolute rationality. But this "all things being equal" account of reality is false. All things are *never* equal. The world is quite simply messy. The rules are not always fair, competition is not perfect, knowledge is sometimes found wanting, and people are often more illogical than rational. In fact, luck—including the luck to be born into a middle-class or rich family—plays an immense role in the real world of the market.

FAIR PLAY OR FAIR SHARE?

Basically, two criteria can be used to judge distributional mechanisms: equity and efficiency. Since the 1950s, the use of efficiency has become predominant. Issues of distribution have been settled by power in a competitive marketplace. As Lester Thurow and Robert Heilbroner state in *Economics Explained,* "The marketplace is efficient, dynamic, and devoid of values."

The necessity of inequality has gained a kind of ideological legitimacy in these times. There seems little question that Americans accept inequality as part of the way things are, at least economically. Although lip service is paid to the concept of political equality, disparities in income have a kind of ontological existence—inherent in the very nature of things. Thus, some conceptual clarity is needed.

The term *economic equality* can be used to mean either equality of opportunity or equality of results. In his book *Equality,* social critic William Ryan distinguishes these uses as the *fair play ideology* and the *fair share ideology.* In the former, the individual is the basic unit of society, and the goal of economic life is to allow unencumbered individuals to fulfill their own purposes and seek their own satisfaction. Individuals differ significantly from one another in terms of their natural endowments and competencies. The sources of those differences may be thought of as inside the person—skill, energy, drive, intelligence, talent, and ambition. Environmental factors are minimized. In the fair play ideology, a fair process is central to legitimacy. In essence, the goal is to level the playing field so as to promote unbridled competition. A fair share ideology, on the other hand, holds that individuals are members of society and that human behavior is social in nature. The strong similarities among humans are believed to be much more relevant than their minor differences. Human behavior is attributed not so much to internal qualities as to the effect of the external environment.

Ryan uses intelligence as an example of these two approaches and, in the end, supports the fair share ideology:

> This can be put another way: given two groups, one relatively poor, one relatively well off, both with exactly the same educational level, we would find that the poor kids with IQ's over 120 would earn just about as much as the rich kids with IQ's below 80. Where does all this leave the meritocracy theory? With regard to IQ as a measure of merit, certainly, the theory is left high and dry. It simply doesn't hold up in real life. A young person's earnings can be predicted best by knowing, first, his or her family's economic status, and second, the amount of education obtained, that is, the number of years he or she was able to stay in school.

Citing the longitudinal study "Five Thousand American Families," Ryan concludes, "Over a period of eight years, although only one in ten families is poor every one of the eight years, over one-third of American families are poor for at least one of those eight years." He goes on to point out that unexpected misfortune or bad luck accounted for much of the economic difficulty encountered by families in the study. These external factors accounted for almost all of the variability in people's economic fortunes. Personal character traits—such as ambition or sloth, intelligence or ignorance, thriftiness or extravagance—which we think have impact in the marketplace, accounted for relatively little of what happened to the people studied. The notion of fair play, esteemed in the American pantheon of values, was not a major factor either. The study found little relationship between these traits and economic position.

And so, equality of opportunity, touted by conventional wisdom and political dogma, may only serve to perpetuate inequality. Environmental conditions—class, sex, race, and social, physical, and educational disabilities—makes the great race of life an unequal contest from the beginning. While equality of opportunity as fair play is a necessary condition for distributive justice, it is not a sufficient condition, as it does not take fully into account the disadvantaged staging platforms from which people are launched into the marketplace, particularly those who are poor. Equal and fair treatment in the marketplace may well produce unequal results that cannot be said to be just. As Herbert Gans writes in *More Equality*, "To treat the disadvantaged uniformly with the advantaged will only perpetuate their disadvantage."

AFFIRMATIVE ACTION
OR REVERSE DISCRIMINATION?

Noted Swedish economist Gunnar Myrdal was wrong—or at least half wrong, which means he was also half right! In *An American Dilemma,* written in 1944, Myrdal set the paradigm for American race relations: The American dilemma was the juxtaposition of the ideal of equality and the reality of inequality. That dilemma has largely defined American racial problems since.

Just as critical, though much less discussed, is the American dilemma of class: the ideal of a classless society versus the reality of sharp class distinctions. Class is the elephant in the room we dare not acknowledge. Race and class are Siamese twin dilemmas so intricately interwoven into American culture that it is hard to distinguish them.

In *Learning to Be White,* theologian Thandeka suggests that race has been used to distract Americans from the realities of class. The obsession with race "makes white working-class and middle-class Americans vote as if their economic interests are identical to the rich." Privilege, she contends, belongs to a tiny elite in society. At the turn of the millennium, one reason the market has been so bullish is that wages have not been increasing correspondingly. American workers are scared to make demands on their employers for fear of losing their jobs. One-fourth to one-third of all U.S. households live paycheck to paycheck. This is not white skin privilege; it is middle-class poverty. Talk of privilege is a distraction from class reality.

Dr. Martin Luther King, Jr., had the right idea when he launched the Poor People's Campaign in 1968. This movement was not as popular among white liberals as was his campaign for civil rights for minorities, for it struck the classist nerve in the American psyche. Relating the rights of poor minorities to the rights of poor people in general produces an explosive mixture. As King wrote in an unpublished manuscript, quoted by biographer David J. Garrow in *The FBI and Martin Luther King, Jr.:*

> The dispossessed of this nation—the poor, both white and Negro—live in a cruelly unjust society. They must organize a revolution against that injustice, . . . against the structures through which the society is refusing to take means which have been called for, and which are at hand, to lift the load of poverty. . . . [This] is much more than a struggle for the rights of Negroes. It is forcing America to face all of its interrelated flaws—racism, poverty, militarism, and materialism. It is exposing evils that are rooted deeply in the whole structure of our society.

Affirmative action has been one of the most controversial remedies for inequality, particularly when applied to situations involving race and gender. In the wake of the civil rights revolution of the 1960s, affirmative action became policy at many levels of government and public institutions. Inevitably, it was immersed in controversy with the charge of reverse discrimination, as white people complained that less-qualified black people unfairly received college admission, jobs, and job promotions. To a lesser extent, men complained of such preferences being granted to women. The moral imperative behind affirmative action was to remedy past discrimination. But in reality, most Americans opposed affirmative action, and a retrenchment of values was underway.

William Bowen of Princeton and Derek Bok of Harvard mount a defense of affirmative action in academia with their book *The Shape of the River.* They argue that granting racial preferences was the best guarantee that outstanding minority individuals would be educated and allowed to enter a truly integrated and therefore better society. Diversity was believed good for its own sake. The authors further argue that merit has very little bearing on who *deserves* to go to college and that an individual's potential contribution to the richness of society should be at least as important as formal measures of ability, such as SAT scores. Bowen and Bok's research points to the fact that when black students with lower SAT scores were admitted to selective colleges, they were more involved than white students in social and community service and political endeavors and more likely to be leaders in these efforts. Conversely, the authors argue, without affirmative action programs, elite institutions might rapidly be stripped of much of their African American presence. In sum, they recommend that the goal should be to select people who are creative, adaptive, reliable, and committed—not just good at taking tests.

William Julius Wilson of Harvard, in a 1999 issue of *The American Prospect,* makes the case for *affirmative opportunity:* a shift from the emphasis on numbers and quotas for the purpose of guaranteeing equality of results to an approach that promotes equality of opportunity, casting a wider net over disadvantaged individuals from various racial and ethnic groups. Other criteria in addition to race would be included: for example, obstacles or hardships an individual had overcome. Wilson argues for broad social programs aimed at disadvantaged people, such as increased employment opportunities and job skills training, improved public education, and better child care and health care services. Wilson contends that actions such as these are needed to help level the playing field.

Racism and classism are both thriving in the United States. They will yield to justice only when American policy and practice accept the idea that the greater the inequality in society, the greater the injustice. The strategy for moving toward economic justice should be a form of affirmative action that focuses mostly on class but is not colorblind, because racism would exist even if classism did not.

THE EQUITY/EFFICIENCY DEBATE

Arthur Okun, a moderate economist, believes that inequality is perpetuated by family status, not merit. In his book *Equality and Efficiency,* he writes, "Clearly, there is some tendency for the affluence or poverty of the father to be visited upon the son." Social scientist Christopher Jencks concurs, reporting in his book *Inequality* that "the sons of families in the top fifth of the socio-economic pyramid have average incomes 75 percent higher than those coming from the bottom fifth."

Okun argues for legally enforced equal employment opportunity, believing it could change economic behavior:

> What is good for equality may be good for efficiency. The narrowing of the racial differentials during the sixties implied a gain of nearly one-fifth in the wages and salaries of blacks. That gain approached 1 percent of the nation's income. When we can have more justice and more real GNP, society should make the most of it.

Daniel Maguire takes a somewhat more radical approach to this issue in *A New American Justice.* He makes an impassioned plea for a strong affirmative action policy:

> Equality of opportunity, for all of the democratic pretensions it exudes, is really the principle of aristocracy. It is . . . the mask of social Darwinism, the cold doctrine of the survival of the fittest. . . . Of what possible value is equal opportunity to those who are physically or socially or educationally handicapped? . . . What equal opportunity thinking does is confirm class structures and class consciousness—the very things against which the ideal of equality was unfurled in American history.

He advocates unequal opportunity so those who have been excluded from equal opportunity in the past may be allowed into the employment process on a fair basis.

Thomas Jefferson invoked the egalitarian ideal when he wrote to Correa, November 25, 1817, "The object is to bring into action that mass of talents which lies buried in poverty in every country." In fact, studies of affirmative action programs, now much on the defensive, indicate that not only do they bring previously excluded persons into the marketplace, they also tend to increase efficiency as a new pool of talent is added to the economy.

The Big Trade-Off

I do not advocate absolute equality of results, for that would be politically unfeasible as well as unresponsive to human differences and needs. Some people, by virtue of their condition—such as a physical disability or sickness—need more than others do to sustain a decent existence. And some people, by virtue of their exceptional talent and responsibility, should receive more to reward their endeavors. I advocate *equity,* which would involve more equality in the end results of the economic process and which would guarantee a basic decent minimum for all.

Philosopher Hugo A. Bedau, in *Justice and Equality,* calls for a *radical egalitarianism.* His goal is to explore ways to remove or at least diminish inequalities. Realizing that it would be an extreme position to claim that all inequalities are unnecessary and unjustifiable and should be eliminated and that it is inherently unjust for some people to have luxuries while others lack necessities, Bedau presents the egalitarian position in these formal principles of equity:

> Justice involves equality. . . .
>
> All men are equal—now and forever, in intrinsic value, inherent worth, essential nature. . . .
>
> Social equalities need no special justification, whereas social inequalities do. . . . (the presumption of equality).
>
> All persons are to be treated alike except where circumstances require different treatment (the principle of equality).
>
> Some social inequalities are necessary.
>
> Some social inequalities are justifiable.
>
> All social inequalities not necessary or justifiable should be eliminated.

To flesh out this formal approach, we need to consider the fundamental tension between equality and efficiency, which Arthur Okun labels "the big tradeoff." He painfully acknowledges the contradictions of capitalism and democracy, in which prizes are awarded that "allow the big winners to feed their pets better than the losers can feed their children." Yet Okun states that these apparent inconsistencies really represent uneasy compromises. Moreover, he believes this is inevitable in a free market economy. "We cannot have our cake of market efficiency and share it equally." He finds the capitalist record of efficiency without parallel. Even though the free market engine knocks and pings from time to time, he would not trade it for any other model. Okun gives capitalism two cheers for its distributive mechanisms. In comparing the market's competitive race metaphor with that of a cooperative dance, he finds the latter morally appealing but unrealistic. He contends,

> A major de-emphasis of competition means forgoing individualistic incentives; and that, in turn, involves either a tremendous sacrifice of efficiency or else the creation of alternative incentives systems. Perhaps people will work and produce in order to save humanity, guided by a love for all mankind, . . . but it remains to be demonstrated that such a spirit can motivate common mortals and not merely saints.

And so Okun concludes that capitalism and democracy need one another "to put some rationality into equality and some humanity into efficiency."

In *Economics Explained,* Thurow and Heilbroner challenge the assumption that the free market is inherently efficient in distributing goods and services. They find the system dynamic but only partially efficient and completely devoid of values. Its central inefficiency is in providing public services for which no price tag exists, such as education, public health, and governmental services. The market society allocates tax money for these services, but citizens tend to view "these taxes as an extraction in contrast with the items they voluntarily buy." This places public goods and services in direct competition with private goods like autos, homes, and clothing. But in fact, they cannot compete, and so we have private opulence and public squalor.

Market efficiency is presumably value free, but in reality, as Thurow and Heilbroner point out, it is "an assiduous servant of the wealthy, but an indifferent servant of the poor." At the turn of the twenty-first century, the free market has put the price of private housing beyond the reach of the poor. At the same time, the availability of inexpensive forms of public housing has declined. This situation is both an economic and a moral failure. While the market measures private affluence as an increase in the GDP, it ignores the basic needs of lower-income people.

Finally, the market is a careless mechanism that produces cycles of inflation, unemployment, poverty, and pollution. To be fair, the market cannot be held solely responsible for these social problems, but their link to the market cannot be ignored.

In *The Economic Illusion*, Robert Kuttner also challenges the idea that equality and efficiency are inimical and that the former must wait on the latter. Writing of the economic recovery of the mid 1980s, he says somewhat sardonically, "It is convenient indeed for the wealthy and powerful that economic recovery should depend on their further enrichment." He continues: "Self-interest is successfully masquerading as a technical imperative. Ideology has appropriated the costume of value-free positive economics."

Kuttner believes the efficiency / equality tradeoff formula is much too simplistic. A wide variety of equality / efficiency bargains are available. For thirty years after World War II, he argues, there was a broad political consensus that equality actually improved efficiency. While this consensus championed policies that preserved political rights, it also extended economic entitlements as a component of basic civil rights. That is, it promoted the concept of *social citizenship*.

In the 1970s, when the economy faltered, a conservative political ideology came to the fore and blamed economic problems on the extensions of the welfare state. Conservative rhetoric traditionally defends efficiency with inequality through the idea of merit: People who rise economically deserve their good fortune. To have is to deserve. Kuttner cites studies by Ryan (already mentioned) and further suggests a series of "thought experiments" that demonstrate that fate and luck are decisive factors in causing many large discrepancies of income and wealth.

Kuttner defends redistributive efforts against the charge that this upsets market efficiency. He indicates that the potential investment of the rich is increasingly superseded by pension funds, representing the deferred wages and savings of wage earners. Okun makes the same point, noting that the savings rate in the United States has remained amazingly constant for several decades. For example, in 1929, when taxes were low and barely progressive, the savings rate was 16 percent of GNP; in 1973, with a presumed "soak the rich" tax rate, the figure was identical. Kuttner concludes, "It is not at all clear that a less equal distribution of wealth enhances the accumulation of capital or its useful investment."

The Question of Incentives

The critical issue in the efficiency/equality debate is that of incentives for production in the marketplace. If income is made more equal, will it stifle the desire to earn and thus to produce more? Is creating income inequality the necessary consequence of rewarding productive behavior?

The critical question in this discussion of incentives is the same question asked rhetorically by the Roman Catholic lay committee in its critique of the Pastoral Letter on the U.S. Economy by the Roman Catholic Bishops: "Who wants to distribute scarcity?" On the one hand, the market gives incentives to risk takers who produce new goods and services more efficiently, and on the other hand, poverty or the threat thereof induces low-income people to work.

It is important that we look at this issue both in terms of the efficiency/equality debate and in terms of policy options. In a 1982 speech at Harvard University, reflecting the style of Anatole France, John Kenneth Galbraith describes the "even-handed majesty of Reaganomics: the poor need the incentive of lower benefits, while the rich require the incentives of lower taxes."

One approach to the question of incentives is couched in purely economic terms: the decline of marginal utility. It is summarized by James E. Meade and Charles J. Hitch in their contribution to *Inequality and Poverty*:

> The larger the income of any one individual in a given situation, i.e., with unchanged tastes, knowledge and needs, the less important it will be for him to receive a given addition to his income. . . . This fact is expressed by saying that the marginal utility of income diminishes as income increases.

In *Towards a New Theory of Distributive Justice,* Norman E. Bowie expresses the same principle somewhat more graphically as he explains the difficulty of measuring economic happiness. He uses the illustration of the poor cereal buyer who experiences a six-cent decrease in its price and the rich candy buyer who experiences a six-cent increase in its price. In sum, "The satisfaction of the poor outweighs the loss of the rich, even though the monetary changes are equal."

Thus, the redistribution of income, dollar for dollar, will greatly increase the satisfaction of the poor without having much effect on the satisfaction of the rich. For example: A $5,000 decrease in after-tax income for someone earning $150,000 would be a small economic annoyance, but an increase of the same $5,000 would put a family of four earning $15,000 above the poverty level. Put another way, the incentive to make $5,000 more at a high income level is very modest, while the incentive to make even $1,000 more at a low income level is quite strong.

Robert Kuttner reports, "Virtually all of the studies of taxation can have two opposite effects on work: an 'income effect' as people actually work harder in order to maintain their pre-tax standard of living; and a 'substitution effect'—people decide to substitute leisure for work." Approaching the topic from a different political perspective, Arthur Okun finds much the same thing: "[Researchers] have uncovered virtually no significant effects of the present (1975) tax system [relatively high marginal rates] on the work effort of the affluent."

In *More Equality*, Herbert Gans cites other studies by Lester Thurow, George Break, and Thomas Sanders of middle- and high-income employees that point to these conclusions:

> People work harder and longer after their taxes go up. Consequently, the $50,000 executive who was taking home less money would not stop working; in fact he or she would probably try to find a better-paying job. At the very highest salary levels, other job attributes such as fringe benefits, prestige, status and power come into play. Candidates for the presidency of General Motors would still step forward even if the job paid less in after-tax income than it does at present.

Daniel Yankelovich, in *New Rules,* his study of American values, finds that people's economic motivations have changed. In the past, the basic motivations were money and recognition, but now, they have more to do with autonomy, creativity, and adventure—what Yankelovich calls "the expressive side of life."

In sum, a greater redistribution of income and wealth is not likely to reduce incentives among the affluent by much. Traditional economics and the law of diminishing marginal utility, as well as a variety of psychological factors, are relevant here. So-called psychic income—a sense of pride, satisfaction, and meaning—at higher levels seems to be more important than marginal increases in monetary income. The role of material incentives as an argument against greater equality of results is not persuasive.

On the other side of the income scale, however—where Abraham Maslow's survival and security needs come strongly into play—incentives play a greater role. In *Do the Poor Want to Work?*, a study on the attitudes poor people have toward work, Leonard Goodwin concludes,

> Poor people . . . identify their self-esteem with work as strongly as the non-poor. They express as much willingness to take job training if unable to earn a living and to work even if they were to have an adequate income. They have, moreover, as high life aspirations as do the non-poor and want the same things, among them a good education and a nice place to live. This study reveals no differences between poor and non-poor when it comes to life goals and wanting to work.

Thus, it seems that the traditional work ethic is so deeply embedded in the American people that many will choose to work even though to do so actually lowers family income.

To sum up the equality/efficiency debate: Conventional wisdom suggests that one quality must be traded off against the other to produce enough goods and services to distribute. But it is not at all clear whether an unfettered free market economy maximizes efficiency. The Gross Domestic Product (GDP) measures the production of luxury and waste equally with providing for people's basic needs. All things being equal, the market is an efficient mechanism, but seldom are all things equal. Many external factors enter into the workings of the marketplace.

The market does provide a rough *quantitative* measurement of goods and services, but it does not provide a measure of *qualitative* production. The efficiency equation should be a function of meeting basic needs for a minimal standard of living for people at all income levels before providing wants for the affluent. Furthermore, on economic criteria alone, it can be argued that greater equality of income will make for greater efficiency, as more people with basic needs will enter the marketplace and "vote" for goods and services.

Even though the market distributes goods and services more efficiently than does a command system, it clearly works best for the affluent and worst for the poor. "A rising tide lifts all boats" is a tempting piece of rhetoric, but the economic facts reveal that the smallest boats are still sitting on the sand. The market mechanism needs to be refined and supplemented by an exterior mechanism to provide some modicum of equity. Thus far in the American experience, government has been that mechanism.

Equity as a Minimum Package

What would true equity look like? Historically, the Roman Catholic tradition has had the theory of a *just wage*, i.e., a wage that is adequate to keep a worker and his/her family at a minimal decent standard of living. Daniel Maguire argues for *minimal due egalitarianism*, suggesting a floor beneath which equity would not allow persons to fall. (We should note that a full-time worker at the U.S. minimum wage in a family of four would fall far short of the government-defined poverty level even with the increase established by the federal government in 1997.) The real value of the minimum wage has declined steadily with only occasional, short-lived increases. Regardless, the minimum wage is too low to act as a strong incentive to work.

It is often said that poor Americans are better off than the poor in the rest of the world, and that is true in absolute terms. However, poverty must be judged in context. When poverty exists in the midst of widespread affluence, it tends to diminish people. The poor do not feel themselves to be members of the society. People need to have economic goods beyond what is required for subsistence, along with some of the free time and convenience that money can buy. Otherwise, they will experience a kind of status starvation. Unless people own a certain number of goods, they cannot be full members of the society.

Lester Thurow, in *The Zero-Sum Solution*, suggests a variation on John Rawls, arguing that "deviations from economic equality must be shown to be beneficial, placing the burden of proof on those who advocate inequality, and that some minimum economic prize is an essential ingredient in economic equity." However, Thurow concludes, "Fair treatment is central to a well-motivated, cooperative, high quality economic team. Equity is the essence of efficiency."

Equity, as a principle of justice, necessitates that all persons are guaranteed a minimal "package," which will meet their basic human needs, at the very least. None should have luxuries while some lack necessities. Furthermore, in an affluent society, it is possible and tolerably efficient for all persons to enjoy a so-called civilizing surplus, which will meet more than basic physiological needs.

The American economy has the capacity to provide not only for basic human needs but also for a civilizing surplus. According to the U.S. Census Bureau, annual per capita income in the nation was $21,181 in 1999. While this income level would no doubt curb the lifestyles of many Americans, it would enhance the quality of life for many more. I am not so foolish as to advocate absolute equality as public policy, but the closer we move to such an egalitarian society without greatly stifling our productive capacity, the greater justice we will create. We are all more human than otherwise, a theological assertion not yet recognized in economic theory. Our common humanity is the basis of human community.

Economic equity is undergirded by a sense of social membership in a community. Repeating the words of Walter Lippmann:

> These differences do not matter, for the best part of him is untouchable and incomparable and unique and universal. Either you feel this or you do not; when you do not feel it, the superiorities that the world acknowledges seem like mountainous waves at sea; when you do feel it, they are slight and impermanent ripples upon a vast ocean.

◆ ◆ ◆

Community and Individualism

To centralize wealth is to disperse the people;
to distribute wealth is to collect the people.

—Confucius, *The Analects*

Proposition Three: The greater the equality in income and wealth, the stronger the sense of community. A third principle of justice is a sense of human solidarity, in which voluntary cooperation interacts with humane competition as an ordering principle.

In this context, we understand *community* to mean more than the aggregate of the individuals of whom it is comprised—a gaggle of customers, so to speak. Rather, *community* denotes an organic entity in which the common good is of paramount importance. This common good is neither individualistic nor collectivistic but understands these as polarities.

Community is in constant tension with individualism, which honors personal uniqueness. In this understanding of community, individuals can be viewed as atoms that are constantly attracted to one another. Individuals are members of a human community, in which self-actualization is understood in terms of the obligations and rights of membership. In fact, serving the community becomes an essential source of individual self-fulfillment.

Alexis de Tocqueville describes this dilemma in his landmark work *Democracy in America*:

> Individualism is a calm and considered feeling which disposes each citizen to isolate himself from the mass of his fellows and withdraw into the circle of family and friends; with this little society formed to his taste, he gladly leaves the greater society to look after itself. . . . Each man is forever thrown back on himself alone, and there is danger that he may be shut up in the solitude of his own heart.

THE WAR OF ALL WITH ALL

The metaphor of the marketplace as a jungle derives from Thomas Hobbes's description of human society as a "war of all with all." Current debate on economic justice focuses on the wars over distribution, as groups struggle for their pieces of the economic pie. As stated by William E. Peacock, former secretary of the army and president of two consulting and research and development firms, in a 1985 interview in *U.S. News and World Report,* "While the stakes may not be life or death as in war, we in business are fighting in a 'zero sum game' for things that are very dear to us—the livelihood of our stockholders, our employees and our families, to say nothing of our own integrity."

This fragmentation of American society is presaged in Richard Titmuss's 1955 essay "The Social Division of Welfare: Some Reflections on the Search for Equity." He warns that the welfare state was already fragmenting into three distinct parts: (1) a *social service state* focused on the poor; (2) an *occupational welfare state* made up of private "perks" that well-off people obtained through their jobs; and (3) a *tax welfare state,* made up of tax deductions (called *tax expenditures*) that are valuable mainly to the affluent.

In *The Economic Illusion,* Robert Kuttner documents the accuracy of this prediction:

> After thirty years, this characterization describes the British and American welfare states all too well. The ratio of tax expenditures to direct expenditures is rising in both countries. The ratio of private, job-based pensions to public social security pensions is also on the upswing. Expenditures of tax subsidies for middle-class mortgages have overwhelmed direct spending on housing for the poor and the elderly. An upper-middle class executive, who pays private college tuition for his children, enjoys first-class medical care thanks to his tax-free corporate health insurance plan, drives a tax-deductible company car, retires in style on a tax-sheltered company pension, and perhaps lives securely in a tax-sheltered exclusive building policed by private guards, enjoys substantial subsidy, but none of it visible. He wonders what his tax dollars are accomplishing— other than coddling the undeserving poor.

That this so-called rugged individualism is not only alive and well but dominant is illustrated in a 1983 *Harvard Business Review* study quoted by Philip Slater in *Wealth Addiction,* which revealed that business executives prefer the individualistic ethos over that of solidarity 2.5 to 1. Almost three-quarters believed a community ideology would dominate by 1985, yet they found it repugnant. Their greatest fear was that of relinquishing control.

That apotheosis of the individual at the expense of the state can be seen in remarks made in the late nineteenth century by Senator Chauncey M. Depew at Vanderbilt University and quoted by Maguire:

> The American commonwealth is built upon the individual. It recognizes neither classes nor masses. . . . We have thus become a nation of self-made men. . . . Commodore Vanderbilt is a conspicuous example of the product and possibilities of our free and elastic condition. . . . He neither asked nor gave quarter. The same . . . open avenues, the same opportunities which he had before him, are equally before every other man.

More recently, such individualism has been cast in the form of a *social Darwinism,* in which the economic survival of the fittest is not a vice but a virtue. Economic life is seen not as a function of human cooperation to ensure the survival of the species but as a function of human competition to ensure the aggrandizement of the market-oriented warrior. Arthur Levitt, Jr., former head of the American Stock Exchange, said at a college commencement in 1981, as quoted in *U.S. News and World Report,*

> Today's fail-safe society seems to have generated a cult of mediocrity—a willingness to settle for whatever life provides instead of exerting every effort to get more, to reach the top, to have it all, or at least more of it than other folks have. The knowledge that no one in this country will be allowed to sink all the way to the bottom, that there will always be a helping hand, or even an entire arm, has . . . taken away one of our most precious rights—the right to fail as well as the right to succeed. Too many of us have lost the spirit of adventure, of risking all we have in order to have more.

In a May 1988 publication of the Unitarian Universalist Church of the Larger Fellowship, the Reverend Marjorie Montgomery quotes from an article titled "The American Phobia—Failure": "Because of the special emphasis we place on success, America is the cruelest country in which to fail. . . . In a society where winning is all, when you lose, you lose everything. Defeat becomes a kind of death."

This atomistic individualism has misinterpreted Darwinism. The phrase *survival of the fittest* refers not to individual creatures but to the species itself. The principle is based not on ruthless individual competition but on the capacity of the species to adapt itself to new ways of life and thus to survive. Cutthroat intraspecies competition has been sanctified in the American ethos at the expense of the cooperation required for building a political and economic community. We ignore the biological base of cooperation for species survival at our peril.

UNIQUENESS AND COMMUNITY

Emphasis on the unique individual is called into question by former Harvard Divinity School church historian Conrad Wright. In an essay called "Individualism in Historical Perspective," he contends that the rugged individualism that was so functional in the glory days of the American republic may well be dysfunctional in the harder times that lie ahead:

> Individualism was all very well on the shores of Walden Pond, but is not nearly as relevant in the slums of Calcutta. Individual initiative was fine as long as there were plenty of codfish on the Grand Banks, but when floating fish factories swarmed over them, overfishing diminished the stock available to all. The social situation that fostered individualism will be a temporary one. . . . [Thus,] the value system that liberals have taken for granted, and have always assumed would be vindicated by history, is in need of overhaul.

Wright claims that the last three centuries of Western culture are an aberration in human history. He calls them

> the product of a unique combination of population, natural resources and technology that can never come again. The individualism that thrived during this period of growth became dysfunctional as limits of growth came into play. We are not so much the little poor kid who got to the top by hard work as the little rich kid who inherited a vast fortune and attributed it to hard work.

Lester Thurow once asked a Harvard alumni gathering from whom they would take income if they were given the task of raising funds to be invested in a plant and equipment from 10 percent to 15 percent of GNP. He describes the alumni's reaction to this proposal in *Generating Inequality:*

> One hand was quickly raised and the suggestion was made to eliminate welfare payments. Not surprisingly, the person was suggesting that someone else's income be lowered, but I pointed out that welfare constitutes only 1.2% of GNP. Where were they going to get the remaining funds—3.8% of GNP? Whose income were they willing to cut after they had eliminated government programs for the poor? Not a hand went up.

In this idolatry of possessive individualism, the value of social solidarity has been sacrificed. Individual property rights have become transcendent to the common good. As the pursuit of market profit has been sanctified, other social values have been subordinated, particularly that of community—the invisible bonds by which a society is held together. Social fragmentation and personal insecurity have been the unfortunate result.

The impact of the free market on the bonds of community has been personalized by political scientists Marc K. Landy and Henry A. Plotkin, writing in a 1982 issue of *Society:*

> The national labor market has become so efficient that, for example, if the demand for spot welders declines in Cleveland and rises in Houston, a man trained in that trade is expected to respond to this market by moving from Ohio to Texas. The market cannot take into account the fact that this spot welder also happens to be an uncle, a church deacon, and a Republican ward committeeman. These other roles do not comprise part of his commodity value and are therefore irrelevant for purposes of market consideration. No means exist for evaluating the loss to the community resulting from the departure of a valued family member, church goer, and citizen. The market has therefore grossly understated the full social costs attendant upon his leave taking.

Measures of market efficiency do not address the resultant fracturing of community, which is a social reality more powerful than the figures of the Gross Domestic Product. The individualism inherent in the operation of the free market needs the occasional rebuke of community consciousness if justice is to be served. Market efficiency—with its stress on personal fulfillment and attendant inequalities in income—fails to address the fact that individual fulfillment is achieved by participating as a member of a community.

Dogmatic economic individualism also forgets that individuals' success depends on the stability and solidarity of the community to which they belong. British economic historian R. H. Tawney reminds us of this in his 1926 book *Religion and the Rise of Capitalism.* He describes the Puritan, the product of the Protestant ethic: "The moral self-sufficiency of the Puritan nerved his will, but it corroded his sense of social solidarity." Personal character was all; social fabric was nothing. Tawney goes on to write somewhat sardonically of the resulting businessman, "Few tricks of the unsophisticated intellect are more curious than the naive psychology of the business man, who ascribes his achievements to his own unaided efforts in blind unconsciousness of a social order without whose continuous support and vigilant protection he would be as a lamb bleating in the desert." Tawney suggests that such rampant individualism would "arm the spiritual athlete for his solitary contest with a hostile world, and dismiss concern with the social order as the prop of weaklings and the Capua of the soul."

In the words of social critic Richard Sennett, from a 1981 issue of *U.S. News and World Report,* American culture has become "drunk on the rhetoric of individualism. We're a very long way from facing the facts of what it would take to put together a more cooperative society." However, one might question the long-term endurance of a nation built on an individualism that is reflected economically in such great disparities of income and wealth.

In a subsequent issue of *U.S. News and World Report* in the same year, financier Felix G. Rohatyn puts the problem trenchantly: "No democracy, not even one as large as ours, can survive half suburb and half slum." And in speaking of the parity issue in *The Zero Sum Society,* Lester Thurow warns, "Unless we can learn to answer such questions and implement our answers, our society is going to both stagnate and be split along group lines. There is no way to avoid the problem. Benign neglect will not solve it."

THE NEW CLASS WAR

In has become politically fashionable in recent years for conservatives to attack liberals for fomenting a class war. The conservatives charge these class mongers with trying to divide the country. The major problem with this accusation is that the growing economic divide has already created a class war, in which the bottom group fights for survival, the middle group struggles to keep its head above water, and the top group accumulates unparalleled income and wealth.

Yet despite these sharp class divisions, the United States has seen relatively few outbreaks of open class warfare. As Jennifer L. Hochschild points out in her book *What's Fair? American Beliefs about Distributive Justice*, even the poorest members of society infrequently challenge the moral assumptions of the society that has placed them at the bottom. Take, for example, the debate over inheritance taxes in the 2000 presidential campaign. If legislated, an inheritance tax would be imposed on only 1 percent to 2 percent of the population—those with a net worth of over $1 million. Yet this policy has been criticized by many who would never be directly affected by it—even though it would add billions to government coffers for antipoverty programs or tax relief for the middle class.

Hochschild provides this summary of her findings:

> We have, then, four explanations for why the dog does not bark, or why poor Americans do not seek downward redistribution of wealth. First, some people do not seek it because they do not want it. . . . They define political freedom as strict equality, but economic freedom as an equal chance to become unequal. . . . Most people do not seek downward redistribution because they cannot imagine it or do not believe in its possibility. . . . A few do not seek redistribution because they strongly oppose it . . . as too egalitarian. . . . A few people do not seek redistribution because they do not care one way or the other about it.

My own view is that Americans foolishly hold on to the American dream of success—the naive view that anyone who works hard can and will make it. They have bought into the mythos of American exceptionalism—that our nation's unique, privatistic economy can work for anyone. They have been seduced by and continue to believe endless promises that are never fulfilled. They have been brainwashed into believing that the United States has a classless society, despite all evidence to the contrary.

In short, the social compact—theologically speaking, the covenant—has broken down in the United States. There is a decreasing sense that "we're all in this together." Even in the boom times, we find that while profits soar, workers' wages are only barely increasing. Instead, increasing competition in the marketplace has brought "down-waging" and "down-benefiting." Full-time workers are being replaced with contingent workers, who work without benefits and move in and out of a company, as need dictates.

Why do these things happen in a time of unparalleled economic prosperity? One reason is that we no longer face the perils that united the nation in times past. During the Depression, most people understood that poverty could happen to them and thus felt sympathy for those in need. Rallying around the country's effort in World War II helped to cement the bonds of community, as people shared a common purpose. Sacrifices were expected as a responsibility of citizenship. But today, we have no national superordinate goals, no sense of national purpose. Instead, we have only the individual purpose to "go for the gold."

Another reason for the fracturing of community is that in a global economy, there is less economic dependence on the locale or region. Self-interest is less tied to the prosperity of the place where one lives. When Henry Ford increased his workers' wages early in the twentieth century, he knew that his company's prosperity depended on having workers who could afford to buy the cars they produced. With globalization, however, money and profit circle the globe with the touch of a key. What happens down the street or on the next block is becoming less and less important. We are insulated from our local milieu by globe-spanning technology.

In today's milieu of prosperity, there is little sense of "It could happen to me." The general prosperity of "the fortunate fifth" effectively separates them and their families from the financial worries that plague millions of people whose economic security is always in doubt. Fewer and fewer social protections like unemployment insurance, health care, and unions are available for working people. Too many seem to feel immune against such uncertainty.

A final reason for the breakdown of community in the United States is that gated communities—either literal or figurative—have isolated economic classes from one another. Quite simply, the "haves" in American society no longer need to associate with or even be aware of the "have nots." It is possible to live in an affluent cocoon. The poor have effectively disappeared from our national consciousness.

HABITS OF THE HEART

The loss of community is not limited to electoral politics, as can be seen in the work of Robert Bellah et al., *Habits of the Heart* (after Tocqueville's term for *cultural mores*). In attempting to "take the moral pulse of America," as Tocqueville did in the 1830s, the authors find a "radical individualism" that is "cancerous." What is deemed *good* has been reduced to what feels good in pursuit of one's private interests, generally economic. Moral decision making is based on serving personal preferences and has no wider community framework by which to justify those values. Quoting Bellah et al.:

> In the vocabulary of one interviewee, active in town politics, the public good is thus defined in terms of the long-range ability of individuals each to get what they have paid for, no more and no less. One's contribution to the community—in time and taxes—is not thought of as a duty but as a voluntary investment.

Today, the rules of the marketplace are the arbiters of living, not the town meeting or the church. Eugene Debs's argument for socialism—that a moral consideration overrides the principles of market exchange, a consideration grounded in the solidarity of the citizens—has little currency today. The litmus test of today's society is how it deals with the problem of economic disparity. The apparent presumption is that the poor will be fed from the crumbs that fall from the table and deserve no more. But in fact, economic prosperity does not trickle down enough to build community.

Creative individualism and healthy community need one another for mutual survival, but many have trouble seeing that the extreme fragmentation that characterizes the modern world really threatens our individuation. What is best about our individualism—our sense of dignity and autonomy as persons—requires a new integration if it is to be sustained.

MONEY AND MEMBERSHIP

Sociologist Lee Rainwater, quoted by Michael Walzer in *Spheres of Justice,* applies this attitude to a money-oriented economy. "Money," he writes, "buys membership in industrial society." Money, however, is not the only economic factor that causes a splintering of community.

In *The Social Limits to Growth,* Fred Hirsch shows the dysfunctional nature of individualism and competitiveness. As he explains, the logic of capitalism leads to an ever-ascending spiral of competition, not only for what he calls *material goods* (consumer products) but also for *positional goods,* which include top jobs, mobility, recreation, services, and leisure. Even as the desire for material goods is satisfied, the desire for positional goods increases. Individuals who are already affluent are caught up in a constantly intensifying pursuit of positional goods, which are, by their very nature, in small supply. As people satisfy their desires for material goods, we might expect them to become more generous. However, each new level of positional goods requires an increased standard of living to achieve the same level of satisfaction. There is thus a growing resistance to redistributing goods among the less affluent.

Economic competition worked as well as it did for as long as it did because there was agreement on communal norms. Adam Smith, for example, felt confident advising people to pursue their self-interests because he assumed that excesses would be countered by law, morality, religion, custom, and education. Instead, those norms have been badly eroded by the compulsive search for positional goods. People's sense of community no longer tempers their individual self-aggrandizement. And so there seems to be no solution except to ask (or to compel) the privileged to yield some of their privileges.

The lack of community solidarity is a prominent theme in Alasdair MacIntyre's *After Virtue*. In sum, our culture has lost the Aristotelian virtues that involve practicing friendship in the context of the *polis,* or "city." The nature of friendship meant that everyone shared in the common project of sustaining public life in the city. Conflict was to be avoided, or at least managed. Today, we are merely a collection of strangers. Quoting MacIntyre, "Modern liberal political society can appear only as a collection of citizens of nowhere who have banded together for their common protection." The Greek term *agon,* which originally meant "a game," now means "a bitterly fought contest." Acquisitiveness, once one of the Seven Deadly Sins, is now celebrated as the greatest value; vice has become virtue. Society has become an arena in which individuals compete for the fulfillment of their own desires. There is no shared vision and little sense of the common good. The only hint of a public good is the summing of individual desires and interests. MacIntyre concludes, "Modern politics is civil war carried on by other means." He summarizes his thesis in these words:

> For what education in the virtues teaches me is with whom I am bound up in human community. There is no way of my pursuing my good which is necessarily antagonistic to you pursuing yours because the good is neither mine peculiarly nor yours peculiarly— goods are not private property. Hence Aristotle's definition of friendship, the fundamental form of human relationship, is in terms of shared goods.

THEOLOGY AND THE COMMON GOOD

American society desperately needs a renewal of the social compact—
a recovery of covenant. For many people, that renewal might prove difficult because they no longer have any notion of what comprises *the
common good*. That point might be illustrated through a story that
addresses whether Americans teach their young to be kind and caring
or fiercely competitive. In a commentary aired on Public Radio's "All
Things Considered," Jim Roberts, a family therapist in Kansas City, told
the following story, as reported by Robert C. Roberts in *Taking the
World to Heart:*

> He was visiting the fourth-grade class of his son Daniel where the
> teacher had organized a "balloon stomp." Each child had a balloon
> tied on his or her leg, and the object was to obliterate everyone else's
> balloon without letting anything happen to yours. It was every man
> for himself and each against all. As soon as somebody stomped you,
> you were "out," and the child who still had a plump, glistening bal-
> loon when everybody else's hung limp and tattered would have the
> winner's glory.
>
> The teacher gave the signal, and the children leapt ferociously
> on each other's balloons, doing their best, meanwhile, to protect
> themselves against the onslaught of others. All, that is, except one
> or two who lacked the spirit of competition. These were just dis-
> mayed by all the hullabaloo, and their balloons were predictably laid
> waste. In a few seconds all balloons were burst but one.
>
> Then a disturbing thing happened. Another class, this time a
> class of mentally handicapped children, was brought in and pre-
> pared to play the same game. Balloons were tied to their legs and
> they were briefed on the rules of play. Said Roberts, "I got a sinking
> feeling in my midsection. I wanted to spare these kids the pressure
> of a competitive brawl."
>
> They had only the foggiest notion of what this was all about.
> After a few moments of confusion, the idea got across to one
> or two of them that the balloons were supposed to be stomped,
> and gradually it caught on. But as the game got under way, it was
> clear these kids had missed the spirit of it. They went about method-
> ically getting their balloons stomped. One girl carefully held her
> own in place so that a boy could pop it, and then he did the same
> for her. When all the balloons were gone, the entire class cheered
> in unison.

These children had mistaken the competitive game for a cooperative one, but their error has some advantages. In the original game only one child could win, but they discovered how to make everybody a winner! In normal balloon-stomping the participants are momentarily alienated from one another (it's you against me), but as these children played it, the game was for camaraderie. Instead of feeling anxious about fellow players, you know the others are there to help you along. In the original game, you wouldn't be likely to learn love. But the play of these children seemed to foster generosity, trust, cooperation, gentleness, and concern for one another. This story is notable for the sense of community and cooperation demonstrated by the second group of children. They showed little, if any, sense of individualism.

We are, by nature, social creatures who create our identity and purpose in a community of other creatures. We are not so much atomistic individuals as we are individual members of a community, with whose fate we are inextricably connected. Thus, the increasing disparity between income levels does far more damage than merely plunging more people into poverty. More and more, this disparity fractures people's sense of community solidarity and weakens their resolve to solve their problems.

Again, what is missing from American society is a sense of community often called *the common good*, a prominent theme in Jewish, Roman Catholic, Protestant, and secular teachings. St. Thomas Aquinas believed, in the words of interpreter Leo Schumacher, that "all material riches belong in common to the human race." There is a creative tension between individual and community, such that the rights of one member cannot override the good of the whole and vice versa.

Political scientist Robert B. Reich observes in "The Liberal Promise of Prosperity,"

> A society that simultaneously offers both the prospect of substantial wealth and the threat of severe poverty surely will inspire great feats of personal daring, dazzling entrepreneurialism, and cut-throat ambition. But just as surely it may reduce the capacity of its members to work together toward a common end.

That communal spirit emerged early in the United States, as indicated in John Winthrop's lay sermon, "A Modell of Christian Charity," given aboard the *Arabella* in 1630. Winthrop advocates a willingness to yield private preference to public necessities:

For it is a true rule that particular estates cannot subsist in the ruin of the public. . . . we must be knit together in this work as one man. . . . we must be willing to abridge ourselves of our superfluities, for the supply of others' necessities. . . . We must delight in each other, rejoice together, mourn together, labor and suffer together . . . members of the same body, so shall we keep the unity of the spirit in the bond of peace.

Winthrop may have taken his ideas from the Book of Acts, which says that the early Christian community, expecting the imminent end of the age, held all goods in common:

And all who believed were together and had all things in common; and they sold their possessions and goods and distributed them to all, as any had need. (4:32–34)

Now the company of those who believed were of one heart and soul, and no one said that any of the things which he possessed was his own, but they had everything in common. (2:44)

While these passages reflect an apocalyptic vision, they also suggest a strong emphasis on human solidarity. This theme was picked up by the seventh-century Diggers community in England, which ignored the law of private ownership and planted grain on unused land. In the words of Gerard Winstanley,

When this universal law of equity rises up in every man and woman, then none shall lay claim to any creature and say, this is mine, and that is yours. This is my work, and that is yours. But every one shall put to their hands to till the earth and bring up cattle, and the blessing of the earth shall be common to all; when a man hath need of any corn or cattle, take from the next storehouse he meets with. There shall be no buying and selling, no fairs or markets, but the whole earth shall be a common treasury for every man, for the earth is the Lord's.

The Declaration of Independence, part of the United States' secular Bible, articulates Americans' right to "life, liberty and the pursuit of happiness" (which was changed from John Locke's version: "life, liberty and property"). While this statement may seem a paean of praise to individualism, there is a scholarly body of thought that interprets *happiness* as public happiness. Public virtue, rather than self-interest, was the beginning principle of republican government. As James Madison puts it in *The Federalist Papers,* "The public good, the real welfare of the great body of the people, is the supreme object to be pursued; and that no form of government whatever has any other value than as it may be fitted for the attainment of this object."

The Preamble to the U.S. Constitution, that other scripture in the democratic canon, is a secular reading of the concept of national community. Its opening words are an affirmation of human solidarity: "We, the people." Moreover, it speaks of "a more perfect union" and the "general welfare."

What Is the Common Good?

We might begin to understand the common good by indicating what it is not. It is not merely the sum of individual happinesses, for we are all members of groups whose realities transcend us: families, religions, nations, a planet. The common good is not the mere aggregation of private wants; rather, it is an expression of our common humanity. The mechanism of the free market does not recognize this; it only supplies the aggregate of personal preferences.

The common good is better understood as a value embodied by a group of people who share in one another's fates and commit themselves to bettering the fate of each individual. In an increasingly interdependent society and world, this kind of collaboration is far more than a religious *desideratum*. It is, in fact, a survival skill. The common good has to do with our need for one another, for we are basically social creatures who find meaning in our interactions with our neighbors. Without understanding ourselves as members of a society over time and space, we forget how much we depend on others, on society as a whole. Music, art, literature—so much that is humanly worthwhile—are inconceivable without understanding individuals as members. We define ourselves essentially by our relationship to the wider community. Even our most personal achievements cannot be understood without realizing our debt to humanity.

The Market Metaphor and Morality

The metaphor of the market as a jungle—or, more currently, as a footrace—is morally limited. In *Equality,* William Ryan suggests that we should consider metaphors for life other than the image of a footrace: "Life is like a collection of craftsmen working together to construct a sturdy and beautiful building. Or, a bit more fancifully, it is like an orchestra—imagine a hundred members of a symphony orchestra racing to see who can finish first!"

The natural resources of the earth, from which our material goods come, are provided free by a nonhuman reality—call it Providence, God, or Nature. And our social benefits have been bequeathed to us by those who have gone before. As many have shared in their creation, so many should share in their enjoyment.

The common good is more than the recognition of our interdependence; it is the commitment to a communal life. This commitment does not require us to sacrifice the totality of our private goods to the public good, for the two are complementary, not contradictory. There is a tension here, but it is a creative one, for we best realize private goods by contributing to the public good.

The statement of the Roman Catholic bishops of the United States is instructive. They recognize private property yet reaffirm the church's tradition that no one has the right to unlimited accumulation of wealth:

> There is a social mortgage on private property. . . . In our increasingly complex economy, the common good may sometimes demand the right to cede to public involvement in the planning or ownership of certain sectors of the economy. The Church's teaching opposes collectivist and statist economic approaches. But it also rejects the notion that a free market automatically produces justice.

Archbishop Rembert Weakland of Milwaukee, reflecting on people's reaction to this statement, says in a 1988 issue of *Christian Century*, "The concept of the 'common good' hardly means anything any more to many of our people." One letter he received from critics said, "I have worked hard for what I got and I am going to keep it. God has been good to me. The lazy slob next door has no rights to what I have earned."

Daniel Maguire describes the individualistic view of justice in *A New American Justice*:

> For the consistent individualist there are no debts to the common good; the common good has no rights. We can have debts only to other individuals; only individuals have rights. We are not a naturally sharing animal in this view—just an animal that might decide to share.

He concludes,

> Any surviving political community has somehow to come to grips with the reality of persons as social individuals. Some forms of social and distributive justice are found in every society. What this signifies is that there are two elements in the meaning of person-hood: individuality and sociality.

Perhaps we should consider the example set by the Saint-Simonians, followers of early-nineteenth-century French socialist Claude Henri Saint Simon. Members of this group each wore a special waistcoat that symbolized community solidarity and mutual support. It could neither be put on nor taken off without the help of a fellow member because it was buttoned up the back. Perhaps we do not wish to go to this extreme to recognize our interdependence, but it serves as a useful symbol of our common lot.

Insofar as inequality divides a people, as would appear to be the case in the twenty-first-century United States, justice is denied. Great disparities in income and wealth violate the integrity of the community. A self-conscious community would do well to emphasize and strengthen the common humanity that unites it rather than perpetuate the class differences that divide it.

A community is more than the sum of its individual parts. It has an organic quality, a life of its own. The meaning of each individual life is not to be found in isolation, individual feats of economic enterprise, or self-aggrandizement. Rather, we find personal meaning by participating in an organic social process of defining and seeking the common good. There is a moral substance in community that overrides the principle of market exchanges.

♦ ♦ ♦

Through the Eye
of a Needle

*Wealthy men are insolent and arrogant; their possession of wealth
affects their understanding; they feel as if they had every good
thing that exists; wealth becomes a sort of standard of value for
everything else, and therefore they imagine there is nothing it
cannot buy. . . . In a word, the type of character produced by
wealth is that of a prosperous fool.*

—Aristotle, *Rhetoric*

Proposition Four: The greater the equality in income and wealth, the greater the potential for moral sensitivity and religious meaning. My perspective has its roots in the Jewish and Christian traditions of theological covenant—a spiritual compact by which human beings make moral and spiritual promises to Life (God). The covenant carries an imperative to do justice. It suggests that human interest transcends self-interest. At the same time, it is a pragmatic perspective, taking into account the realities of human nature and society as well as economic problems.

Self-interest is inherent in human nature and serves to drive economic activity. The need for solidarity is also inherent in human nature and moves us to compassion. In considering this last proposition attacking great economic disparities, I draw again on Lord Acton's famous dictum, "Power tends to corrupt, and absolute power corrupts absolutely." Paraphrasing and expanding these words, "Affluence (and poverty) tend to corrupt, and absolute affluence (and poverty) corrupt absolutely." Conversely, I believe that economic equity enhances the potential for moral and spiritual development.

THE MORAL CORRUPTIONS OF AFFLUENCE

Is it true, as the late philosopher Ayn Rand said, that capitalism and altruism are incompatible? For Rand, enlightened self-interest was the supreme good. Believing that to be true, would we condemn the Massachusetts businessman who lost $1.5 million by paying wages and benefits to his employees after his factory burned down? Maybe he just does not get it—or does he? These contrasting philosophies illustrate the relationship between making money and morality.

The notion that affluence tends to corrupt is found in Plato's *Laws*. Plato held to moderation in all things, from health of body to accumulation of riches:

> The same holds good of the possession of goods and chattels, and they are to be valued on a similar scale. In each case, when they are in excess, they produce enmities and feuds both in States and privately, while if they are deficient they produce, as a rule, serfdom. And let no man love riches for the sake of his children, in order that he may leave them as wealthy as possible; for that is good neither for them nor for the State.

Washington Post columnist David Broder updates that scenario, writing in July 2000 about the debate over eliminating the inheritance tax. At the time he wrote his column, a federal inheritance tax was levied only on estates in excess of $675,000; couples could double that limit to $1.35 million by careful estate planning. Broder writes,

> The $28 billion in inheritance taxes came from the 2% of very large estates. Rep. Pete Stark, a California Democrat who built a successful banking business before he came to Congress, addressed his five children and 10 grandchildren in personal terms in explaining, during House debate, why he was not going to vote to give them a "seven-figure business" entirely tax-free. Under existing law, he said, "you are going to get a down payment from your mother and me of $1.35 million (tax-)free. You have not worked a day in your life for that." While the excess value of the estate will be taxed, Stark said, "you are going to get 10 years to pay that off at below-prime-rate interest rate. If you are so dumb that you cannot run that business with over a 50% down payment given to you and 10 years to pay off the balance at a low rate, you do not deserve it."

This is a prime example of how the marketplace gives some a head start in the race for riches. The Stark children and grandchildren, through no effort of their own, will have a head start on millions of children, who will begin the race with virtually no resources. Even with the inheritance tax, the Stark family will reap a reward that has not been earned. This result flies in the face of the American work ethic, which says that one is entitled only to what one has earned.

In *Spheres of Justice,* Michael Walzer credits Thomas Hobbes for the image of the race in a competitive society—a race in which there are no spectators, in which everyone must run. He quotes Hobbes at this point:

> To consider them behind, is glory
>
> To consider them before, is humility
>
> To be in breath, hope
>
> To be weary, despair
>
> To endeavor to overtake the next, emulation
>
> To lose ground by little hindrances, pusillanimity
>
> To fall on the sudden, is disposition to weep
>
> To see another fall, is disposition to laugh
>
> Continually to be outdone, is misery,
>
> Continually to outgo the next before, is felicity
>
> And to forsake the course, is to die.

Other values, beyond basic economic and ethical issues, are at stake in a distributional mechanism that creates the disparity in wealth currently seen in the United States. A society that so distances the affluent from the poor is in danger of causing moral insensitivity among the affluent. Those who excel in the race also seem at risk in the spiritual dimensions of life.

AFFLUENCE AND SELF-RIGHTEOUSNESS

The danger of self-righteousness is omnipresent: "I have worked hard and been properly rewarded. I deserve everything that has come my way. Let others do the same." Consider a *New Yorker* cartoon showing three fish swimming, one behind the other. The first, a small fish, says, "There is no justice." A larger fish swims immediately behind the first fish, ready to swallow it. This fish says, "There is some justice in the world." Finally, the third, a very large fish, prepares to swallow both and says, "The world is just."

As John D. Rockefeller said, "The good Lord gave me my money." He believed the old shibboleth "God helps those who help themselves." Historic belief in the Puritanical notion that wealth and poverty are the results of people's moral desert is one of the reasons the United States has been the most reluctant of all the welfare states to provide a minimum economic package as a right of citizenship.

This view is in sharp contrast with the wisdom of Ecclesiastes:

> Wise men do not always earn a living, intelligent men do not always get rich, and capable men do not always rise to high positions. (9:11)

> I have also learned why people work so hard to succeed: it is because they envy the things which their neighbors have. But it is useless. It is like chasing the wind. They say that a man would be a fool to fold his hands and let himself starve to death. Maybe so, but it is better to have only a little, with peace of mind, than be busy all the time with both hands, trying to catch the wind. (4:4–6)

Economic well-being is generally attributed more to effort than to luck, blind fate, or the workings of impersonal social forces. Yet Robert Kuttner, in *The Economic Illusion,* suggests that a good many of the outcomes produced by the market reflect little more than these causes:

> An investor happens to hold the right stock at the right time; an autoworker finds himself in the wrong trade in the wrong decade. The unexpected passing of a rich aunt produces a windfall for one family, while the untimely death of a husband produces hardship for another. Prudent citizens who save and invest sometimes lose their shirts; diligent and loyal workers often lose their jobs. People reap fortuitous windfalls or suffer devastating reverses that have nothing to do with their social contribution or their personal effort.

The hubris and sense of entitlement that often characterize the affluent have a long history in Western religion. The biblical prophet Amos said,

> Woe to those who are at ease in Zion, and to those who feel secure on the mountains of Samaria, the notable men of the first of the nations. . . . Woe to those who lie upon beds of ivory . . . who drink wine in bowls, and anoint themselves with the finest oils, but are not grieved over the ruin of Joseph. (6:1–7)

Take away from me the noise of your songs; to the melody of your harps I will not listen. But let justice roll down like waters, and righteousness like an everflowing stream. (5:23–4)

German writer Bertolt Brecht, a twentieth-century prophet, protests against the corruption of Nazi society in *A German War Primer*:

Those who take the meat from the table teach contentment.

Those for whom the taxes are destined demand sacrifice.

Those who eat their fill speak to the hungry

Of the wonderful time to come.

Those who lead the country into the abyss call ruling too

Difficult for ordinary folk.

THE BLUNTING OF SOCIAL CONSCIENCE

In the early 1990s, a story circulated about then President George H. Bush after he expressed amazement at the workings of an electronic checkout scanner at a supermarket. He was ribbed for being so out of touch with everyday American life. Anthony Lewis, in a 1992 *New York Times* column, finds in this episode an even larger and more disturbing truth:

> Upper-income Americans generally . . . live not just a better life, but one quite removed from that of ordinary families. They hardly experience the problems that weigh so heavily today on American society. And that fact has dangerous political consequences. . . . It is not a recipe for a healthy democratic society.

Using the vernacular of the times, we might say many rich people are "empathy challenged." A great divide in material prosperity tends to blunt the social conscience. According to a survey in a 2000 issue of *Modern Maturity*, the monthly magazine of the American Association of Retired Persons,

> Four out of five of those surveyed said they feared that wealth would turn them into greedy people who consider themselves superior, and three-fourths said that wealth promotes insensitivity. Even those who said they would like to be wealthy shared that negative view of how the rich behave.

Accounts of the recession of the early 1980s indicate that while wages and profits were down and unemployment was up, corporate executives continued to receive hefty salary increases and increased "perks." The phenomenon of *golden parachutes,* or generous termination agreements for corporate executives deposed by corporate takeovers or shake-ups, became ubiquitous. In the 1990s and into the twenty-first century, we observe the same phenomenon on an even larger scale.

Affluence is morally problematic. As the Roman Catholic bishops said in their pastoral letter on the economy, "Greed is moral underdevelopment." Its very existence strains our moral capacity. Take, for instance, the case of Imelda Marcos. She and her husband became rich through illicit means while the reasonably prosperous Philippine economy became a debtor nation with rapidly escalating poverty. Mrs. Marcos set a standard for conspicuous consumption and moral insensitivity. Campaigning for political office, she said to a Philippine audience of Negrito tribal people who had lost their mountain homes and hundreds of children to the eruption of Mount Pinatubo in June 1991, "I have suffered like you; I know pain as you do; I, too, am homeless." She then returned to her $2,000-a-day hotel suite in Manila.

Or take the case of Phil Knight, the founder of the Nike Corporation, who is high on the Forbes 400 list of richest Americans. Despite documentation of low wages paid to Nike workers in foreign nations, enormous Nike contracts, and huge payoffs to Nike hustlers such as Michael Jordan and Tiger Woods, Knight refuses to be disturbed by antisweatshop critics. The 1997 Forbes 400 issue reported, "An unrepentant Phil Knight blasts his sweatshop critics. 'This isn't an issue that should even be on the political agenda today. It's just a sound bite of globalization.'"

The *Rochester Democrat and Chronicle* reported in 1998 that Paul A. Allaire, then Chairman of Xerox, took home nearly $21 million in salary, bonuses, exercised stock options, and other compensation, almost quadrupling his pay package from 1996. President and Chief Operating Officer G. Richard Thoman received a package worth $10.2 million. These disclosures came two days after the company said it would cut nine thousand employees as part of restructuring to reduce costs. A Xerox spokesperson said the layoffs were a "painful but necessary" step and that the compensation packages had been determined well before the restructuring took shape. Thoman was consequently fired after Xerox stock plummeted, but he walked away with a severance package of $800,000 a year. Other Xerox employees, however, continue to worry about their future with "America's document company." They must wonder at the rewards given to management even in the wake of clearly inept corporate planning.

Individuals who are part of the machinery of corporate America can be compelled to act against their consciences. Alan Downs is a management consultant who was once hired by a Silicon Valley business to plan a major workforce reduction. He includes in his book *Corporate Executions* an example of the standard speech to laid-off workers:

> We regret to inform you that due to a recent reorganization, your job no longer exists. We made every effort to find a place for your skills in the new organization but have been unable to do so. This decision is not a reflection on your job performance or skills but the result of business changes. It has been reviewed at the highest level of organization and will not be reversed. You will be escorted to your desk and allowed to pack your personal belongings. You are to be off the premises within the period of one hour and are not to return. Should you have forgotten any personal belongings, they will be mailed to you. The company has provided an outplacement center at another location to which it is suggested that you report at 8:00 a.m. tomorrow. Your supervisor will now provide you with a packet that explains your severance pay and benefits. Included in that packet is a letter of final settlement (absolving the company from any further liability), which you must sign in order to receive your severance pay. If you choose not to sign it at this time, please be aware that this offer of severance pay expires at the end of business today.

Downs agonized about playing God: "In my head I knew this was a necessary pruning, but in my heart I saw myself sitting on the other side of the table stunned at the news that the job to which I had given so much was seen as unnecessary and discarded." One secretary he knew pleaded, "What am I supposed to do? . . . I am a single mother, my parents are gone, and I just closed on a house two weeks ago. I need my job." For Downs to show sympathy was against company policy. Four hundred jobs were eliminated that day.

But at the so-called executioners' party, there was a surprise. The vice-president of human resources, with whom the down-sizing team had worked, thanked the group for its performance and proceeded to pass out pink slips to many of them. Six months later, the company's CEO resigned. Many suspected it was his mismanagement that had thrown the company into a mess. Nevertheless, he received a $4-million golden parachute, roughly the savings recouped from all of the layoffs for the first year.

That was the day Downs decided to put his hatchet away. "I learned the hard way that while the initial cut of a layoff is painful, the aftermath can be deadly." It was a cure that can kill. Since then, he has been studying "corporate executions" and finds what others are beginning to discover: Down-sizing in the wake of roaring profits and soaring CEO salaries may not, in the long run, even help the bottom line. First, the fat is sliced, then the muscle, and then the brainpower. Business analysts are also learning what Henry Ford figured out decades ago: You will not sell many cars to the unemployed.

In a 1996 issue of the *Washington Post National Weekly Edition*, David M. Jones, chief economist at Aubrey G. Lanston & Co., a New York securities dealer, points to the celebrations on Wall Street that follow announcements of major corporate layoffs: "You begin to wonder when 20,000 workers are fired and everyone stands up and cheers." The celebratory response makes economic sense: Layoffs mean higher unemployment, less upward pressure on wages, lower interest rates, and easier business borrowing. Nonetheless, it is morally repulsive.

William Simon, benefactor of the Graduate School of Business Administration at the University of Rochester, writing in the *Times Union* in 1996, bemoans those who seek a more progressive taxation system, charging that they want to penalize success. Simon wants a flat tax: "It's wonderful idea: Keep the money you make." At one time, he says, his combined federal and state income tax rate reached 88 percent, but now he is able to keep most of what he earns. He further says that the U.S. poor "are the envy of the world." One wonders what poor people he has spoken with.

HOMO FABER OR HOMO SPIRITUS?

A young Andrew Carnegie wrote in a memo to himself in 1868, "To continue much longer with most of my thoughts wholly upon the way to make more money in the shortest possible time, must degrade me beyond hopes of permanent recovery." His self-reflection raises this basic question: As human beings, are we *homo faber*—workers and economic creatures—or are we *homo spiritus*—spiritual creatures? I suspect we are both. The problem is how to achieve the proper balance.

I recognize the self-interest in me and in all of us; it is part of our human nature. I realize the efficiency of the market's productive power. But I also recognize in all of us a loftier sensibility—a sense of mystic oneness with all people, poor and rich alike. We who are prosperous cannot in good conscience say to the poor, "Your end of the rowboat is sinking."

Sociologist Philip Slater, in his 1983 book *Wealth Addiction,* identifies character flaws in the very wealthy people he studies. He finds them myopic in their understanding of the world, not at all generous (even their philanthropic efforts had virtually no impact on their fortunes), and power hungry. The sin of pride is apt to be a particularly powerful force in the affluent.

In Arianna Huffington's "Reinventing Charity," an online column of June 24, 1999, she reports a study of the most generous charitable givers published in *Slate* magazine. The largest contributor was Audrey Jones Beck, who gave forty-seven impressionist and postimpressionist paintings valued at more than $80 million to the Houston Museum of Fine Arts, for which she will have a building named in her honor. Huffington quotes Harvard sociologist Francie Ostrower from her book *Why the Wealthy Give:* "[The wealthy] take philanthropy and adapt it into an entire way of life that serves as a vehicle for the cultural and social life of their class."

In Robert Coles's study of children of wealth and poverty, *The Moral Life of Children,* he observed "that since wealthy children are treated as if they were the center of the universe they tend ultimately to believe it." In the self-portraits of rich American children, for example, the figure of the child fills up the whole page, while in those of Hopi children, the figure is merely a dot in a rich landscape.

Affluence tends to infect people with a kind of moral insensitivity. Anecdotes do not prove the point, but they do serve to illustrate it. Clare Booth Luce, journalist, playwright, and former U.S. Ambassador to Italy, made these remarks in *U.S. News and World Report* in 1982 about providing aid to developing countries: "I believe charity begins at home. . . . I repeatedly see pictures in the papers of a starving mother with her child holding out its hand. I think it would be hypocritical if I didn't say that I would feel a little more compassion if one of my pet birds had broken a leg."

In a 1987 article, *Washington Post* columnist David Broder quotes New Jersey state Republican Party chairman Frank B. Holman, who calls the younger generation "the hope of the Republican Party." Holman elaborates on his point, saying, "That's where we can eat them up. These young people are very ambitious. They want it all and they want it now, and they don't want to see it taxed away. They don't care if Aunt Tilly is being taken care of in the nursing home or not; Aunt Tilly better take care of herself."

The creation of so many new millionaires and billionaires in Silicon Valley has driven up housing costs in Woodside, California, to an average of $1,515,065. David A. Kaplan's *The Silicon Boys* indicates that these *nouveau riche* are imparting their values to their progeny. There is a program in the local junior high curriculum called "How to Be a Millionaire." The first math assignment in the seventh grade has a child spend a hypothetical $1 million and learn about spreadsheets. The children can make only fifteen purchases and can spend only $700,000 on a house and buy two cars. No more than $25,000 can go to charity.

For most millionaires, charitable contributions hardly make a dent in their wealth. This has traditionally been the case, despite the generosity of billionaires such as George Soros, who has donated millions to various causes, including rebuilding the Russian economy; Ted Turner, who will give $1 billion to the United Nations over a decade; and Bill Gates, whose foundation has provided millions for AIDS prevention and treatment in Africa. As we enter the twenty-first century, however, there appears to be a growing movement among Silicon Valley millionaires to turn to philanthropy to find meaning in their lives. One hopes that will become the dominant ethos of that unique economic enclave.

But generally, as people become affluent, they do not become more generous in their contributions to philanthropic or charitable groups nor do they seem to take on an attitude of *noblesse oblige*. Surveys of charitable giving in the wake of the 1981 federal income tax cuts did not suggest increased generosity. A 1985 study by the Rockefeller Brothers Fund found that Americans with incomes of $1 million or more in 1962 gave away nearly one dollar of every five dollars they earned. People in the poor and middle classes gave proportionately more of their incomes. In *Wealthy and Wise,* financial consultant Claude Rosenberg, a veteran manager of rich people's money, says that while those with over $1 million in earnings saw their incomes jump 80 percent from 1980 to 1991, their charitable contributions dropped 57 percent. In 1993, the *New York Times* reported that of the 205,623 households that filed tax returns claiming incomes of more than $500,000, 10 percent (20,354) made no deductions for charity.

Along with its list of the sixty most generous givers, the December 1996 *Slate* magazine reports, "When wealthy Americans give, they tend to give to universities, medical research centers, and cultural institutions—not organizations to help the poor." This statement confirms the view of the late theologian James Luther Adams, who said in a 1977 lecture, "The New Narcissism," at the Winter Institute of Meadville/Lombard Theological School, "Business and professional people, so far from breaking through class and race barriers, more deeply entrench themselves in their own class perspectives by participation in philanthropic and service organizations."

Syndicated columnist James Glassman, quoted in the Winter 1997 issue of *Too Much,* a publication of United for a Fair Economy, reports that families with incomes of more than $1 million donate only 8.5 percent of their incomes, according to one study. Apparently, the reason for the decline in charitable giving is the decline in the marginal tax rate.

In his 1985 essay "How We Get the Poor off Our Conscience" in *Harper's Magazine,* John Kenneth Galbraith traces the history of human indifference to the plight of the poor. The modern attitude seems rooted in *utilitarianism,* the notion of providing the greatest happiness for the greatest number. The sad result is that the happiness of many will not be served. In 1830, Thomas Malthus declared that poverty was the fault of the poor; i.e., the high birthrate among this group caused shortages of food, space, and clothing. From this view, it was a short step to social Darwinism, "the survival of the fittest." Herbert Spencer, for instance, believed that eliminating the poor was nature's way of improving the human race.

According to Galbraith, the New Deal of the Franklin Roosevelt era marked a distinct turnaround for Americans. They could ease their consciences with the belief that the government was taking care of the poor. The modern process of conscience clearing is more complicated. Four rationales persist:

1. Government welfare programs are marked by incompetence and thus make the plight of the poor worse.
2. Providing public help only hurts the poor (though no proof is offered).
3. Providing public welfare has an adverse impact on individuals' incentive to support themselves.
4. Attempts to help the poor have impinged on the freedom of the affluent to control their own money.

In the last analysis, says Galbraith, all of these excuses add up to nothing more than denial. People simply choose not to think of unpleasant things such as poverty in the midst of plenty.

On October 15, 1981, as I was leaving a meeting of the Unitarian Universalist Service Committee Board of Trustees, contemplating how to fulfill its mission to work for justice, I read in my daily paper that the United Nations International Children's Emergency Fund (UNICEF) had reported that 42,000 children around the world die needlessly each day. The same day, the *Wall Street Journal* reported a Gallup survey of top executives, who said they were deeply worried about the adequacy of their personal wealth. These executives had six-figure incomes, yet they admitted to severe anxiety about their financial security. The juxtaposition of these facts jarred me into a kind of cognitive dissonance that motivated me to write this book.

Conspicuous Consumption Revisited

In *Luxury Fever,* Robert Frank points out that Americans' spending on luxury goods grew by 21 percent from 1995 to 1996 while overall merchandise sales grew only 5 percent. Perhaps the most blatant example of luxury spending is the purchase of so-called trophy homes— mansions with more than 10,000 feet of living space. There are nineteen such homes along one short stretch of the Florida coast near Palm Beach. And in Seattle, Microsoft co-founder Paul Allen built a 74,000-square foot house—about the same size as the building that houses Cornell University's Johnson Graduate School of Management, which provides space for one hundred faculty and administrative staff and six hundred students every day.

Gift giving among the affluent provides more examples of what Thorsten Veblen labeled "conspicuous consumption." The *Robb Report's Fifteenth Annual Ultimate Gift Guide* for December 1998 advertises a unique way of giving a gift of thirty-one diamonds weighing sixty-nine carats: One could fly on a chartered jet to Worth Avenue in Palm Beach, Florida, to decide on the setting. One would then stay in the Imperial Suite at the five-star Breakers hotel, play a round of golf with a PGA pro, shop some more on Worth Avenue, and return home via chartered jet. And the cost of this outing? $1,050,000. High-end retailer Nieman Marcus, known for its unique but pricey gift items, sold a $1,500 designer Raj doll replicating a street urchin.

Thus, the conspicuous consumption during the recession of the early 1980s cannot hold a candle to that of the 1990s. One wonders what the new century will bring.

The moral insensitivity of the affluent emerges from a destructive self-centeredness. The superabundance of goods and services satisfies material needs but creates wants that can never be met. Whereas needs rise in arithmetic proportion, wants seems to rise geometrically. Hence, the wealthy are caught in a never-ending search for self-gratification with spiritually numbing results. One generation's luxury becomes the next generation's necessity.

Ralph Waldo Emerson suggested that people are most conservative after dinner; that is, when their own needs have been satisfied, they tend not to worry about others. This moral callousness has been cryptically restated by twentieth-century theological ethicist Clarence Skinner: "A stuffed prophet sees no visions."

Symbolic of the potential for corruption and callousness among the affluent is the following story told by Larry L. Greenfield, former president of Colgate Rochester Divinity School, in the Fall 1986 school bulletin. At his hotel near the Philadelphia airport, he spotted a beautiful, new, red Porsche. Its owner had paid a few extra dollars for a so-called vanity license plate that read "IOU 000." The invisible hand of the market often comes in the shape of a fist.

As we contemplate the frenetic economic machine and the values that fuel it, we should keep in mind three of the seven deadly sins: pride, covetousness, and gluttony.

THE SPIRITUAL CORRUPTIONS OF AFFLUENCE

Erich Fromm has discussed the spiritual price we pay in a society where the acquisition of goods has become a preoccupation. In *To Have or To Be,* he points to the American tendency to find satisfaction in consuming and "taking in commodities." Everything is available for consumption, and the world is the object for our appetites. Even spiritual pursuits can be reduced to material objects, subject to exchange and consumption. Given the explosion of American religious and quasi-religious expression, this has come to be called the "spiritual marketplace." A variety of self-proclaimed spiritual gurus offer sure-fire routes to spiritual bliss, often accompanied by temporal wealth. This is the *having* mode of existence, which stands in clear contrast to the *being* mode of existence, wherein human experience is cherished as a spiritual value.

R. H. Tawney, in his 1920 book *The Acquisitive Society,* brings an *aesthetic judgment* to bear on the disparity between rich and poor:

It is said that among the barbarians, where wealth is still measured by cattle, great chiefs are described as hundred-cow men. The manager of a great enterprise who is paid $400,000 a year, might similarly be described as a hundred-family man, since he receives the income of a hundred families. It is true that special talent is worth any price, and that a payment of $400,000 a year to head a business with a turnover of millions is a bagatelle. But economic considerations are not the only considerations. There is also the point of honor. And the truth is that these hundred-family salaries are ungentlemanly.

Is *ungentlemanly* a strong enough term to describe wealthy people whose incomes are several times the salary of the president of the United States and exceed the Gross Domestic Products (GDPs) of some developing countries? One must wonder about the spiritual life of someone who lives in extravagance and luxury while people in his/her own nation go to bed hungry and thousands of children around the world die every day. I think of Tolstoy's evocative essay on czarist Russia, "How Much Land Does a Man Need?" with its stark contrast between the aristocracy (of which he was part) and the peasantry. To paraphrase Tolstoy, how much income or wealth does a person need to live the good life? How much is enough?

MONEY AND MEANING

There is a yet deeper religious problem in this life of endless getting and spending. It has to do with the meaning of human existence itself. A preoccupation with accumulation from the marketplace can have strange manifestations. One new psychic disease has been labeled "affluenza" by San Francisco's C. G. Jung Institute. Its symptoms are "lack of motivation or self-discipline, suspiciousness, boredom, guilt, low self-esteem and alienation." *Washington Post* columnist Robert J. Samuelson wrote in 2000 about a contemporary manifestation called the "sudden wealth (or loss) syndrome," characterized by "excessive guilt" and "identity confusion." These conditions may be related to a sense of apathy in the lives of those who face no challenges. An emptiness of the soul can result from a surfeit of things. Beyond a certain economic sufficiency, there is no correlation between happiness and affluence. The mantra "I shop; therefore, I am" does not express an adequate spiritual basis for living a full life. Countless possessions have not made anyone's cup run over. Rather, it seems there is a hole somewhere.

In 1987, Ivan Boesky, the legendary stockbroker, was found guilty of insider trading and fined for his crime. Today, no longer able to derive satisfaction from speculating in takeover stocks, the new Boesky is described as deeply philosophical, always asking those around him what it takes to be happy. Sometimes, he asks the question directly and almost out of the blue: "You seem to be a happy, stable person—what is it you do that makes you so?"

Surprisingly, wealth and happiness are only moderately correlated, according to a study from the National Opinion Research Center of the University of Chicago and reported by Robert J. Samuelson in a 1994 issue of the *Washington Post National Weekly Edition* (see Table 2).

| Annual | Individuals Who Reported Being . . . | | |
Income	*Very Happy*	*Pretty Happy*	*Not Too Happy*
$0–14,999	21%	58%	21%
$15–24,999	31%	56%	13%
$25–34,999	32%	60%	8%
$35–49,999	36%	59%	5%
$50–74,999	34%	60%	6%
$75,000+	45%	49%	6%

TABLE 2   *Relationship of Happiness to Income*
Source: Data from *Washington Post National Weekly Edition*, January 17–23, 1994.

Excluding people in the highest and lowest income groups, the study found that around 30 to 35 percent of individuals reported being "very happy." Rates for individuals who considered themselves "pretty happy" were even more consistent: around 55 to 60 percent. Yet rates for those who were "not too happy" were considerably higher among individuals in the lowest two income groups.

Spiritual insensitivity can also produce "poor talk," in which affluent people perceive their relative poverty compared to their personal aspirations and often find themselves on a "hedonic treadmill." As John Kenneth Galbraith puts it in a 1975 *Harper's* essay: "That the love of money is the root of all evil can conceivably be disputed. What is not in doubt is that the pursuit of money, or an enduring association with it, is capable of inducing not only bizarre but ripely perverse behavior."

This point is illustrated by an exchange between George B. Leonard and a member of a group of industrialists to whom he was speaking. As quoted in the *Intellectual Digest* of October 1973, Leonard remarked that "hot competition is far from inevitable in the future." One of the industrialists, noting "a look of real anxiety" on some of the faces around him, finally spoke up, asking: "If there is to be no competition, then what will life be all about?"

That is a valid question. What is the point of all this striving, this frenetic acquisition? If there were an apparent goal—say, to establish social justice or world peace or to create a community of contemplation—one might see some point in the compulsion to win the economic race. But the purpose of striving and getting and having seems merely to do more of the same. Money ceases to become a means to a more meaningful existence and instead becomes the purpose of that existence.

How else can we explain the illicit behavior of Wall Street traders, who are already millionaires yet take pride in the headline proclaiming "Wall Street Is Bullish on Greed"? Aristotle's concept of *eudaimonia,* which means blessedness, happiness, and prosperity—a state of being well and well-being—is foreign to the current American pattern of achievement. Aristotle argued against identifying the good with money, honor, or pleasure. In *After Virtue,* Alasdair MacIntyre succinctly summarizes what he believes Aristotle had in mind: "We strive in order to be at rest, rather than in order to struggle ceaselessly from goal to goal, from desire to desire."

The religious question is about the meaning of life. But in our culture, that issue is increasingly dwarfed by the marketplace. The acquisition of wealth tends to corrupt. Life should be more than an enlarged scoreboard on which to record wins and losses.

THE MORAL AND SPIRITUAL CORRUPTIONS OF POVERTY

It may be clear that affluence and its twin, power, tend to corrupt. But it may not seem so clearly the case with poverty and its twin, powerlessness. Theodore Parker, in his mid-nineteenth-century sermon "The Perishing Classes," writes,

> Now consider the moral temptations before such [poor] men. Here is wealth, food, clothing, comfort, luxury, gold, the great enchanter of this age, and but a plank between it and them. . . . In the midst of all this, what wonder is it if they feel desirous of revenge; what wonder that stores and houses are broken into.

The poor are thus isolated from the warmth and hope of ordinary life. With "dinners without appetites" at one end of the table and "appetites without dinners" at the other, the stage is set for societal indigestion.

James Luther Adams has suggested a corollary to Lord Acton's dictum on power. In an essay from the Midsummer 1996 *Unitarian Universalist Register-Leader,* Adams writes,

> Impotence tends to corrupt. Absolute impotence corrupts absolutely. When persons or groups lack power to influence the society of which they are a part, there ensues corruption of the spirit, loss of a

sense of self, loss of a sense of historical participation. The poor, limited in power in a monied society, are hard pressed to participate in those decisions that affect their lives.

Adams cites a small, all-white Appalachian community, Granny's Hollow, in eastern Kentucky: "Having become the castoffs of a technological society, being powerless to change their condition, disease, filth, malnutrition, illiteracy, inbreeding and its consequences, drunkenness, and religious fanaticism were rife among them." These people's poverty and powerlessness had eroded both their pride and their will to live.

Whereas people who are poor suffer from a paucity of choices, the affluent have an overabundance of choices, which may drain them spiritually. And while the wealthy may have too much control over their lives, the poor do not have enough.

The contrast in views on human nature between psychologist Carl Rogers and theologian Reinhold Niebuhr is instructive in this context. Niebuhr focuses on the sin of pride, Rogers, on the lack of self-love. The two views are seemingly contradictory, but in fact, they suggest the broad spectrum on which human nature can be understood. Could it be that the affluent among us tend toward the sin of pride and the poor among us tend toward the sin of self-hate?

Self-esteem is an essential ingredient in the religious development of every person. When one is poor, when the culture in which he/she lives suggests that poverty is deserved, when it has become more blessed to judge than to help, when benevolence is given in condescending private charity or in begrudging public welfare, that person's self-esteem must suffer.

Perhaps the classic literary description of the moral and spiritual struggle with poverty is Victor Hugo's novel *Les Miserables*. The protagonist, Jean Valjean, is a poor worker who has stolen bread to feed his hungry family and subsequently been jailed for many years. In describing this character's "inwardness of despair," Hugo illuminates the heart of the poor. Valjean has admitted committing the crime and the wrongfulness of it. But does the punishment fit the crime?

> "Had not the scales of justice been over-weighted on the side of expiation? . . . Did not the penalty . . . become in the end a sort of assault by the stronger on the weaker, a crime committed by society against the individual and repeated daily for nineteen years? [Did society have the right] to grind a poor man between the millstones of need and excess—need of work and excess of punishment?

Given his experience, Valjean passes judgment on society:

> He condemned it to his hatred. . . . During the years of suffering he reached the conclusion that life was a war in which he was one of the defeated. Hatred was his only weapon, and he resolved to sharpen it in prison and carry it with him when he left. . . . He took it upon himself to pass judgement on the Providence which had created society, and this, too, he condemned. . . . His spirit both grew and shrank.

Quite interestingly, an adaptation of Hugo's *Les Miserables* for the musical theater has for years played to packed and affluent audiences on Broadway and around the world.

THROUGH THE EYE OF A NEEDLE

In his seminal essay "The Eye of the Needle," economist Robert Heilbroner explores the ambivalence Americans feel about wealth. On the one hand, he extols the acquisitive drive and profit motive—even though these qualities may not represent the best of human nature—because they seem to serve the market better than more altruistic motives. Yet he places at least modest sanctions on making "too much" money. This drive, says Heilbroner, is not inherited biologically but is a social manifestation with deep psychological roots: "Acquisitiveness is a means of fortifying and enlarging the Self by projecting it into objects that will expand in social value." Heilbroner concludes,

> Thus modern psychology emphasizes the ease with which the accumulation of wealth becomes the vehicle for the expression of childhood needs and longings, whether for love or security or for other primitive satisfactions. Behind the voracious acquisitor we now see not a wicked adult, but a hungry and importunate child. . . . The typical obsessive-compulsive attributes of the money-oriented character, with its social blindness and its self-destructiveness, can now be seen, not in moralistic terms, but as symptoms of a personality that has not overcome its infantile demands and which therefore pursues external goals with a childish selfishness or with a near-autistic intensity.

Heilbroner believes this juxtaposition of rich and poor, whether among individuals or among nations, is fundamentally unjust. Each step that "widens the gap between rich and poor—that is, every act of the rich to grow richer—worsens a condition that is already profoundly wrong."

Not only is it wrong but it is also dangerous in terms of its effect on the social fabric. The chasm between the rich and the poor is simply unjust. It remains for us to formulate principles and policies that will begin to redress this wrong. We need canons of economic justice that seek, in the words of Christopher Jencks from his book *Inequality,* to reduce the "punishments of failure and the rewards of success."

I am terribly afraid that the capitalistic marketplace has been infected with a bit of Marxist philosophy. For Karl Marx, economics was the chief determinant of human action and meaning. I fear that the dominance of the marketplace over all other human considerations simply repeats one of Marx's mistakes. Our obsessive pursuit of money is actually a misplaced religious quest in which Mammon becomes God.

✦ ✦ ✦

Muddling toward
the Beloved Community

*The Rev. John E. Smallwood [played by Peter Sellers] arrives as
vicar of Holy Trinity Church in Orbiston Parva, an English village
contentedly thriving under the aegis of the wealthy Despard family
and the pill it manufactures—sedative, pepper-upper and laxative
combined, a perfect trinity. Smallwood takes Biblical injunctions
literally and persuades rich Lady Despard to do likewise. Lady
Despard freely distributes food to those who will take it, driving
butcher, baker and candlestick maker out of business. And when
Smallwood pronounces that the trinity of Father, Son and Holy
Ghost is more efficacious than the triple-actioned pill, sales go
down, unemployment goes up and mob violence ensues. . . .
Culture, we learn, maintains its precarious balance only so long as
everyone is committed to the ideology of profit-sharing and of it-is-
better-to-receive-than-to-give; whereas an authentic Christian
unless he is able to win everyone to his reversal of ideals, simply
succeeds in giving impetus to riotous anarchy.*
—William Mueller, "Review of the film *Heaven's Above*"

It will no doubt be argued that this case for distributive justice is simply one more liberal scheme to soak the rich and give to the poor. There
was a similar wailing and gnashing of teeth as Congress enacted the
progressive income tax. What is the moral basis of this ability-to-pay
principle? On the surface, it seems to be Robin Hood morality writ
large. I contend, however, that this principle recognizes that we are
members of a community seeking the common good. Democracy at

its best is not the individual freedom to get rich but the common pursuit of "liberty and justice for all."

Americans seem to hold individuality above all other values, yet at our best, we realize that our personal good is caught up in that of the commonweal. Years ago, I read a column by then Ohio Senator Stephen Young about a wealthy constituent who bemoaned providing governmental help for the poor. This man had attended free public schools and a land grant public college. He had borrowed money for his successful investments through government-guaranteed loans. On and on it went, the story of apparent Horatio Alger–type success. Yet in reality, Young's story is that of a man taking full advantage of the benefits of living in a society.

With generous tax expenditures for the middle and upper classes and gaping holes in the "safety net" for the poor, this pattern of the "haves" ignoring the "have nots" is well established. The most critical problem in American culture is the elevation of greed, once considered a moral defect, to first place in the pantheon of virtues. It is New Hampshire's coming of age: "Don't tread on me!" We have become drunk on the rhetoric of individualism. Concern for community takes a poor second place to unrestrained individualism in political debate, or what passes for it in our time.

Our individualistic economic system evaluates career paths solely by what they command in the marketplace. But the marketplace is amoral; there is no moral rationale for remuneration. Doctors, lawyers, accountants, and business managers do important work and are generally well remunerated. Nurses, social workers, teachers, and many others also do important work but for modest incomes. Outstanding high school math and science teachers are lured to corporations for two, three, or four times what they are paid to teach. Are these individuals worth more to society in industry than in education, especially as the United States seeks to become more competitive in the world economy? How do we evaluate and remunerate a nurse in an intensive care unit, a counselor who works with drug addicts, or a teacher in a ghetto school? Or dare we even raise the moral issue behind this problem?

In a perfect society, persons might be remunerated on the basis of effort, sacrifice, and contribution to the common good, however hard these qualities might be to measure. In the real world, it is up to social policy, shaped by human conscience, to compensate for the limitations of the market and move us closer to justice. However, these measurements for economic distribution barely make the radar screen in a market economy. Introducing such topics is akin to heresy in a society that deifies the marketplace. Nevertheless, a moral substance overrides the principles of the market. The public interest is more than the aggregation of individual interests. As the Roman Catholic bishops write in their pastoral letter on the economy, "There is a social mortgage on private property."

I believe we best understand ourselves not as atomized individuals, heroically making our own way in some "survival of the fittest" arena, but as social members who feel obligated to the commonweal. Good fortune obligates, as Albert Schweitzer suggested. Those of us who prosper are morally obliged not to further feather our nests, not just to dole out charity, but to work for public policies that will lead to a society in which resources are more equitably shared, in which everyone has a stake in the success of the enterprise.

American society has become increasingly fractured as the income and wealth disparity between classes has grown. There is little to stop this corrosion of social solidarity except to make an appeal to the "better angels of our nature." I fear that the past several years have witnessed a serious erosion in our collective conscience. "To have is to deserve" is our moral motto. Yet for some, service is still more important than acquisition and the public good still transcends the private good. Our compulsive pursuit of self-interest needs the tempering vision of the common good if our democracy is to survive and prosper. Such a vision is scarcely popular now, but justice has never been determined in the voting booth. Good fortune obligates. How does this basic ethical stance work out in the canons of distributive justice?

THE CANONS OF DISTRIBUTIVE JUSTICE

Is it possible to present a distributive ethic that will be fair to all people and at the same time produce abundance to be shared? I believe it is, and I suggest several *canons of distribution* that serve as middle axioms between the principles of justice—freedom, equity, community, meaning—and social reality—poverty in the midst of plenty.

The Canon of Need

All human beings have the inherent right to have their basic human needs met before any economic surplus is distributed to others. This, of course, assumes a society capable of producing such a surplus, a condition clearly met by the United States. Simply stated, the basic needs of the poor transcend the superfluous desires of the rich in moral importance.

This principle is affirmed in religious and philosophical traditions from Plato to the Jewish and Christian scriptures. Grounded variously in the beliefs that every person is a "child of God" and in the "reverence for life" and the "inherent worth and dignity of every person," there is an inalienable right to "life, liberty and the pursuit of happiness." Thus, this first canon has religious, philosophical, and democratic secular sources. It is based on the idea that all human beings are worthwhile. That is, while some things are to be used for some instrumental purposes, human beings are not to be used as means to some higher end; they are ends in themselves.

Further, the canon of need recognizes the individual as a center of freedom, a freedom understood not only as liberation from arbitrary outside restraints but also as human possibility to make choices from viable alternatives. Self-determination requires a minimal economic package to be realized. To meet human needs a society requires an approximation of equity or fairness in human distributional schemes. The world is inherently neither just nor unjust in terms of economic status. Recognizing the roles of fortune, genetic inheritance, and social factors over which persons have little or no control, the canon of need recognizes and respects the dignity of those judged as "losers" by a competitive society.

We are more than mere individuals; we are individuals within a community. We are members of a social, political, economic entity by virtue of our very humanity. To exclude some members from that community because they have not produced enough is to erode the community's foundation in human solidarity.

Our moral sensitivity is enhanced as we meet the needs of society's weakest members. This should not be done condescendingly; in our best moments, we know it is right to "do unto the least of these" with compassion. A community that strives to meet the needs of its poorest members enhances its members' quest for spiritual meaning. I would define this as the struggle for love and justice in community. A society may be judged by how it treats its poorest, weakest, and most vulnerable people.

Daniel C. Maguire, in his book *A New American Justice,* provides a personal example of the concept of worthwhileness. His son, Danny, has an incurable degenerative disease that will preclude his ever making a contribution to the economic well-being of the community.

Yet the community provides, at taxpayer expense, a whole range of services, from bus transportation to specialized schooling. As Maguire points out,

> There is no public utility in this. . . . Danny can lay claim to no distinctive merits, works, rank, or earned entitlements. . . . The polity is investing enormously and will never get a productive citizen. . . . His own worth is the reason why he has a right to the essential care he needs. . . . People have rights because of their needs. . . . Danny's case is particularly illuminating in this regard since his intrinsic worth is the only justification for meeting his essential needs.

It is this attention to meeting needs based on the intrinsic worth of the individual that sets the civilized society apart from the barbarian society, in which the sacrifice of expendable human lives is the norm. Moreover, it is what sets the democratic society apart from the totalitarian, in which the interests of the individual are totally subsumed in the interests of the state.

Clearly, the concept of *need* requires definition. Some believe they need luxury goods to live meaningfully. I believe a community has no obligation to provide for that kind of need. But a community is obliged to provide for essential needs that are required for a humane existence. In American society, this humane existence is defined officially by the poverty level, although other definitions at a higher standard of living could be defended as more just.

For the ancient Greeks, the difference between freedom and slavery was whether or not a person was caught up in the struggle for mere survival. The free person was not engaged in the "tyranny of survival" but had sufficient means not only to survive but also to pursue the good life. Economic security was the prerequisite for the realization of other values.

Michael Walzer points out that in Athens, public payments were made to all citizens who held office, served on the Council, or sat on a jury. This policy allowed every citizen to participate in public life. The purpose was "the maintenance of a vigorous democracy." Public funds were distributed so as to balance somewhat the inequalities of Athenian society. This was particularly the case with regard to payments to elderly citizens, who would not have been working anyway. We might even attribute to this distributive effect the virtual absence of civil strife or class war throughout the history of democratic Athens. Perhaps this was an intended result, but it seems more likely that the reasoning behind the payments was a certain concept of citizenship. To make it possible for each and every citizen to participate in political life, the citizens as a body were prepared to lay out large sums.

Drew Christiansen, in *Human Rights in the Americas,* suggests two corollary principles:"(1) The decency principle requires that no one be forced to endure degrading living conditions because of a correctable maldistribution of resources. (2) The dignity principle requires that people not be denied the means to satisfy their basic needs." Christiansen cites the "ranking of harms" concept: "An actually injurious condition should outweigh a mere change in a harmful direction." He goes on to illustrate,

> An entrepreneur may suffer loss of some financial advantage because of his government's price supports for food, but the unemployed slum dweller suffers more directly when inflation in food prices leads to hunger and disease for himself and his family. The first is merely a decline in potential wealth, the second is a direct and real harm.

Morally, providing economic freedom is contingent on first meeting the basic human needs of all persons in the economic order. The problem in a purely market-based economy is that essentials such as food, clothing, and shelter compete in the same market with luxury goods. Productive resources tend to be allocated in such a way as to produce greater profits, which may simply force up the prices of essential goods. For instance, it is the high profit margins on large automobiles like sports utility vehicles (SUVs) that drain productive resources from manufacturing low-cost cars with narrower profit margins. All prices then tend to rise. A variation of this overreliance on the market is the urban phenomenon of closing nonprofitable food stores in low-income areas and opening them in more lucrative settings. This is the dictate of the market, but it deprives some of the opportunity to meet basic human needs in a convenient way. Thus, the "just deserts" of one person may have to be sacrificed for the urgent need of another. There is a moral substance in society not defined by market forces.

Justice according to need must have priority over other claims; otherwise, there will be no basis for community and no stable context for individual self-actualization. The goods of the earth are the common property of all; we are merely human stewards of this largesse, which we have done nothing to deserve. As human beings, we do not own anything. Goods are merely loaned to us for our use.

One historical perspective on this issue is from the 1917 "Declaration of Social Principles" of the Universalist Church of America. The statement advocates "An Economic Order which shall give to every human being an equal share in the common gifts of God, and in addition all that he shall earn by his own labor." This kind of moral guarantee is not part of modern American mores. I would affirm the principle simply and powerfully enunciated by the Roman Catholic bishops of Canada in their "Ethical Reflections on the Economic Crisis" that "the needs of the poor have priority over the wants of the rich." In liberation theology, this has been called *the preferential option for the poor.* It corresponds most closely to John A. Ryan's concept of the Canon of Human Welfare.

But can this understanding be objectified? A number of authors have proposed establishing an income floor that is between 50 percent and 70 percent of the median income—with 50 percent providing the minimum for meeting bare physiological needs and 70 percent providing a so-called civilizing surplus. Establishing this income floor would provide an equality of results at the lowest income levels. It would require allocating differential amounts, however, as even people's most basic needs vary. For instance, persons with disabilities, physical or mental, would require more resources than others. Thus, this formula would not mean equal shares for everyone.

What would absolutely equal shares mean in the United States? According to a September 2000 report from the U.S. Census Bureau, per capita personal income in the United States in real terms was $21,181. This income level clearly cannot be the goal of redistribution, but it indicates that there is sufficient income and wealth in our nation to meet the basic needs of all people. The canon of need argues for public and private policies and practices that will guarantee a basic income for everyone as a matter of right, a citizen's wage.

The Canon of Proportional Equality

Every human being should be limited in his/her consumption of income and wealth by the principle of sufficiency. This is an ethic of limits, a floor based on need and a ceiling based on proportionality, as articulated in Plato's *Laws.*

In his book *Religion and the Rise of Capitalism,* Richard Tawney observes that allowing great disproportions of income is simply ungentlemanly. The contrast cited at the outset of his study is operative here: A professional basketball player can make $121 million a year while a child lives on welfare.

Robert Reich, writing in *The American Prospect* of May 8, 2000, points out that the annual average pay of a chief executive in the United States rose 18 percent in 1999 to $12 million. He then offers these examples of people at the other end of the pay spectrum:

+ Four hundred janitors in Los Angeles protesting their wages of less than $16,000 a year

+ More than 2 million Americans who earn between $7 and $8 an hour working in nursing homes, "bathing and feeding frail elderly people, cleaning their bedsores, lifting them out of bed and into wheelchairs, and changing their diapers"

+ Some 700,000 home health care aides, who average between $8 and $10 an hour

+ Hospital workers, most of whom are earning less than they did fifteen years ago, adjusting for inflation

+ An estimated 2.3 million child care providers whose median wage is $6.60 an hour—less than that of funeral attendants ($7.30 an hour) and pest controllers ($10.60 an hour)

By comparison, Reich says that many law firms pay first-year associates $120,000 plus a signing bonus and that Wall Street investment banks pay more than $75,000 a year for financial analysts. Then, with undisguised irritation, he writes, "Setting a new example for college students across America, the president of Brown University, not content with a meager $300,000 salary, just jumped ship after only a year and a half for another university that offered three times as much." Reich indicates that the policy of the Federal Reserve Board, which raises interest rates to check inflation, makes life harder for the people on the bottom rungs of the ladder, who end up paying more for first mortgages, car loans, and other borrowing. "This year the richest 2.7 million Americans, comprising the top 1 percent, will have as many after-tax dollars to spend as the bottom 100 million put together, and they'll have 40% of the nation's wealth."

In Third World countries, it is commonplace to find huge mansions with walls and guards in the same neighborhoods with shanties. I have seen such mansions in Kenya, in the Philippines, and in Mexico that are only short distances from shanty towns with the most despicable conditions. In the United States, the process of *gentrification*— replacing low-cost tenements in urban areas with high-cost housing units—is increasingly causing a similar pattern, such that whole communities of prosperous people are sealed off from the surrounding less affluent communities. Gated communities also have become common-place throughout the land. In fact, there are more private security guards than police in the United States.

These examples of extreme inequality attack the democratic egal-itarian ideal as well as common-sense standards of decency. The class warfare underway in the United States undermines the principles of proportion and balance one might expect to see in a truly prosperous society and violates our sense of aesthetics as well as ethics.

Such a concept responds to Thorsten Veblen's theory of *conspicu-ous consumption* and the corrupting potential of excessive income and wealth. It is based on an ethic of *enough;* that is, beyond a certain level, income is not only superfluous but can be morally and spiritually cor-rupting. Such a distributive system could be implemented through a progressive tax system.

The advocacy group United for a Fair Economy proposes the *ten times rule* in setting compensation: That is, the highest-paid executive can make no more than ten times the salary of lowest-paid employee in a company. This rule is spelled out in Sam Pizzigati's book *The Maximum Wage*. Plato believed that the ratio between the richest and the poorest person in the ideal state was 4 to 1, and Aristotle believed it should be 5 to 1. The Roman Plutarch wrote, "An imbalance between rich and poor is the oldest and most fatal ailment of republics."

However, as we know, good ethics does not necessarily make good politics. This ten times rule is not merely populist rhetoric, however. Establishment business guru Peter Drucker thinks a CEO's salary should be capped at twenty times that of the average worker in a large company and fifteen times that in a small company. Over a century ago, J. P. Morgan declared that no CEO of any company he controlled would be allowed to earn more than twenty times the wages earned by any other employee in that organization. Republican social critic Kevin Phillips has for years warned of the economic and social danger caused by the widening gap between rich and poor in his books *The Politics of Rich and Poor* and *Boiling Point*. This is an idea whose time has come.

The Canon of Contribution to the Common Good

The canon of contribution to the common good is a far more subjec-tive measure than the first two canons, yet some rough evaluations can be made. The calculation of social value is difficult, as William Ryan points out in *Equality*. He cites a study by the National Opinion Research Center (NORC), in which ninety occupations were evaluated and then compared by levels of remuneration. Physicians, who were ranked second, and college professors, who were ranked seventh, would seem to hold roughly the same level of social values and work in professions that require about the same amount of education and training. Yet physicians, on the average, earn more than twice as much as professors. Similar comparisons can be made between ministers (ranked fourteenth) and dentists (seventeenth), welfare workers (forty-sixth) and undertakers (forty-seventh), and many other anomalous pairs. On the other hand, we find that architects (fifteenth) have approximately the same average income as police officers (fifty-fifth).

In an intriguing essay entitled "The Economics of Superstars," which appeared in a 1983 issue of *The American Scholar*, Sherwin Rosen asks if the principle of payment by contribution has been abandoned. He cites the work of Italian economist Vilfredo Pareto, who discovered that while the curve depicting the distribution of intelligence quotients (IQs) is bell shaped, the curve depicting the distribution of income is not. Specifically, the right-hand side (high income) falls much more slowly than the equivalent curve on the left (low income). According to Rosen, this means "that the distribution of earnings is far from proportionate to the distribution of ability." Rosen then asks, "How can it be that many a mediocre free agent [in professional sports] earns far more than the Secretary of State and the President of the United States combined?" Yet these income levels are the current allocations of the market. A more deliberate attempt to define one's contribution to the common good could hardly do worse. The average family can hardly afford to attend professional sports' games, which are often held in stadiums built using tax dollars, because the ticket prices are too high.

The controversy over comparable worth/pay equity provides an opportunity to achieve some sense of proportion. While this effort is intended to wipe out the effects of discrimination against women and minorities, it is an instructive tool for exploring the problems and possibilities of an intentional system of distributive justice. In looking at the comparable values of various work positions, the worth of a given economic task becomes subject to public debate.

Granted, it is demonstrably difficult to define contributions to the common good, yet it is possible to make a start. I suggest that contributions that can be shared by the citizenry at large should take precedence over those enjoyed by the elite. Thus, creating public parks would more aptly suit the common good than building private swimming pools. Human service occupations would have priority over those directed toward luxury consumption. Child care workers would earn more than sanitation workers, teachers would be paid more than fashion designers, and social workers would receive more than professional athletes. Providing public transportation would be more important than satisfying private desires to drive big cars. Positions in government would be more highly compensated than comparable positions in the private market.

While I defend the ethics of this view, I am not so naive as to believe it has a chance of becoming public or private policy. Nonetheless, the issue must be engaged. At the very least, it would prompt a fascinating exercise in values clarification.

The principle here is that those people who work in the service of the community must be rewarded more generously than those who work to further competitive self-aggrandizement. In her book on moral development, *In a Different Voice*, Carol Gilligan spells out this contrast in terms of the predominantly male ethos of individualistic competition versus the predominantly female ethos of social connection. The U.S. economy is currently based on the perspective that the world is comprised of individuals in conflict with one another over claims to resources. This represents the male ethos. The feminist view, however, sees the world as an arena not for conflict resolution so much as for preserving connections. This ethos is grounded in human attachment, the principle of caring.

A distributive ethic needs to factor in this community-building value. Contribution to the common good is an imperfect but necessary consideration in the allocation of resources in a just society—a radical but appropriate consideration in the democratic dialogue about resource allocation in a free society.

The Canon of Productivity

The canon of productivity is the basic economic concept of compensation reflecting production—that is, you can take out what you put in. This canon has been seen by some as a kind of divine dispensation, rooted in the fundamental nature of things. More cautious students of economics deny that distribution based on productivity is necessarily *just* distribution. For example, how is it possible to justify that the incomes of CEOs and professional sports stars are many times the income of the President of the United States, who arguably has the largest impact on total production of goods and services of the nation? It is clear, however, that any formula for economic reward must consider the importance of productivity as a vital incentive.

My purpose here is not to discard the canon of productivity but to put it in its rightful place as one of several ways to allocate economic resources justly. My practical assumption is that productivity is well established in the American economic and moral psyche and needs mainly to be *disestablished* as a canon of divine right. It is a useful and important principle of distribution—but not a sacred one.

There are a number of problems with this canon. To the extent that one's remuneration is based on the skills he/she has acquired through a lifetime, this canon gives an unfair advantage to those who have backgrounds conducive to acquiring those skills. For example, growing up in a middle-class family provides a wide range of educational, cultural, and occupational opportunities. Thus, we tend to reap what others have sown.

In the race metaphor, this means that some people are given a head start as well as better training, while others are held back at the start and even handicapped. Economists Samuel Bowles and Herbert Gintis report in a 1997 issue of the *Washington Post* that children from the wealthiest 10 percent of the population are twenty-seven times as likely as children from the bottom 10 percent to be in the top 10 percent in terms of income.

Natural abilities are a second component of productivity. Clearly, the economic system is not responsible for the effects of different genetic endowments on people's abilities to succeed. This does not mean the race should not be run, but it does mean that society should seek to ameliorate, not to compound, this natural inequity. One might consider the intriguing idea of reversing the current pattern of income distribution to compensate for the fact that unequal endowments have resulted from accidental and unmerited advantages. This is the *principle of redress,* which is, in effect, the application of affirmative action to even out the odds. Society must, therefore, give more attention to those persons with fewer natural abilities than to those with more.

"From each according to ability, to each according to need" is an apt moral expression when properly qualified. A just economy will encourage productivity among all its citizens who are able to produce economically. American society stresses incentives for the affluent at the expense of incentives for the poor. The plight of the working poor, the relatively high tax burden on the poor, and the social welfare system, which still tends to discourage people from working by dropping medical and other benefits for those who take jobs—all contribute to a reduction of productivity. A just society will maximize the abilities of its least-advantaged citizens and thereby more effectively meet human need. At the same time, such a society will recognize that people with limited ability, who are thus limited in productivity, nevertheless deserve to have their needs met because they are likewise members of the community.

The Canon of Effort and Sacrifice

Generally, it seems fair to reward effort, leisure being a form of income. But what about those individuals who, by virtue of genetics or environment, are unable to work? Should they be excluded from the benefits produced by the others' productivity? Should we follow the words of the Apostle Paul, who said, "Let him who does not work, not eat"— an early statement of the Protestant work ethic?

This position neglects the fact that in any given society, there is a group of citizens who, for very good reasons, are not and cannot be productive. The very young and the very old, for example, are able to contribute relatively little economically, yet they should not be excluded from the community. Likewise, people with disabilities, both mental and physical, are generally thought worthy of compensation, even though they may not be able to work effectively. The Americans with Disabilities Act, passed in 1990, testifies to the general public support for people who have disabilities and cannot work. Caregivers in the family are not typically compensated for productivity, yet they perform the tasks of maintaining a home and caring for children and elders, the costs of which would be enormously expensive on the open market. Yet workers in these fields are at the low end of the income scale.

Effort can be measured in many ways. The difficulty of some kinds of work—mental or physical—requires different kinds of effort. In addition, some kinds of labor place workers in great danger; others allow people to operate in safe environments. Some work is dirty; some seems like play. In this connection, I think of Gandhi's practice of cleaning latrines as a reminder of how unpleasant some kinds of necessary work can be. Effort should be rewarded, but these practical conditions, not often noted, must be considered.

The Canon of Scarcity

At any given time, certain kinds of skills are in demand while others are not. A college professor, for instance, may worry that students' desire to hear him/her lecture may wane and cause a drop in his/her income. Would this individual deserve a cut in pay? Is it ethically just for income levels to be founded on the shifting sands of technology and taste?

Rewarding the scarcity of a particular talent fails to recognize the *joint inputs* that mark so many economic endeavors. In professional sports, one superstar may be highly rewarded when his/her team wins a championship, but in most cases, there is a "kitty" that is shared equally by all team members. The profit-sharing plans of some businesses could be said to follow a similar system of economic reward.

Clearly, people with valuable skills must be rewarded. The work done by the surgeon, the airplane pilot, the business executive, and the national politician cannot and should not be rewarded at the same level as work involving more mundane skills. Moreover, given the realities of human nature, incentives must be included in any realistic economic scheme.

I only suggest that the canon of scarcity find its proper place. Given an affluent society, such as that of the United States, it is quite possible to remunerate people by means of the other canons and still have a surplus from which to reward those who have rare skills.

THE MARKET IS NOT GOD

It is tempting to yield to the pragmatic argument of market efficiency. To be sure, it is a powerful argument. Yet it can be countered with the argument set forth in *Economics Explained* by Lester Thurow and Robert Heilbroner that reduction of the income gap to a ratio of 5 to 1 appears to be efficient for full-time working white males. This argument is at least worth exploring.

Even if efficiency is somewhat compromised through redistribution, one can argue that economic efficiency is not the sole goal of a democratic society. Other values are at stake here, as well. Economists such as Arthur Okun seem to make a polite bow in the direction of the normative and then continue to speak and act as if ethics and economics are irrelevant to one another at best and antithetical at worst. If, indeed, economics is to be the servant of humanity, then efficiency should be only one dimension of human valuation, not the sole measure of economic worth.

Clearly, the free market has a vital role in allocating resources according to certain abilities in a just economic order. As the Eastern bloc countries have painfully discovered, it is preferable to be a command economy, in which a state elite prescribes production and distribution. What must be corrected, however, is the reliance on the market as the only mechanism for distributing resources. It is an imperfect system, for a number of reasons:

+ The market often discriminates on irrelevant bases, including race, gender, disability, sexual orientation, and ethnic background.
+ The market does not take into account economic externalities—for instance, generally speaking, pollution is created through private enterprise but cleaned up using public resources.
+ The market unfairly places the wants of the affluent in competition with the needs of the poor.
+ The market is preoccupied with the canon of productivity to the exclusion of all others.
+ The market allocates in such an uneven manner as to create a situation of class tension, at best, and class warfare, at worst.
+ The market overemphasizes incentives at the upper income level while virtually ignoring them at the lower.

Current national policy does overemphasize the role of the free market, which requires structural attention as well as recognition that other means of economic distribution (including governmental action) can also be used to mend its inevitable flaws.

Without question, these canons will be controversial and criticized. Regardless, they are worthy of consideration, insofar as the marketplace system of allocation is fraught with injustice when allowed to operate exclusively. What mechanisms might be required to implement these canons as social policy is not quite clear, but at least, proposing such a framework might serve to deepen public debate on the question of economic justice in both the private and public sectors. Poet Robert Frost, in his play *Masque of Reason,* may ultimately be right in saying that "there's no connection man can reason out between his just deserts and what he gets." It may well be time to come just a bit closer in the operative world, however.

These canons, or middle axioms, seek to flesh out a philosophy of distributive justice. They strive to balance the lofty requirements of economic ethics and the hard requirements of an efficient economic system. At present, these canons and economic realities exist in creative tension. Unfortunately, economic reality has come to dominate normative considerations in recent times. These canons of economic justice seek to redress the imbalance. When freedom is primarily the freedom to get rich, when justice is equated with the acquisitive spirit, when greed is good, and when values are tied to fulfilling purely private hopes and wishes, it is time for a new look at distributive justice. Professor Jeffrey Kovac, writing in the Summer/Fall 1997 issue of *Religious Humanism,* provides an anecdotal challenge to the conventional wisdom in response to the question "How much do we deserve?" The radical nature of this challenge will create cognitive dissonance for all those seriously engaged in the debate about distributive justice.

Kovac writes of a friend who worked in a professional position at San Francisco State University:

> To have adequate time for her job and her family, she employed a part-time housekeeper. She paid the housekeeper exactly the same hourly wage that she earned as a professional. The reasoning was that the housekeeper was allowing her employer to do the professional work that she enjoyed, so the housekeeper's time was worth the professional rate.

The effect of this arrangement on the woman's income must have been considerable, and perhaps not many could afford to do it. But the effect of this arrangement on our ethical consideration of economic and moral worth is even more substantial. How much do we deserve?

◆ ◆ ◆

Policy Implications for the United States

In a competitive society, there have to be losers.
We haven't faced up to what we are going to do about the losers.
—William Sloan Coffin, "Morality USA"

What might we do to lessen the vast disparities of income and wealth in the United States? Without application such theoretical discussions are self-indulgent and dull. Let justice roll down like waters, of course, but someone must establish the irrigation system. Informed by the canons of distributive justice, let us consider basic strategies for reducing inequity, including the free market and its variations, government transfer programs, taxation reforms, and some form of guaranteed annual income.

THE FREE MARKET

The maritime metaphor that a rising tide lifts all boats—popularized by President John F. Kennedy to justify his administration's tax cuts—has been conventional wisdom in virtually all efforts to reduce inequality and end poverty. It is assumed, particularly among supply-side economists, that the free market is the single most effective means to effect economic justice. But redistributing scarcity neither reduces inequity nor ends poverty. When the market flourishes in freedom, everyone benefits. Such is the assertion made by advocates of the free market as an antipoverty program. Does that assertion stand up under scrutiny?

Despite the longest peacetime economic expansion in U.S. history and despite strong gains in hourly productivity, the American economy is still characterized by poverty in the midst of plenty and economic stagnation in the middle quintiles of the population. To be sure, poverty has decreased slightly over the past few years of expansion. But even when the poorest segment of the population is not considered, there are sizable gaps in income and wealth among Americans. How do we account for the stubborn persistence of this pattern when the economy is on a roll? What will happen when the inevitable downturn in the economy comes?

Why is this so? Macroeconomic conditions can reduce poverty for households with able-bodied working heads or even two workers, but they have relatively little effect on the many poor heads of households who are either not active or only partly active in the labor force or who are quite simply not paid enough. There are too many poor households that do not and probably cannot benefit directly from improved market conditions. For example, according to 1999 U.S. Census Bureau data, 9.7 percent of the poor were elderly, 18 percent were children under six, and many more poor households were headed by people who were normally not expected to work full time—that is, the elderly, students, disabled, or women with children under age six. Of the poor, over one-quarter worked less than full time. One in every two children under six lived in a female-headed household.

The U.S. *Census Brief* of December 1997 reports some sobering findings about the lives of people with disabilities. Among persons aged twenty-one to sixty-four, 82 percent of those without disabilities had jobs compared to 77 percent of those with nonsevere disabilities and 26 percent of those with severe disabilities. More than three-quarters (77.4 percent) of disabled Americans aged twenty-two to sixty-four do not receive public assistance.

Despite the provisions of the Americans with Disabilities Act, the market has had only a modest effect in moving people with disabilities out of poverty. For example, an Urban Institute study, referenced on February 29, 2000, by the Center on Budget and Policy Priorities, found that over one-third of current recipients of TANF (Temporary Assistance to Needy Families, formerly known as AFDC, or Aid to Families with Dependent Children) scored low on a standard mental health scale while close to one-fourth scored as having very poor mental health. One-fifth of former recipients who were not working scored in the bottom 10 percent nationwide. Clearly, helping these people to benefit from a vigorous marketplace will not be easy.

A second operational factor is that increasing the mean (average) income of families does not necessarily reduce poverty. The average income has been increasing for the upper two quintiles (or 40 percent), but there has not been a corresponding increase in the bottom three quintiles. A roaring stock market may well lift the mean income by raising the incomes of those who benefit from such phenomena but leave untouched people from the lower income brackets, who are only marginally affected by such activity. A growing economy with increasing employment is holding inequality steady and may help some of the poor (those close to the labor market), but it does not help many poor households that are not in this position.

In the long historical view, the free market has been the most effective antipoverty mechanism ever. The sheer productive might of the American system has created such a huge economic pie that even those living on the crumbs are physically better off than people in the Third World. Still, the free market economy is prone to create vast disparities in income and wealth. Poverty has persisted, despite enormous growth in the Gross Domestic Product (GDP). Disparity has increased along with economic growth.

Another water metaphor associated with another president is the trickle-down theory that characterized Reaganomics. This theory assumes that wealth created at the top of the economic pyramid by a burgeoning economy will eventually improve the lot of those below. As John Kenneth Galbraith once said, "In my youth, we called the 'trickle-down' theory the 'horse-and-sparrow' theory. If you feed the horse enough oats, some will pass through to the road for the sparrows." The metaphors may differ, but the result is the same: The market is a limited mechanism in terms of income redistribution. How much actually trickles down to how many? The least criticism that can be offered is that the trickle-down process is very slow and very imperfect.

A sober, nonideological assessment would suggest that the free market's functioning efficiently is a *sine qua non* for just distribution of wealth, especially for the top two quintiles of the population. Few would exchange the dynamism of the market, even with its inequities, for the stultifying, if sometimes egalitarian, policies once employed by the Eastern bloc nations. Even so, the late Michael Harrington, a passionate socialist, suggested that capitalism has effectively organized the means of production to create an abundance of goods. In his book *Socialism*, however, Harrington, points out that the free market leaves much to be desired in the fair distribution of those goods.

Beyond its productive capability, the market co-exists in a climate of freedom, in which other distributive mechanisms may operate with minimum deleterious impact on the market itself. Thus, the market implies a democratic milieu, and this is the condition that makes possible significant redistributive mechanisms to guide the market and remedy its faults. The free market, then, is a necessary but insufficient condition for establishing a just economic community.

GOVERNMENT TRANSFER PROGRAMS

Government transfer programs, as we now know them, came into existence as antipoverty measures to counter the Great Depression. Along
with public works projects, the major efforts have been in the area of
social security: unemployment insurance, retirement and disability benefits, and formerly, Aid to Families with Dependent Children (AFDC).

Lyndon Johnson's Great Society programs of the mid 1960s constitute the most recent incarnation of government transfers with the
goal of eliminating poverty and alleviating inequality. A look at the
poverty rate during the late 1960s and early 1970s indicates that these
programs had a positive impact (despite two recessionary periods during that time), even though the nation was bogged down in the Viet-
nam War. The poverty rate climbed again in the late 1970s and 1980s
due to economic recessions and reductions in government transfer payments. Nevertheless, these transfers, more so than taxes, are responsible for reducing poverty to the extent that it has been reduced.

During the presidency of Ronald Reagan, government transfer
programs came under serious assault and benefit reductions were the
order of the day. Rhetoric about "welfare queens" (young women with
a proliferation of babies) and people on welfare driving expensive cars
became part of the political assault on public welfare. Facts to the
contrary did not deflect the attacks. People who were not receiving
benefits but working for marginal incomes became angry, and the politics of resentment came into full play. The result was the Personal
Responsibility Act of 1996. Its proponents call it "the end of welfare as
we know it," and its critics call it "welfare deform." Regardless, it is the
most recent attack on what has been called the "welfare state."

Leading the charge was Charles Murray, whose book *Losing
Ground: American Social Policy 1950–1980* was a virtual bible for the
Reagan administration's assault on welfare in the 1980s. Its influence
carried over well into the 1990s and is operative even today. An examination of this book is a useful way of evaluating the efficacy of transfer
programs to build a more just society.

Murray has been called the "thinking man's George Gilder." He
extols the free market economy and savages government welfare
spending, like Gilder, but with statistics. Murray surveyed the period
from 1950 to 1980 and discovered that while life was good for most
Americans in 1950, by 1980 it had become decidedly worse for a number of them, particularly those who were supposed to be helped by government welfare programs.

Murray theorizes that the lives of poor people got worse while the
economy thrived and welfare quadrupled and that welfare programs

were the cause of this decline. The error, he claims, was strategic. The "haves" made it possible for the "have nots" to behave in destructive ways by changing the rules of the economic game and subsidizing irretrievable mistakes. In what he calls "the generous revolution," Murray points to a major paradigm shift in the 1960s—from giving the poor a helping hand, not a handout, to blaming the system and exonerating the poor from responsibility for their plight. Thus, it was *the system* that had to be righted. This "elite wisdom" shifted the policy focus from equality of opportunity to equality of results, from welfare as a privilege to welfare as a right, or affirmative action. This elite wisdom became national policy.

Murray claims that the poverty rate stopped declining at the very time antipoverty programs dramatically increased. He writes, "Perversely, poverty chose those years to halt a decline that had been under way for two decades." Using African Americans as a proxy for people who are disadvantaged, he writes that the unemployment rate among this group increased throughout the War on Poverty / Great Society period. While African Americans above twenty-five years of age were doing better, those below twenty-five found their situation worse. Murray summarizes the pattern: "A growing number of blacks seemed to give up on getting ahead in the world just as others were demonstrating it was finally possible to do so." And he describes similar situations in the areas of education, crime, and the family. In sum, things were getting worse for people who were poor and disadvantaged at the very time they should have gotten better due to improved economic conditions. Interestingly, Murray concludes, "This is of course a hazardous assertion. It is not susceptible to proof."

Murray believes that the popular wisdom against welfare programs should be taken seriously, given these realities of human nature:

1. People respond to incentives and disincentives.
2. People are not inherently moral or hard working. In the absence of countervailing influences, people will avoid work and be amoral.
3. People must be held responsible for their actions in the proximate world.

He concludes with this realistic word: "The tangible incentives that any society can realistically hold out to the poor youth of average abilities and average industriousness are mostly penalties, mostly disincentives."

From these observations, Murray argues for a wholesale scrapping of the welfare system. He labels government programs as counterproductive and suggests replacing them with a voucher system in education, with private philanthropy and voluntary local groups to care for the pauperized. Accordingly, Murray believes, most poor people would pick themselves up by their own bootstraps, make their way, and gain new dignity. Reform would come not because stingy people had won but because generous people would stop kidding themselves about the effects of their philanthropy.

We can critique Murray's *Losing Ground* thesis in three areas: methodology, theology/ethics, and program. Michael Harrington, in a 1985 issue of *The New Republic,* finds fault with "crunched numbers," referring to Murray's selective use of statistics. For example, Murray does not include the dramatic decline in poverty among the elderly, one of the great government achievements of the past thirty-plus years. His claims also run contrary to the positive evaluations of such programs as Head Start and the Job Corps. Harrington also challenges Murray's use of African Americans as the prototype for the disadvantaged, pointing out that poor black males aged sixteen to sixty-five made up barely 10 percent of the poor population. Murray also ignores externalities that impinge upon statistics: for instance, technological change, "stagflation" (recession with inflation), the flight of corporate capital, the rising levels of normal unemployment, cultural shifts, and the revolution in occupational structure, as detailed in Harrington's book.

Murray's *Losing Ground* fails to establish a cause/effect relationship between government programs and an increase in poverty; he resorts to the argument of *post hoc ergo prompter hoc* ("after this, therefore because of this"). Murray excoriates affirmative action programs, but several studies give them high ratings, including that outlined in *Shape of the River,* by William Bowen and Derek Bok. These authors demonstrate the utility of affirmative action programs in increasing black participation in the labor force.

Contrary to Murray's view, antipoverty measures do work. Cash transfers lifted 5.1 percent of Americans out of poverty in 1967 and 9.1 percent out of poverty in 1981—both years in which the poverty rate was 14 percent. In *Fighting Poverty,* Sheldon H. Danziger and Daniel H. Gottschalk come to this simple and startling conclusion: "The main effect of welfare is to raise the income of the poor."

According to a study by the Center on Budget and Policy Priorities, reported in March 2000 but covering the year 1998, the number of people living in poverty before the provision of social insurance, means-tested cash, and noncash benefits less federal taxes declined from more than 54 million to just over 28 million. That is, before various government programs were put in place, 20.1 percent of people were poor;

after these programs were implemented, the rate dropped by nearly half to 10.5 percent (using the most conservative poverty measurement).

The safety net created by these programs brought about some amazing results. It reduced child poverty from about 15 million to 10 million, or from 21.5 percent to 14.3 percent. Among individuals aged eighteen to sixty-four, the number of people living in poverty fell from about 23 million to 15 million, or from 14 percent to 9.1 percent. Among elderly persons, the figures are even more dramatic. The number of poor elderly was reduced from over 15 million to not quite 3 million, a reduction from 48.2 percent to 8.8 percent. Despite dramatic changes in safety net programs, they remain a major factor in reducing poverty among Americans.

Murray's theological/ethical view is a pessimistic one, bordering on the Malthusian and the Hobbesian. Economic facts dispute his characterization of people who prefer the dole to work, who work toward their own self-destruction, and who are easily undermined by government engineering. And his theology of human nature is questionable. One can contrast his view of original sin with Paul Tillich's view of human nature as finite freedom, which seems more in keeping with observable reality. We are free and self-actualizing creatures, and even though we ever strive to be gods, we are always prone to demonstrate our finitude. We may indeed be sinful, but in the Old Testament sense of "missing the mark," we are not inherently demonic creatures who want only to be given the goods of life. Even Adam Smith held to humanity's fundamental altruism in economic matters. He believed human generosity would smooth the hard edges of economic competition.

Murray's characterization of the political economy as a spiritual entity in which penalties are all pervasive strikes me as unduly pessimistic as an observation and decidedly counterproductive as a policy. Every community depends on a minimum of decency, altruism, and cooperative behavior. Yet little, if any, such behavior seems to exist in the Murray political/economic universe. Leon Wieseltier, in a 1985 article in *The New Republic*, observes that even Adam Smith allowed for two government interventions in the free market economy: government relief for the poor and taxation for such purposes. Wieseltier continues,

> The argument that it is morally and intellectually more correct to celebrate the good fortune of the many than to condemn the bad fortune of the few is really an argument for the delegitimation of social conscience. It is made by those of little faith in our order. Those with faith fasten on the few.

Wieseltier concludes that conservatives have always been able to live with the fact of poverty—someone else's. "At least it can be said of the bleeding-heart liberal that his heart really bled."

In relying on private philanthropy and local charity, Murray ignores the hard evidence of the twentieth century. The Christian Coalition's 1995 Contract with the American Family, for example, relies heavily on the private sector (predominantly religious organizations) to end poverty. Ralph Reed, former Coalition organizer, said, "I think the American people have an almost endless reservoir of generosity."

That is not the reality, however. There are about 32.3 million poor people in the United States, and some 258,000 religious groups: churches, synagogues, mosques, temples, and similar institutions. That means that every group should, on average, be responsible for about 125 poor people, providing income maintenance, health care, child care, moral support, and the rest. But many of these religious groups have fewer than one hundred members; most have difficulty meeting their current expenses. Charitable giving is grossly inadequate, and three-fourths of these religious groups are already involved in providing community service. And what if the government were to supply the money to these groups? The issue of church/state separation would likely be a thorny one.

Labor economist Rebecca Blank, in *It Takes a Nation: A New Agenda for Fighting Poverty,* estimates that every one of these religious groups would have to raise an additional $300,000 per year *forever* to assume the support burden. She writes, "Alternatively, if this giving is done through private charitable organizations that serve the poor, it would require those groups to raise over *seven times* more in private donations than they currently receive."

If this privatization of social welfare is a serious program, why has it not yet been implemented? The reason is too obvious: It is impractical. How would the money be raised? If the funds came from government in the so-called charitable choice provision of the 1996 welfare reform legislation, how would the separation of church and state be addressed? Who would administer this vast network of private sector groups? Who would set policy? Would antiabortion groups take only people who were chaste as members? Would Christian Coalition congregations serve children of unwed parents? Would poor people who are gay or lesbian have to find sympathetic congregations to belong to? The private sector is simply not equipped to handle this vast welfare system.

The religious community, of course, should do more. It already fills many of the holes in the safety net, and it has a vital role to perform in educating the community about public needs and moral obligation. For example, it might be helpful to insist on comprehensive evaluations of current welfare reform instead of accepting the raw data of reduced welfare roles without knowing what has happened to those no longer receiving government aid. Today's attitude of political correctness—that the phrase *good government* is an oxymoron—has been foisted on us by those who never saw a government program they did not want to cut. This attitude is dogmatic and undermines serious reform. Eliminating programs and reducing welfare roles is not the same as ending poverty. We need to debunk the limited perspective of those who, having only a hammer, see every problem as a nail. We need to learn that government programs reduce poverty at a rate five or six times faster than economic growth. A valuable role for religious groups would be to advocate for the powerless in the halls of power.

It is not clear why a private sector welfare program that did not work in the past to eliminate poverty would work now. Nonetheless, Murray's critique serves to remind welfare state liberals that utopianism of any stripe is off the mark. What is required is a balanced and honest investigation.

That kind of evaluation is available in *Fighting Poverty: What Works and What Doesn't,* perhaps the most comprehensive study of antipoverty programs of the 1980s. The editors of this work, Sheldon Danziger and Daniel H. Weinberg, identify three basic kinds of programs to help equalize incomes and eliminate poverty: means-tested income transfer payments, social insurance, and education/training programs.

Means-tested programs distribute goods, services, and cash to poor and near-poor families based on entitlements, but only certain groups of people qualify. Three dollars out of ten are transferred in the forms of food, housing, and energy; four dollars represent an investment in medical care; and only three dollars are transferred as cash. While one study found only 23 percent of the April 1979 poverty gap was reduced in this way, Gary Burtless of the Brookings Institute writes, "Nonetheless, means-tested transfers are the nation's least costly mechanism for reducing the gap between market-provided incomes and the resources required for a standard of living above the poverty level." Burtless adds a note of sober realism when he concludes, "Means-tested assistance by itself is simply not sufficiently generous to eliminate the poverty of these families."

Social insurance is more important than means-tested programs in reducing the poverty gap. According to one estimate, 64 percent of Social Security and Medicare payments go to families whose pretransfer incomes are below the poverty line. Approximately one-third of these benefits go toward reducing the poverty gap, and one-half of the pretransfer poverty gap has been eliminated by them.

Investment in *education and training,* the third category of government grants, has a decidedly mixed record. In comparison to the enormous confidence during the early War on Poverty days that this investment in human capital would end poverty, current assessments are much more guarded. Danziger and Weinberg summarize the effect of such programs: "The lesson to be drawn is not that targeted education and training are valueless; they are modestly useful. But unfortunately they are unlikely to make a crucial difference in the lives of most people who participate in them."

It is safe to say that the welfare state, as we know it, has fallen short of the expectations of its advocates but has done better than its detractors would like to admit. That is hardly a satisfactory summary, but it seems not far off the mark. It should also be said, however, that the welfare state in the United States, like Christianity, has not really been tried. That is, spending on human resources has been so sparse and so reluctantly undertaken that it is not surprising Americans have secured so little of the "general welfare" promised by the Preamble to the Constitution. Our promotion of the common good as a nation has been, in a word, *niggardly.* Our spending on social programs is far less than that of most of the other Western democracies. We are the only one among them with no universal health insurance. Welfare in the United States is understood more as a privilege than as a right.

To personify the pre-1996 welfare reform program, let me share a story of a friend whom I will call SR. She is a self-described "middle class mom . . . [with] two great kids and a job I loved, working with kids with physical disabilities." Getting out of a bad marriage had taken any excess funds she had, but she owned (along with the bank) a small home and "was blessed with children who thought shopping at thrift shops was more of an adventure than the malls. . . . We were the poor folks in a rich suburb, but we managed, and were happy."

However, SR's teenage daughter had cystic fibrosis, a debilitating and ultimately fatal illness. When her daughter's condition deteriorated quickly, SR felt she needed to be home with her to provide the increasingly time-consuming therapies that were her daughter's only hope of staying alive until donor lungs were found. "Within 6 weeks, I had completely run through my savings, and applied for public assistance." Since both her children were special-needs kids, she also received Supplemental Security Income (SSI) for both and about $60 a month in food stamps; her son was eligible for free school lunches.

In SR's words,

> We made it, but just barely. We could cope with our very reduced circumstances because we knew this was a temporary situation. . . . Public assistance did not save my daughter's life, but it gave us the chance to give her the best shot possible. I was able to spend her last year with her, and at the same time meet the needs of her brother. Without public assistance to enable me to be home, there is no doubt in my mind [she] would have died much sooner. But taxpayers would have paid a horrendous bill in the meantime for the 24 hour nursing care she required. I can't begin to imagine what the stress of having to work, instead of being with [her], would have done to me physically and emotionally. I am very grateful for public assistance, but receiving it was neither pleasant nor easy.

SR detailed problems with case workers, lack of privacy in welfare offices, and humiliation in using food stamps at suburban grocery stores. Her daughter died in 1993, and SR stayed on public assistance for another year while beginning grad school. Having found grant money and a loan program, she chose to stop receiving welfare benefits, although as a student, she was still eligible. Since then, she has moved from the area and is working in a not-for-profit clinic providing health care to poor children.

Again, quoting SR,

> I am once again part of the middle class, and expect to be out of debt soon. When I hear people gripe about people on welfare, I quietly say that I was a welfare Mom, too, and that I was not an aberration, but absolutely the norm, two years and off. Two of the nurses I work with have also needed public assistance at one time in their lives. I suspect that the experience of being in need, and receiving help, is part of why they are working for low pay, and providing wonderful care to a difficult population.

The new welfare reform legislation is not quite as compassionate. Charles Murray's proposals, which seemed so radical at the time, have to a disturbing extent been implemented in the 1996 federal welfare reform legislation designed "to end welfare as we know it." The major elements of the Personal Responsibility and Work Opportunity Reconciliation Act are devolution of responsibility to the states, creating a whole patchwork of programs, a lifetime five-year time limit for receiving benefits, work requirements, and support programs such as child care, educational benefits, health care, and some cash payments.

It is hard to say how SR's story would have turned out under the new welfare reform program. Many of the props that supported her and her family are missing now. According to a 1997 story in the *Rochester Times Union,* about 135,000 children were reclassified as not disabled and would lose their SSI benefits—especially those with multiple problems but none of which was serious enough to qualify under the new and more stringent requirements. Food stamps and child nutrition programs have been cut, often because families leaving welfare do not know they may still be eligible. Outreach programs by government officials, preoccupied by saving public money, are spotty at best.

Interestingly, Medicaid has not suffered such severe cuts. Why? Perhaps because many middle-class people have parents in nursing homes paid by Medicaid. For example, New York State Governor George Pataki's father lived for many years in a fireman's retirement home, paid for by taxpayers through Medicaid.

On the positive side, current welfare reform seeks to end dependency and put welfare recipients to work. Work is good for both body and soul. However, it is fascinating to see those who have insisted that women stay home to raise their children now want to require poor women to work or else. But are there enough family-sustaining jobs for the wave of new job seekers?

Robert Edelman, former adviser to President Bill Clinton, resigned in anger when the president signed the welfare reform bill. He writes in a 1997 issue of *The Atlantic Monthly,* "We have been reduced to the politics of the waitress mom. She says, all too legitimately, 'I bust my tail. I don't have decent child care. I don't have health coverage. Why should 'these people' get what I don't have?'" The answer, of course, is that we need to help not only the desperately poor but also the working poor, who are just barely making it.

As noted earlier, the Personal Responsibility and Work Opportunity Reconciliation Act of 1996 provides a lifetime five-year time limit for receiving public assistance, after which a person is placed at the tender mercy of his/her state legislature. This provision undermines human dignity by using a stick, not a carrot. There are some exceptions to this policy, but it has rightly been called the "drop dead" provision of the act.

Such a rule is arbitrary. No justification has been given for specifying this particular period of time. While the average recipient receives welfare for two years or less, this penalty falls hardest on those least able and least likely to make the transition from welfare to work. Furthermore, it takes no account of the job market in a particular region, the circumstances in which a recipient finds himself/herself, or one's individual capabilities. This is especially distressing when positive motivations to work are having promising results. The federal Earned Income Tax Credit (EITC), the states' Income Tax Disregard (the state version of EITC), and the child assistance programs have all successfully enabled many to leave poverty.

The current version of welfare reform is morally repugnant in its too often punitive policies and practices. Its understanding of human nature is that people are inherently lazy and dependent and that they wish to exploit the public and will cheat to do it. The reality is that less than 2 percent of participants fit this description. Moreover, the program is arbitrary in forcing people into a Procrustean bed, with its five-year time limits and its stress on employment at any cost, paying little attention to human individuality or circumstance. The program's provisions for child care, work training, and education are, in most cases, grossly inadequate. It was initially estimated that this legislation would push more than 1 million children into poverty and that 11 million families will lose income, including 8 million families with children. Millions more will lose Medicaid, since many mistakenly believe that once they leave welfare, they are ineligible for this supplementary program.

At its worst, the 1996 welfare legislation was called "legislative child abuse," mean spirited, ideologically driven, and draconian. It was said that this "prune and punish" philosophy had compromised the United States' commitment to its poor. Apparently, women and children were to come last in America.

At the time, I shared those sentiments, and I continue to be deeply troubled by this policy. Let me illustrate my concern. In 1999, I attended a program at the Rochester, New York, Children's Collaborative at the YWCA with the director of Monroe County's Department of Social Services. Having heard the director assure us that children would not be hurt when adults lost their eligibility for assistance, I asked him what would happen to me and my children if I were a parent who had used up my five years? How does my cut-off not hurt my children? How much collateral damage to my children would be tolerated in order to punish me? He didn't know—but thought these were good questions.

Current evaluations of 1996 welfare reform are preliminary and decidedly mixed. A rough summary would be that the worst predictions of its critics have not been realized nor have the highest hopes of its supporters. It is true that welfare roles have dropped dramatically. Nonetheless, the incidence of poverty has dropped only slightly, and evidence pours in of increasing numbers of persons at soup kitchens and in homeless shelters and of declining health coverage for poor families. It seems that where there has been increased public support, poor families near the poverty line and close to the workforce have, in many cases, moved out of poverty. Yet many of them stand to lose important benefits, which raises the question as to whether they were better off on welfare than they are in the workforce. The data are sketchy but worth noting as we approach September 2002, when the first individuals will lose their five-year eligibility and be cut off.

According to "The Initial Impacts of Welfare Reform on the Incomes of Single-Mother Families," a study by the Center on Budget and Policy Priorities, released on August 22, 1999, the average income of very poor families fell during the early years of welfare reform. The poorest 20 percent of female-headed families with children—namely, 2 million families with 6 million people—fell an average of $580 per family. Even when food stamps, housing subsidies, the EITC, and other such benefits are included, these families' incomes remain below three-quarters of the poverty line. The study concludes that most of these losses can be attributed to the erosion of safety-net programs.

The average earnings and overall incomes of low-income families with children rose substantially between 1993 and 1995 as the economy expanded. But the average incomes of the poorest 20 percent of female-headed families with children fell from 1995 to 1997 despite continued economic growth, as welfare system changes took effect on a large scale due to state reforms and enactment of the 1996 federal welfare law. As summed up by Wendell Primus, the study's lead author, "It is disturbing that substantial numbers of children and families are sinking more deeply into poverty when we have the strongest economy in decades and when substantial amounts of funds provided to states to assist these families are going unused."

Despite some gains, the Center on Budget and Policy Priorities report cautions against "pronouncing welfare-reform an unqualified success." The number of people on public assistance has plummeted to half its peak level (1994). But the authors conclude that "too much emphasis has been placed on caseload reduction and insufficient attention paid to income and poverty outcomes." With a strong economy and the lowest unemployment rate in decades, these poor families should not be losing ground. "Welfare reform should not be pronounced a success until the outcome among these poor families with children is one of consistent income gains rather than of income stagnation or losses."

Currently, at least six states are using surplus federal welfare funds to pay for tax cuts or general fund programs. Relatively little of the surplus is being used for child care, training, education, or transportation subsidies to help low-income people find living wage work. Welfare advocate Frances Fox Piven, in a 2000 issue of *The Nation*, points to the "irrationality of yanking poor women out of college to sweep the streets in abusive workfare programs or of cutting paltry cash grants to punish families for breaking any of the new and mindless rules that welfare departments are generating."

Robert Reich, former secretary of labor, writes in a 2000 issue of *The American Prospect* that the nation should make three moral commitments based on an individual's willingness to work:

> First, any adult needing to work full time deserves a full-time job. Second, that job should pay enough to lift that person and his or her family out of poverty. Third, people should have the opportunity to move beyond this bare minimum by making the full use of their talents and abilities.

Based on these moral commitments and the basic criterion of making work pay, there is a mixed record of welfare reform evaluation now available (2000):

+ The Minnesota Family Investment Program has had major success in creating affordable housing along with welfare reform.
+ Illinois, unlike many other states, has plowed every dollar it saved from the reduced welfare lists into social services, especially an expanded daycare program. It has consolidated its social services bureaucracies, coordinated with community-based organizations, and reduced welfare roles by 50 percent, compared to 30 percent for New York and California. The state has received two performance bonuses from the federal Department of Health and Human Services, and Secretary Donna Shalala said, "Illinois is the first big state with a very big city that has done very well."
+ Wisconsin instituted a good child care program.
+ Oregon was conscientious about job placement.
+ Washington's Work First program—"a job, a better job, a career"— is targeted to every low-wage worker who wishes upward mobility, not just those who have been on welfare. An effective job preparation program with "coaches" has been put in place.

+ Vermont is trying a "kinder, gentler" approach to welfare reform based on gaining waivers from the federal government to modify the rules and make them less onerous.

+ South Carolina, on the other hand, has taken a "tough sanctions, tough luck" approach that ends support to the entire family for a single instance of noncompliance.

In the same issue of *The American Prospect*, Michael Massing reports, in "Ending Poverty as We Know It," that nationwide, more than 1 million people have lost their Medicaid and only 10 percent to 15 percent of families eligible for federal child care subsidies actually get them.

A 2000 edition of the *Washington Post National Weekly Edition* reports a Brookings Center study by Bruce Katz that found that cities are lagging far behind rural and suburban areas in welfare reform because of the concentration of poverty, lack of entry-level jobs, and inadequate transportation and other services. Marcia K. Meyers, social work and public affairs professor at Columbia University, points out that welfare offices themselves often undermine welfare reform. Also writing in the June 19–July 3, 2000, issue of *The American Prospect* she notes,

> [Congress] left the delivery of these support services to a welfare system that has neither the incentives nor the organizational capacity to advertise and deliver them. As a result, many working families are not getting the help they need to achieve self-sufficiency on low wages. This is not inconsistent with the reluctance of many elected officials to spend money on the poor. But it is also not inevitable. Rather, it means that lawmakers committed to real reform of the system will need to consider changes not only in the rules and regulations, but in the delivery system as well.

The Unitarian Universalist Service Committee (UUSC) launched a welfare reform monitoring project in 1995 and found many problems:

+ Lack of knowledge of the new rules by state officials and condescending attitudes toward clients

+ Pressure to reduce roles rather than improve the lives of people

+ Closing cases on technicalities

+ Depriving clients of educational opportunities because of zeal to get them into any kind of jobs, no matter what the pay and benefits

+ Punitive enforcement of family caps in some states

The UUSC today recommends elimination of the five-year cumulative limit of benefits or a more flexible exemption policy, increasing the minimum wage and indexing it to inflation, rewarding states for helping recipients achieve self-sufficiency rather than reducing welfare roles, and involving recipients in welfare design and evaluation.

In sum, the welfare reform enacted by the 1996 legislation is here to stay. It has not been as disastrous as its critics claimed it would be, but it has problems its advocates have not admitted. It needs serious evaluation, not the exploitation of reduced welfare roles by politicians. The criterion for evaluation should be how well the program brings people who are poor above the poverty line, not just an arbitrary reduction in welfare cases. More, not less, funding will be required if adequate services are to be provided to enable poor people to become self-sufficient.

Critiques of welfare reform are getting underway at the grassroots level. In New York City, Community Voices Heard and other groups pushed through a public jobs program over Mayor Rudolph Giuliani's veto. Other groups are coming together under the National Campaign for Jobs and Income Support (www.nationalcampaign.org). Ending poverty as we know it will require a massive citizens' effort to reform current welfare reform and give it a human face.

THE STAKEHOLDER SOCIETY

Yale Law School professors Bruce Ackerman and Anne Alstott, writing in the July 17, 2000, issue of *The American Prospect,* suggest a *stakeholder approach* to reducing inequality. They propose giving every young adult American a stake of $80,000 as a birthright of citizenship, which would be financed by an annual wealth tax equal to 2 percent of every individual's wealth in excess of $180,000 with an $80,000 exemption for each taxpayer. Each stakeholder would be free to use this money as he/she saw fit: to start a business, go to college, raise a family, or save for the future. If possible, the stake should be paid back in full by the time of the individual's death. Some restrictions would apply—namely, a high school education and others for special circumstances.

The authors note that the annual cost of this program in 2000 would be about $255 billion, a little less than the United States spends on national defense. Admitting this is a large number, they point out that after World War II, wealthy taxpayers were much poorer and were paying heavier taxes, yet they helped pay for the GI Bill of Rights to give postwar veterans a fair start in adult life. The authors acknowledge the proposal's political problems yet identify parallels to programs in other nations and the Permanent Fund in Alaska, in which every Alaskan receives $1,000 a year out of revenues from North Slope oil. Beginning with the assumption that "all Americans have a fundamental right to start off as adults with a fair chance at making a decent life for themselves," the authors ask: "Is America more than a libertarian marketplace? Can we make this a place where all citizens have a fair shot at the pursuit of happiness?" Clearly, this is a radical proposal, but it is founded on the basic American value of equality of opportunity.

OTHER ALTERNATIVES TO LESSEN INEQUALITY AND END POVERTY

One of the tried and true methods of increasing the dispersion of income is unionization. Conversely, one of major reasons for the stagnation of wages over the past three decades is the decline of the labor movement. American business management has been almost universally antagonistic to organized labor. For reasons perhaps similar to those cited by Jennifer Hochschild in *What's Fair?*—in which she explains why socialism has never played a major role in American politics—organized labor has never had the power of its counterparts in Western Europe. It is no coincidence that the wages of the average American worker have not matched the growth of the GDP or productivity.

Historically, unions have been very successful in advocating for better wages. Lawrence Mishel, Jared Bernstein, and John Schmitt, in *The State of Working America,* cite data showing that union workers made an average of $23.48 per hour compared to $17.28 for nonunion workers, including wages, insurance, and pensions. On average, organized workers receive more than 25 percent more in hourly pay than nonunion workers. AFL-CIO President John Sweeney has energized organized labor and brought about a reversal in the downward trend of membership. Low-income service workers are the next group with potential for effective organizing. Those who seek more equality will see the labor movement as a strong ally.

THE LIVING WAGE CAMPAIGN

In 1995, Robert Blanchford wrote *The Living Wage and the Law of Supply and Demand.* In it, he makes this recommendation to his readers:

> Whenever you hear a speech or read a paper which tells you that the "living wage" is against the "economic law," ask the speaker or writer

these questions: (1) What is the actual working of the economic law? (2) In what book on political economy can that law be found? In every case . . . the speaker or writer will be unable to tell you.

The *living wage campaign* is based on the assumption that any person who works full time and year round should earn a wage that is sufficient to support a family. This notion goes back to St. Thomas Aquinas, who argued for the same sort of wage centuries ago in a much less prosperous time.

The new living wage campaign has been undertaken in an effort to persuade government agencies to do business only with those firms that pay their employees a living wage. That living wage is determined locally, based on the cost of living for a family, and is implemented through a local ordinance. The living wage campaign is a logical extension of the minimum wage, which has fallen in value over the years and can never truly have been considered a living wage. This campaign has been successful in a number of large cities, including Baltimore in 1994 and, more recently, New York, Los Angeles, Boston, Milwaukee, Minneapolis, Portland, and Rochester, New York, among others.

Robert Pollin and Stephanie Luce detail this campaign in *The Living Wage: Building a Fair Economy*. Pollin notes that, as an economist, he was at first opposed to the idea, but as his research developed, he became a staunch supporter. Likewise, many government officials and businesspeople were initially opposed to the plan but came around when they saw the overall positive impact it had on the community. In Los Angeles, for example, the living wage plan has had quite positive results. Low-wage workers have enjoyed, on average, a 33.5-percent increase in pretax earned income and a 13.5-percent increase in disposable income and nonindigent health coverage. And the taxpayers have enjoyed a decline in the total government subsidy of nearly 40 percent.

TAXATION AS AN INSTRUMENT OF EQUITY

According to former president Ronald Reagan, the idea of a progressive income tax came from Karl Marx, "who designed it as the prime essential for a socialist state." Now we know the shocking reality that Thomas Jefferson had the idea first. In a letter to James Madison, dated October 18, 1785, Jefferson said that one way to lessen inequality in wealth "is to exempt all from taxation below a certain point and to tax the higher portions . . . in geometrical progression as they rise." The question is: Was Jefferson a Marxist, or was Marx a Jeffersonian?

Government taxation is an area that has historically helped to produce a more egalitarian income distribution, regardless of the original
intention. A progressive income tax rate has, in theory, and to a lesser
extent, in practice, served to take money from the affluent and redis-
tribute it to the poor through welfare programs.

Contrary to conventional wisdom, the overall burden of federal
taxes has not changed dramatically in recent years. According to the
authors of *The State of Working America,* it was 17.8 percent of GDP in
1950, 19.8 percent in 1979, and 21.2 percent in 1997. But the structure
of taxation has changed appreciably, not to the benefit of the poor. As
a percentage, the federal *corporate* income tax has fallen from just over
30 percent of federal revenue in the 1940s to less than 10 percent in the
1990s while the federal *individual* income tax has gone from about 40
percent in the 1940s to 75 percent in the 1990s. Thus, while corporations have been far less heavily taxed, individuals have seen their taxes
rise to the point that they are now carrying the greatest burden of federal tax revenue.

The payroll tax, or Social Security, has also increased markedly,
representing a drastic shift that places the tax burden on the poor, most
often the working poor, for whom the payroll tax is the most burdensome (see Figure 9). The lowest 20 percent (or quintile) of Americans
saw their payroll tax rate jump from 5.5 percent in 1977 to nearly 8 percent in 1999. Yet during the same time frame, the top 1 percent experienced a hardly discernible increase from 1.5 percent to just over 2
percent. Since payroll is taxed at a fixed rate on earnings up to a cap
(which is far above poverty levels), it is a strongly regressive tax. And
the overall federal tax burden, while progressive, is not markedly so
when one considers the variations in income and wealth.

Robert Kuttner, in *The Economic Illusion,* summarizes the failure of
the U.S. tax system as a mechanism of income redistribution: "Taking
the tax system as a whole, despite nominal elements of progressivity,
the effective tax burden was roughly proportional to income for about
80% of the population. That is, it scarcely redistributed income at all."
Kuttner uses the "Parable of the Racquetball Club" to illustrate the
inequity of the tax system:

> An old mill building is renovated by a developer who gets a tax credit
> equal to 25% of renovation costs by virtue of the 1981 tax amend-
> ments. The investment is depreciated to provide artificial tax losses.
> No expense is spared in making this a luxury sports club, with low
> membership rates made possible by the effective subsidy of other

taxpayers. Consider the distributive effects. Here is an affluent clientele enjoying a reduced rate on a luxury facility, thanks to subsidies in the tax code. The same tax preferences also serve to lower the taxes paid by other affluent people, in their role as investors. For symmetry, one could even imagine an investor joining his own club—and reaping subsidy both ways, as he polished his backhand. Imagine the outcry if Congress directly appropriated cash subsidies for members of racquetball clubs. Further, consider the contrast between this luxury club and the ragged condition of public recreation facilities for the non-rich. . . . The illusion that subsidizing the rich is more 'efficient' is purely an artifact of the present tax code. Whom to subsidize, if anyone, is nothing but a political choice. Subsidies that flow from tax preferences often have extreme distributive bias, but the bias is rarely made explicit or addressed as a conscious policy choice.

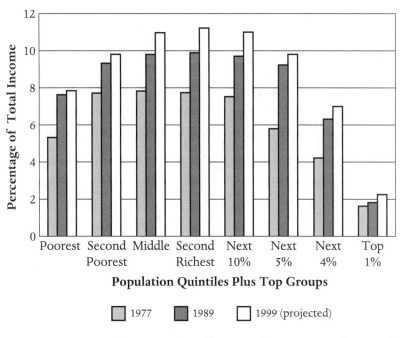

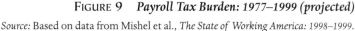

FIGURE 9   *Payroll Tax Burden: 1977–1999 (projected)*

Source: Based on data from Mishel et al., *The State of Working America: 1998–1999.*

The pattern of effective federal tax changes on family tax payments changed only slightly from 1977 to 1998 (including income, Social Security, excise, and share of corporate income tax). According to data from Citizens for Tax Justice, the poorest quintile of the population actually saw a decrease, due primarily to the effect of the Earned Income Tax Credit (EITC). The EITC remains one of the most effective and least controversial income redistribution plans, since it is granted only to working families who file tax returns. Federal taxes for most Americans actually decreased over the period. The top 1 percent of taxpayers saw the largest decrease in effective federal taxes. It is the regressive nature of so much taxation, particularly at the state and local levels, that is especially hard on low-income people.

Despite most Americans' complaints about burdensome taxes, the fact remains that the United States is one of the most lightly taxed of all industrial democracies. Of course, it is also true that the residents of other more highly taxed nations get more services from their governments, including universal health care and better unemployment and retirement benefits. In 1995, while tax revenue as a percent of GDP was 27.9 percent in the United States, it was 28.5 percent in Japan, 39.2 percent in Germany, 44.5 percent in France, 41.3 percent in Italy, 35.3 percent in the United Kingdom, 37.2 percent in Canada, 30.9 percent in Australia, 42.4 percent in Austria, 46.5 percent Belgium, 51.3 percent in Denmark, and 49.7 percent in Sweden.

Taxation remains one of the most powerful tools for redistribution. The problem in the United States has been that the redistribution effected most recently has been to the benefit of the affluent, not the poor. The top marginal tax rates plummeted from 91 percent in 1959 to a nominal 39.6 percent in 2000, with an effective rate of 34.4 percent for the wealthiest 1 percent of Americans.

What is required is a taxation system somewhat akin to those of Japan and West Germany, which apply relatively steep tax rates to individuals yet seem not to discourage their work effort. Germany has demonstrated that the public sector can tax and transfer as much as 45 percent of the national income without disrupting personal motivation and economic growth, as long as individual tax rates are not confiscatory. Japan effectively does not tax the bottom third of the workforce. But these nations have more progressive taxation of personal wage and salary income, providing social services such as universal health care without greatly affecting economic efficiency.

The U.S. Tax Reform Act of 1986 was a major step in this direction. It effectively reduced taxation on the poor and near-poor, and it closed a number of tax loopholes for the affluent. Even so, it did not do much for the progressivism of taxation, given its two rates of 15 percent and 28 percent. (It also provided a temporary 33-percent rate for upper-income taxpayers.) The 1993 and 1997 federal tax legislation added more tax rates at the upper end of the income level without greatly hurting economic efficiency.

Nothing has been done to change the regressive payroll tax by raising it at the upper levels, like any other income. Consider what happened to after-tax income distribution from 1969 to 1999, despite cries of onerous marginal tax rates on the most affluent. According to U.S. Census Bureau data, the mean income of the poorest quintile rose the least during this period, from $1,957 to $9,940. The second-poorest quintile did somewhat better, enjoying an increase from $5,216 to $24,436. But the real gains were seen in the upper-income brackets. The richest quintile saw its mean income increase from $20,520 to $135,401, and the richest 5 percent saw an increase from $31,586 to $235,392. By any standards (and despite some modest increases in the top marginal tax rates), this segment of the population has been getting richer and richer while those in the middle and on the bottom have seen their shares either stagnate or decrease.

Is the Wealth Tax an Un-American Activity?

Since wealth is even more unevenly distributed than income, it stands to reason that a wealth tax may be one important means of creating greater equity. Taxation should be based on ability to pay, and the wealthy, who have seen their share of wealth increase dramatically the past few years, are in a good position to contribute to the greater good of the community.

Many of the advanced industrial democracies of Europe (including Austria, Finland, Germany, Luxembourg, the Netherlands, Norway, Spain, Sweden, and Switzerland) levy a wealth tax at comparatively modest rates of 1 percent to 3 percent. This kind of tax in the United States might raise $50 billion a year, which would be enough to fund a variety of programs that would help level the playing field—full funding of Head Start, for example. Unfortunately, the Constitution prohibits such a direct tax on individuals based only on their wealth. Article 1, Section 9(4), reads, "No capitation or other direct tax shall be laid, unless in proportion to the census or enumeration herein before directed to be taken." In fact, the Sixteenth Amendment was added to the Constitution in 1913 in order to levy an income tax.

Writing in a 1996 issue of *Boston Review,* Edward N. Wolff proposes a wealth tax modeled after that of Switzerland. He begins by defining *wealth* (or *net worth*) as being composed of four parts: (1) homes; (2) liquid assets, including cash, bank deposits, money market funds, and savings in insurance and pension plans; (3) investment real estate and unincorporated businesses; and (4) corporate stock, financial securities, and personal trusts. Wolff's proposed wealth tax would work as follows: "All household effects, pensions, and annuities would be excluded from the tax base with a $10,000 exemption on automobiles" (only expensive cars—this proposal was made in 1996—would be subject to the tax).

The rationale for such a tax is based on the ability to pay. However, it also recognizes that income is a measure of economic resources that understates the disparity of resources among people. As described by Wolff,

> Two families with identical incomes but different levels of wealth are not equivalent in terms of their well-being, since a wealthier family will have more independence, greater security in times of economic stress, and additional liquidity for advantageous purchases. Wealth gives a family greater ability to pay taxes, and in the interests of equity, it is justifiable to tax current wealth in addition to income.

Wolff also believes that an annual wealth tax might induce individuals to transfer their assets from less to more productive uses. For example, instead of investing in cars, which yield no money income, persons might invest in income-yielding assets. Taxes on land might inhibit the avoidance of income taxes by encouraging investors to switch assets into income-yielding forms. Finally, Wolff believes that total household wealth is so concentrated that such a tax would affect only a very small part of the population. It would be irrelevant to the vast majority of taxpayers.

Clearly, a wealth tax would be controversial, and the affluent would wield their considerable power against it. Politicians would certainly shy away from such a proposal, since they are so beholden to the wealthy.

Regardless, a wealth tax is not now under serious consideration in the United States, even among reformers and activists. But discussion of such a proposal should raise these ethical questions: In a democracy, how do we justify the concentration of such enormous wealth (and power) in the hands of so few? And is the United States a democracy or an oligarchy?

THE NEGATIVE INCOME TAX AND GUARANTEED INCOME

And so, we move now to the final strategy proposed for reducing the income disparity in the American economy: the so-called *negative income tax,* along with its cousin the *guaranteed annual income.*

The guaranteed income idea appears to have been initiated during the 1940s by Lady Juliette Evangeline Rhys-Williams, who proposed that a flat grant or "social dividend" be given to all English citizens regardless of their economic circumstances. And in the United States, a 1946 article by economist George Stigler introduced the idea of a negative income tax. John Kenneth Galbraith made mention of it in his well-known book *The Affluent Society* in 1958, and Robert Theobold developed it still further in his 1967 book *The Guaranteed Income.*

Most surprisingly, however, the idea was given support from an unlikely source, conservative economist Milton Friedman, in his 1962 book *Capitalism and Freedom.* In 1971, Senator Daniel Patrick Moynihan, then domestic advisor to President Richard Nixon, proposed a similar concept with his Family Assistance Program. It was defeated in Congress by a coalition of conservatives who opposed any such guarantee and liberals who thought the guarantee provided was too low.

The notion of a guaranteed annual income remains an intriguing one, even though its chance of adoption is slim to none under current U.S. political conditions. Nonetheless, it merits continued discussion until the political climate is ripe for legislative implementation. Toward that aim, I would call it a *citizen's wage.* The current system too often penalizes work effort—for instance, through the loss of income or health and child care benefits—and it encourages cheating to survive. Under a system of *negative* income tax, working would always leave one better off than not working, much like the federal Earned Income Tax Credit (EITC) or the state Earned Income Disregard.

In *Capitalism and Freedom,* Friedman begins with the proposition that government is justified in setting a floor under the standard of life of every person in the community. The target population is the poor; that they are poor is the only thing to note, not why they are poor. This floor would have to be established in such a way so as not to distort the free market. The mechanism Friedman prefers is the negative income tax. A floor would be established below which no one would be allowed to fall. If an individual's earnings went below this floor, the government would make up the difference, providing essentially a guaranteed annual income. As their earnings increased, people would be taxed at progressive levels, following the rule that the more one earns, the greater percentage one pays. Likely calculations of gross income using a guaranteed income/negative income tax are shown in Table 3.

Friedman believes, as I and as most economists do, that self-interest is a powerful motivator. His plan combines the best features of the safety net and economic incentives. Its advantages include the following:

+ It is directed specifically at poverty.
+ Cash goes directly to the poor, thus avoiding the paternalism of a means-tested welfare bureaucracy.
+ The plan provides incentives to earn more.
+ It is less expensive than a "rag bag" of antipoverty measures.

Friedman, as a highly regarded economist, is to be credited for this advocacy; as a conservative, his word carries weight. However, certain defects in his program are immediately evident. For instance, he assumes that poverty can be eliminated simply by putting money into

Family's Gross Income	Grant to Family	Total Income
$0	$9,000	$ 9,000
$2,000	$8,000	$10,000
$4,000	$7,000	$11,000
$8,000	$5,000	$13,000
$12,000	$3,000	$15,000
$15,000	$1,500	$16,500
$18,000	$0	$18,000

TABLE 3   *Potential Impact of a Guaranteed Income/ Negative Income Tax by Income Group*

the hands of the poor, thus enhancing their freedom. But poverty may not be simply the absence of money; it may be only a symptom of other problems, such as lack of education, training, and skills. Moreover, Friedman's plan makes no structural changes in the social conditions that facilitate, if not create, poverty. And while his negative income tax mechanism makes a useful contribution, it is only one useful weapon in the war against poverty.

A variation on Friedman's program is that of *family allowances*— grants for families according to the number of children they have. Programs of this nature are in place in more than sixty countries. The United States is the only industrialized nation in the Western world that does not provide a family allowance. But such a program, while worthy, is simply too narrow in scope and ignores millions of nonchildren and nonparents who live in poverty.

More recently, such a proposal has been made by Herman E. Daly, former World Bank economist, and John B. Cobb, Jr., a theological ethicist, in their 1992 book *For the Common Good*. They fault the old welfare system for inducing a culture of dependency. They would replace it with a negative income tax that would have four criteria:

A preferred system should

1. require that the truly basic needs of all be met;
2. be simple and inexpensive to implement;
3. require a minimum of information from recipients and impose a minimum of special conditions upon them;
4. provide strong incentive to work.

Although the details of this plan can be complex, the basic idea is that the government would send checks to those individuals whose reported incomes were below a certain amount. The checks would become smaller as the individuals' incomes increased but not to the full extent of the increase, so that there would always be a positive incentive to earn more.

No doubt, technical problems can be found with any form of negative income tax/guaranteed income program and the transition required to implement it. The obstacles to a guaranteed income plan, however, would probably be moral, social, and political rather than economic. Yet this plan does meet the basic criteria established by the canons of distributive justice. It would provide an income floor for the poor, and it would reduce income disparity. It would also preserve incentive and maximize freedom while increasing equity. Finally, it would maintain the power of the marketplace while combining it with a strong program of income maintenance.

A MULTIFACETED STRATEGY

The optimal plan for a more equitable distribution in the American economy would be multifaceted. The means for implementing economic justice are currently in hand, given the unprecedented budget surplus anticipated over the next decade and beyond. Sufficient funds would presumably be available to end poverty and to reduce the growing divide in American economic life.

While I cannot with any precision propose what a grand strategy should be, surely it should include the following, moving from proximate doable programs to the more difficult long-range solutions:

+ Increase the Earned Income Tax Credit (EITC) to bring the working poor up to the poverty level . Even President Ronald Reagan endorsed this antipoverty program, which was bipartisan until the ultraconservative congressional class of 1994 took over the Congress.

+ Transform the minimum wage into a living wage. Living wage campaigns across the nation are successfully moving low-income people up the payscale without jeopardizing community resources.

+ Implement a welfare reform that will end the cruel arbitrariness of a five-year time limit and put more emphasis on the "carrot" (programs for education, child care, health coverage, and job training) than on the "stick" (that is, attitudes and actions that regard getting people off welfare roles as more important than getting people out of poverty).

+ Develop an affirmative action program that stresses class more than race or ethnicity but still recognizes the underlying discrimination in American culture, even after all classism has been screened out.

+ Create a social policy that is "front loaded," one that recognizes that investing in human resources early on makes far more sense than applying draconian sanctions later. Full funding for Head Start would be such an example. Despite the almost universal regard for the program from both major political parties, full funding has thus far eluded federal leaders. Government transfer programs have been a vital stopgap and have saved many from misery. But with a bureaucracy developed to ensure against cheating, means-tested programs have become inefficient (hence, Arthur Okun's "leaky bucket"). Government responsibility should be shifted away from means-tested income programs to those that recognize the rights of citizenship and provide basic public services for all citizens, including children's allowances (like those provided by most other Western nations), an equitable and well-funded public school system at all levels, social services that provide counseling and other support services, public transportation and recreational facilities, and universal health insurance.

+ Institute tax reform that guarantees true progressivity, that seeks to maintain a ratio of top quintile to bottom quintile of not more than five to one (in keeping with the Heilbroner/Thurow discussion), and that makes the payroll tax more progressive by raising the upper limit on which these taxes are paid.

+ Create more effective taxes on wealth. This would involve maintaining the inheritance tax but indexing it for inflation. A wealth tax that reduces income superfluity and redistributes excess resources more broadly, as is done in the European countries cited earlier, should be explored.

+ Legislate a negative income tax, a system of income maintenance that operates through the Internal Revenue Service and provides a floor under all Americans while also providing strong incentives, particularly at the lower income levels.

Together, these proposals meet the canons of distributive justice:

+ *The canon of need*—Clearly, this is at the heart of a needs-based system as supplemented by basic public services. There should be no holes in this "safety net."

+ *The canon of proportional equality*—This canon would be fulfilled through a rigorously progressive tax system that would exclude income at the lower levels in coordination with a negative income tax.

+ *The canon of contribution to the common good*—This canon would be difficult, if not impossible, to build into legislation. Job comparability is already roughly established in the public sector. Comparable worth legislation would encourage it in the private sector, as well.

+ *The canon of productivity*—The proposals above clearly continue to rely on the free market as the basis for economic activity. The rough efficiency of the market would help support this canon by providing rewards for greater productivity.

+ *The canon of effort and sacrifice*—Here again, one can hardly rely on government structures. One must count on the market as being open to persuasion on this point.

+ *The canon of scarcity*—The market seems to do a reasonable job here through the law of supply and demand. Distortions would exist, but a progressive income tax would help moderate them.

Clearly, there is not a perfect match between the articulated canons of economic justice and list of proposals I have outlined. But then, ours is a far from perfect world. I can only hope that these canons of distributive justice might inform policies that move in the direction of more equitable distribution.

That is only part of the task, however. Before these canons can influence public policy, the United States needs a serious conversation on the value of fairness and equity. It must be more than a conversation about ethics; it must be substantially an ethical conversation.

THE COMMUNITY OF THE DIALOGUE

What remains, at this juncture, is what theologian Paul Tillich called "silent interpenetration," in which people committed to more equitable distribution enter the lists to debate those who claim the market settles all the really important economic questions. I hope that the foregoing discussion might make a contribution to what the late Robert Hutchins called the "community of the dialogue," which is democracy at its best.

I have tried to show that poverty in the midst of affluence is a moral scandal; that great disparities in income and wealth cannot be justified, morally or economically; that the principles of freedom and trusteeship, equity and efficiency, community and individualism are decisive economic issues; that both poverty and wealth are morally and spiritually corrupting; and that a program for meeting economic needs in the United States does not require moral compromise.

I suspect such ideas will not receive a warm welcome in our society among those who already benefit from the economic order. It has not been my purpose to be popular but to be prophetic in the sense of laying down a plumbline by which we might measure ourselves—in other words, to get a "God's eye view" of our lives and our world.

Robert Heilbroner, in *The Nature and Logic of Capitalism,* provides a sardonic summary of this inquiry:

> If the rich man—or better yet—the rich society—finally wins admission to heaven, I suspect it will be not because capitalists have pure hearts, but because scientists will have succeeded in breeding exceptionally thin and agile camels, and because technology has succeeded in making needles with very large and very wide eyes.

In my more pessimistic moments, I believe we, as Americans, have ceased to be a nation of citizens and have instead become a self-righteous collection of taxpayers. There is a moral chasm between the two, but in my more hopeful moments, I have faith in the basic decency of the American people that Heilbroner's cynicism will be proved unfounded.

What might motivate Americans to create policies that reduce inequality and end poverty? One alternative has been described as a "theology of relinquishment." Without question, many, if not most, of us live more comfortably than nearly all the people in history have lived, not excepting royalty. We live more comfortably than the vast majority of people in our country and even our world. Yet we often feel impoverished—not because we are needy but because our expectations continually outstrip our resources. *Enough* seems always to be a little more than we have. Such an effort will require sacrifice, not only economically but also in terms of social time and political effort.

Ethically, I propose an act of class betrayal. Politically, I must act against my apparent self-interest. That may seem foolish until I realize that my true self-interest lies in creating a just society. As long as I believe self-interest is defined by personal acquisition and as long as a large number of affluent people follow their narrow self-interest, we are in for class warfare, from which no winners will emerge.

Certain signs suggest that this larger view of the common good is upon us. Recently, five CEOs of large American corporations lobbied Congress for full funding for the WIC program, which provides pre- and postnatal care for poor women and children. The positive impact of this program has been demonstrated. But why were these normally conservative, "limited government" businessmen lobbying for social welfare legislation? They knew that the well-being not only of their corporations but also of their nation depended on the good health of the children who will be the citizens and workers of tomorrow. These individuals can tell the national interest (and incidentally, their own) when they see it.

Perhaps if enough people are willing to relinquish enough of their affluence, the proverbial "eye of the needle" will become larger or "the camel" will become smaller. If enough people have the courage to commit acts of class betrayal, perhaps we can be needled into the kingdom of heaven.

How much do we deserve? There is no more important social or moral question before us as we move into the new century. Our problem is not that we do not have the economic resources to end poverty and reduce inequality. Even before the economic expansion of the 1990s, there were adequate resources. We lacked something then as we do now. Former president George Bush once bemoaned that in facing these social problems the nation had more will than wallet. I beg to differ. Our problem is that we have more wallet than will.

Author Robert Fulghum highlights both the problem and the possibility of the American economy. In his book *Maybe (Maybe Not)*, he creates an arresting image that aptly describes our society. He invites his high school–age students to play musical chairs, which they do with gusto. The competition is ferocious but finally won by a member of the high school wrestling team. Upon winning, the winner has a look of triumph on his face and raises his hands in the familiar victory salute, "Number One, Number One."

But games are supposed to be fun, and this game has become much too competitive to be fun. Fulghum invites the students to play musical chairs again. Only this time, if they cannot find a chair when the music stops, they are to sit in someone's lap. The students play, but the mood is changed. There is laughter and giggling. No one is in a hurry. Only the winner of the first game has a hard time.

There is one more step in this process: The music plays, the students march, and Fulghum takes away the last chair. When the music stops, the students are to sit down in each other's laps. Despite youthful protestations that it cannot be done, Fulghum shows them how by carefully standing sideways in a circle, each taking a step into the middle to shrink the circle, and by carefully sitting down on the count of three, they can—and do—accomplish it.

Fulghum concludes,

They all sat. No chair. I have played the chair game with many different groups of many ages in varied settings. The experience is always the same. It's a problem of sharing diminishing resources. This really isn't kid stuff. And the questions raised by musical chairs are always the same: Is it always to be a winners-losers world, or can we keep everyone in the game? Do we still have what it takes to find a better way?

There is no more important issue for the twenty-first century than for us to find that better way. The question is: How much do we deserve? The answer is still blowing in the wind.

Selected Bibliography

Albelda, Randy, Elaine McCrate, Edwin Melendez, June Lapidus, and The Center for Popular Economics. *Mink Coats Don't Trickle Down: The Economic Attack on Women and People of Color.* Boston: South End Press, 1988.

Aquinas, St. Thomas. *Summa Theologica.* Translated by Fathers of the English Dominican Province. 5 vols. Allen, TX: Thomas More Press, 1981.

Aristotle. *The Nicomachean Ethics.* Translated by David Ross. 1925. Reprint, New York: Oxford University Press, 1998.

———. *The Politics of Aristotle.* Edited and translated by Ernest Barker. New York: Oxford University Press, 1962.

Arthur, John. *Justice and Economic Distribution.* 2nd ed. Edited by William H. Shaw. Englewood Cliffs, NJ: Prentice-Hall, 1991.

Atkinson, Anthony Barnes, ed. *Wealth, Income and Inequality.* 2nd ed. Oxford: Oxford University Press, 1980.

Bagby, Meredith E. *Annual Report of the United States of America.* 1998 ed. New York: McGraw-Hill, 1998.

Beatty, Jack. *The World According to Peter Drucker.* New York: Free Press, 1998.

Bedau, Hugo A. *Justice and Equality.* Englewood Cliffs, NJ: Prentice Hall, 1971.

Bellah, Robert Neelly, ed. *Habits of the Heart: Individualism and Commitment in American Life.* Berkeley: University of California Press, 1996.

Benne, Robert. *The Ethic of Democratic Capitalism: A Moral Reassessment.* Philadelphia: Fortress Press, 1981.

Birch, Bruce C., et al. *The Predicament of the Prosperous.* Philadelphia: Westminster Press, 1981.

Blank, Rebecca. *It Takes a Nation: A New Agenda for Fighting Poverty.* Princeton, NJ: Princeton University Press, 1998.

Bowen, William G., et al. *The Shape of the River.* Princeton, NJ: Princeton University Press, 1998.

Breton, Denise, and Christopher Largent. *The Soul of Economies: Spiritual Evolution Goes to the Marketplace.* Wilmington, DE: Idea House, 1991.

Brown, Lester R., Christopher Flavin, and Hilary French. *State of the World 2000.* New York: Norton, 2000.

Budd, Edward C., ed. *Inequality and Poverty: An Introduction to a Current Issue of Public Policy.* New York: Norton, 1967.

Campbell, Joseph, and Bill Moyers. *The Power of Myth.* Edited by Betty Sue Flowers. 1988. Reissue, Landover, MD: Anchor, 1991.

Cauthen, Kenneth. *The Passion for Equality.* Totoma, NJ: Rowman and Littlefield, 1987.

Childress, James F., and John MacQuarrie, eds. *The Westminster Dictionary of Christian Ethics.* Philadelphia: Westminster Press, 1986.

Coles, Robert. *The Moral Life of Children.* Boston: Atlantic Monthly Press, 2000.

Collins, Chuck, and Felice Yeskel. *Economic Apartheid in America: A Primer on Economic Inequality and Insecurity.* New York: New Press, 2000.

Collins, Chuck, Betsy Leondar-Wright, and Holly Sklar. *Shifting Fortunes: The Perils of the Growing American Wealth Gap.* Boston: United for a Fair Economy, 1999.

Daly, Herman E., and John B. Cobb, Jr. *For the Common Good: Redirecting the Economy Toward Community, the Environment, and a Sustainable Future.* 2nd ed. Boston: Beacon Press, 1994.

Danziger, Sheldon H. *Fighting Poverty: What Works and What Doesn't.* Edited by Daniel H. Weinberg. Cambridge: Harvard University Press, 1986.

Downs, Alan. *Corporate Executions: The Ugly Truth About Layoffs—How Corporate Greed Is Shattering Lives, Companies, and Communities.* New York: American Management Association, 1995.

Ehrenreich, Barbara. *Fear of Falling: The Inner Life of the Middle Class.* New York: HarperPerennial, 1990.

Ferguson, Thomas. *Golden Rule: The Investment Theory of Party Competition and the Logic of Money-Driven Political Systems.* Chicago: University of Chicago Press, 1995.

Folbre, Nancy, and James Heintz. *The Ulitmate Field Guide to the U.S. Economy: A Compact and Irreverent Guide to Economic Life in America.* New York: New Press, 2000.

Frank, Robert. *Luxury Fever.* Princeton, NJ: Princeton University Press, 2000.

Freeman, Richard B., et al. *The New Inequality: Creating Solutions for Poor America.* Boston: Beacon Press, 1999.

Friedman, Milton. *Capitalism and Freedom.* Chicago: University of Chicago Press (Phoenix Books), 1963.

Fromm, Erich. *To Have or To Be.* New York: Continuum, 1996.

Funiciello, Theresa. *Tyranny of Kindness: Dismantling the Welfare System to End Poverty in America.* New York: Atlantic Monthly Press, 1993.

Galbraith, John Kenneth. *The Affluent Society.* Boston: Houghton Mifflin, 1998.

Gandhi, Mohandes. *The Essential Gandhi: His Life, Work, and Ideas.* Edited by Louis Fischer. New York: Vintage, 1983.

Gilligan, Carol. *In a Different Voice: Psychological Theory and Women's Development.* 1982. Reprint, Cambridge: Harvard University Press, 1993.

Gordon, Scott. *Welfare, Justice, and Freedom.* New York: Columbia University Press, 1980.

Harrington, Michael. *The New American Poverty.* New York: Holt, Rinehart and Winston, 1984.

———. *Socialism: Past and Future.* 1972. Reprint, New York: NAL/Dutton, 1992.

Heilbroner, Robert L. *The Nature and Logic of Capitalism.* New York: Norton, 1986.

———. *Between Capitalism and Socialism: Essays in Political Economy.* New York: Vintage Books, 1970.

Hirsch, Fred. *The Social Limits to Growth.* Campbell, CA: iUniverse.com, 1999.

Hightower, Jim. *There's Nothing in the Middle of the Road but Yellow Stripes and Dead Armadillos.* New York: HarperCollins, 1997.

———. *If the Gods Had Meant Us to Vote They Would Have Given Us Candidates.* New York: HarperCollins, 2000.

Hobbes, Thomas. *Leviathan.* Edited by Richard Tuck. Cambridge: Cambridge University Press, 1996.

Hochschild, Jennifer L. *What's Fair? American Beliefs about Distributive Justice.* Cambridge: Harvard University Press, 1981.

Jencks, Christopher. *Inequality: A Reassessment of the Effects of Family and Schooling in America.* New York: Basic Books, 1972.

Jones, William. *Is God a White Racist? A Preamble to Black Theology.* Boston: Beacon Press, 1998.

Kaplan, David A. *The Silicon Boys and Their Valley of Dreams.* New York: Harper-Perennial, 2000.

Kaufmann, Walter. *Without Guilt and Justice.* New York: Peter H. Wyden, 1973.

Korten, David C. *Globalizing Civil Society: Reclaiming Our Right to Power.* New York: Seven Stories Press, 1998.

Kozol, Jonathan. *Amazing Grace: The Lives of Children and the Conscience of a Nation.* New York: HarperPerennial, 1995.

———. *Rachel and Her Children: Homeless Families in America.* New York: Crown, 1988.

———. *Savage Inequalities: Children in America's Schools.* New York: Crown, 1991.

Kuttner, Robert. *The Economic Illusion: False Choices between Prosperity and Social Justice.* 1984. Reprint, Philadelphia: University of Pennsylvania Press, 1987.

———. *Everything for Sale: The Virtues and Limits of Markets.* 1996. Reprint, Chicago: University of Chicago Press, 1999.

Lalone, Emerson Hugh. *And Thy Neighbor as Thyself: A Story of Universalist Social Action.* Boston: The Universalist Publishing House, 1959.

Lao Tso. *Tao Te Ching.* Translated by Gia-Fu Feng and Jane English. New York: Vintage Books, 1997.

Lekachman, Robert. *Greed Is Not Enough.* New York, Pantheon Books, 1982.

Levy, Frank. *Dollars and Dreams: The Changing American Income Distribution.* New York: Russell Sage Foundation, 1987.

Lucash, Frank S., ed. *Justice and Equality Here and Now.* Ithaca, NY: Cornell University Press, 1986.

MacIntyre, Alasdair. *After Virtue: A Study in Moral Theory.* 2nd ed. Notre Dame, IN: University of Notre Dame Press, 1997.

Maguire, Daniel. *A New American Justice*. Minneapolis: Winston Press, 1980.

Maslow, Abraham Harold. *The Farther Reaches of Human Nature*. 1971. Reprint, New York: Arkana, 1993.

Meeropol, Michael. *Surrender: How the Clinton Administration Completed the Reagan Revolution*. Ann Arbor: University of Michigan Press, 2000.

Mill, John Stuart. *Utilitarianism*. Edited by George Sher. 1861. Reprint, Indianapolis: Hackett, 1979.

Miringoff, Marc L., and Marque-Luisa Miringoff. *The Social Health of the Nation: How America Is Really Doing*. New York: Oxford University Press, 1999.

Mishel, Lawrence, et al. *The State of Working America: 1998–99*. Ithaca, NY: Cornell University Press, 1999.

Myrdal, Gunnar, and Bok Sissela. *An American Dilemma: The Negro Problem and Modern Democracy*. Piscataway, NJ: Transaction, 1996.

National Conference of Catholic Bishops. *Economic Justice for All: Pastoral Letter on Catholic Social Teaching and the U.S. Economy*. Washington, DC: U.S. Catholic Bishops, 1986.

Newman, Katherine S. *Declining Fortunes: The Withering of the American Dream*. New York: Basic Books, 1994.

Nozick, Robert. *Anarchy, State and Utopia*. New York: Basic Books, 1977.

Okun, Arthur M. *Equality and Efficiency: The Big Tradeoff*. Washington, DC: Brookings Institute, 1975.

Pasquariello, Ronald D. *Tax Justice: Social and Moral Aspects of American Tax Policy*. Lanham, NY: University Press of America, 1985.

Phillips, Kevin. *The Politics of Rich and Poor: Wealth and the American Electorate in the Reagan Aftermath*. New York: Random House, 1990.

———. *Boiling Point: Democrtas, Republicans, and the Decline of Middle Class Prosperity*. New York: Random House, 1993.

———. *Arrogant Capital: Washington, Wall Street, and the Frustration of American Politics*. Boston: Little, Brown, 1995.

Pizzigati, Sam. *The Maximum Wage: A Common-Sense Prescription for Revitalizing America—By Taxing the Very Rich*. New York: Apex Press, 1992.

Plato. *Five Great Dialogues: The Republic*. New York: Walter J. Black, 1942.

———. *The Laws*. Cambridge: Harvard University Press, 1942.

Pollin, Robert, and Stephanie Luce. *The Living Wage: Building a Fair Economy*. New York: New Press, 1998.

Powers, Charles. *Can the Market Sustain an Ethic?* Chicago: University of Chicago Press, 1978.

Rawls, John. *A Theory of Justice*. 1971. Reprint, Cambridge, MA: Belknap Press, 1999.

Reich, Robert B. *Tales of a New America: The Anxious Liberal's Guide to the Future*. New York: Vintage Books, 1987.

Reiman, Jeffrey H. *The Rich Get Richer and the Poor Get Prison*. 5th ed. Needham Heights, MA: Allyn and Bacon, 1997.

Rosenberg, Claude, Jr. *Wealthy and Wise: How You and America Can Get the Most Out of Your Giving*. New York: Little, Brown, 1994.

Ryan, John A. *Distributive Justice: The Right and Wrong of Our Present Distribution of Wealth*. New York: MacMillan, 1916.

Ryan, William. *Equality*. New York: Vintage Books, 1981.

Samuelson, Paul A., and William D. Nordhaus. *Economics*. 16th ed. New York: McGraw-Hill, 1998.

Schor, Juliet B. *The Overworked American: The Unexpected Decline of Leisure*. 1991. Reprint, New York: BasicBooks, 1993.

Schorr, Lisbeth B., and Daniel Schorr. *Within Our Reach: Breaking the Cycle of Disadvantage*. New York: Doubleday, 1989.

Schumacher, E. R. *Small Is Beautiful: Economics as if People Mattered*. New York: Harper and Row, 1989.

Sennett, Richard, and Jonathan Cobb. *The Hidden Injuries of Class*. 1972. Reprint, New York: Norton, 1993.

Shue, Henry. *Basic Rights: Subsistence, Affluence and U.S. Foreign Policy*. 2nd ed. Princeton, NJ: Princeton University Press, 1996.

Slater, Philip. *Wealth Addiction*. New York: Dutton, 1983.

Smith, Adam. *The Wealth of Nations*. Edited by Andrew Skinner. New York: Penguin USA, 2000.

Tawney, R. H. *Religion and the Rise of Capitalism*. Piscataway, NJ: Transaction, 1998.

————. *The Acquisitive Society*. New York: Harcourt, Brace, 1948.

Thandeka. *Learning to Be White: Money, Race, and God in America*. New York: Continuum, 2000.

Thurow, Lester. *The Zero-Sum Society: Distribution and the Possibilities for Economic Change*. New York: Basic Books, 1980.

Thurow, Lester, and Robert Heilbroner. *Economics Explained: Everything You Need to Know About How the Economy Works and Where It's Going*. 1982. Reprint, New York: Touchstone Books, 1998.

Tocqueville, Alexis de. *Democracy in America*. Edited by J. P. Mayer. Translated by George Lawrence. New York: HarperPerennial, 2000.

Unitarian Universalist Service Committee. *Welfare and Human Rights Monitoring Report*. Boston: UUSC, 2000.

Wachtel, Paul L. *The Poverty of Affluence: A Psychological Portrait of the American Way of Life*. Philadelphia: New Society Publishers, 1989.

Walzer, Michael. *Spheres of Justice: A Defense of Pluralism and Equality*. New York: Basic Books, 1983.

Weber, Max, et al. *The Protestant Ethic and the Spirit of Capitalism*. Philadelphia: Routledge, 1993.

Wesley, John. "On the Use of Money." In *The Westminster Dictionary of Christian Ethics*, edited by James F. Childress and John MacQuarrie. Philadelphia: Westminster Press, 1986.

Wilson, William Julius. *When Work Disappears: The World of the New Urban Poor.* New York: Knopf, 1997.

Wogamon, J. Philip. *Guaranteed Annual Income: The Moral Issues.* Nashville, TN: Abingdon Press, 1968.

———. *The Great Economic Debate: An Ethical Analysis.* Philadelphia: Westminster Press, 1977.

Wolff, Edward N. *Top Heavy: A Study of the Increasing Inequality of Wealth in America.* New York: Twentieth Century Fund Press, 1995.

World Watch Institute. *The State of the World 2000.* New York: W. W. Norton, 2000.

Note: Statistics in this book are generally from 1999, the latest year for which most data is available. For up-to-date factual information, please refer to these and other relevant websites:

American Enterprise Institute	http://www.aei.org
Brookings Institute	http://www.brookings.edu
Bureau of Labor Statistics	http://www.BLS.gov
Center on Budget and Policy Priorities	http://www.centeronbudget.org
Children's Defense Fund	http://www.childrensdefense.org/index.html
Congressional Budget Office	http://www.CBO.gov
Electronic Policy Network	http://www.epn.org
U.S. Bureau of the Census	www.census.gov/hhes

Index